THE FIRST MASTER

THE FIRST MASTER

John Allen Giles and
The City of London School

✳

Terry Heard

THE FIRST MASTER – John Allen Giles and The City of London School
First Published 2021 by
T.J.Heard
c/o John Carpenter Bookshop
City of London School
Queen Victoria Street
London EC4V 3AL

Text and Compilation © Terry Heard 2021.

British Library Cataloguing in Publication Data:
A catalogue record for this publication is available
from The British Library Bibliographic Database.

ISBN (13): 978–1–9168762–0–0

For permission to reproduce any part of this publication
please contact the Publisher.

PRINTED IN GREAT BRITAIN
Swallowtail Print, Norwich

CONTENTS

Foreword

'The schoolmaster is abroad and I trust to him with his primer against the soldier in full military array'. With these words, Lord Brougham, sometime Lord Chancellor, threw down a challenge and a manifesto. The modern foundation of the City of London School, with Brougham as active supporter and attended by such leading figures of the Radical intelligentsia as Dr Birkbeck and George Grote, was part of this British ferment of reform, to which these three, two with Scottish experience and one self-taught, brought enthusiasm for the value of education. A decade before the old boarding schools began to change, here was a proposal for affordable middle class education, science based and geared to the practical needs of urban life, with an entry not limited by a religious test but open to Dissenters and Jews from the very beginning. Within a generation, the success of this project was attested by the glowing reference in the Report of the Taunton Commission, a Parliamentary tribute by Richard Cobden to the School's example of religious tolerance, and by the remarkable range of distinction Old Citizens were achieving in public life.

Brougham's skill with the trowel as he laid the foundation stone in 1835 was considered worthy of a member of the Plaisterers' Company. In fact, relations with the City were not so smooth; the Lord Mayor had earlier threatened to arrest the mercurial Brougham. The key figure in all this is Warren Stormes Hale, the tallow chandler whose initiative made CLS possible but whose doubts about the suitability of Dr Giles helped to bring down its first Headmaster. Drawing on archives of the School (which he has done so much to recover and organize), of the City, and on Giles's extensive diary and memoirs, Terry Heard brings alive the issues and characters of this formative period with particular emphasis on the hitherto little known Dr Giles.

The author, with his experience as an Old Citizen and a former Second Master, guides us expertly through relations with the Corporation and the conflict of cultures that Giles was not the last headmaster to find challenging. Posterity has judged Giles unsuited to teaching, but his subsequent career must surely qualify this. Among the two hundred volumes he wrote are dozens of translated classical texts – 'cribs' to censorious classicists – and dozens more of edited medieval chronicles. Almost all are now forgotten, judged as hasty popularizers. But in their day they opened up swathes of great writing and obscure history to several generations of students. Terry's researches bring vividly before us Giles's family and social life, his correspondence with many well-known figures of Victorian public life, his humour and open-mindedness and the personal flaws which were his undoing. There is an extraordinary twist in his life, as the reader will discover. As with the best biography, we are left with the sense that Giles's personality has become familiar to us yet remains enigmatic.

Lionel Knight, MBE

Preface

My interest in John Allen Giles and the early days of the City of London School (CLS) started more than 50 years ago, when I was a relatively new member of the CLS teaching staff. At lunch one day Giles came up in conversation, I don't remember why, and the Bursar, Denis Stenhouse, remarked "There are some old papers about Giles in my cupboard." He later lent me a brown paper parcel containing some 80 documents, ranging from short lists or notes to lengthy reports. Intrigued by the story these tell, which was new to me although I had been at CLS as a boy, I took them home to sort and summarise. I also began consulting the School Committee minute books, first in the Guildhall Records Office, and more recently in the London Metropolitan Archives.

Nearly twenty years later the school moved from the Victoria Embankment to its present home on the riverside near St Paul's. By then I was the Second Master, and was much involved with planning the move. We took that opportunity to gather together the school's records, historic documents and artefacts, which were scattered in cupboards all around the old building, and created an archive with its own accommodation.

In 2006, nine years after I retired from CLS, I was invited to return as part-time archivist. During the ten years I worked in the archive more and more Giles material came to light, and most importantly I discovered that the Giles *Diary and Memoirs*, in which Giles's view of some events differs substantially from the official record, had been published by the Somerset Record Society in 2000. Nicholas Railton's 2002 biography of the extraordinary Friedrich Bialloblotzky was also an eye-opener. So after my second retirement in 2016 I felt that it was time to investigate further and draw all these threads together: here is the result.

Terry Heard, June 2021

Acknowledgements

At the City of London School my researches were encouraged by David Rose, the Librarian, and by my successor as Archivist, Katherine Symonds, to both of whom I give thanks for friendship and practical help. Other Corporation records, particularly the School Committee Minutes, were formerly at the Guildhall Records Office and are now at the London Metropolitan Archives; I am indebted to their staffs for their unfailing helpfulness over many years. Similar thanks go to the Archivist of the Mercers' Company for access to the Company's records and the minutes of the Joint Grand Gresham Committee. For help in obtaining illustrations I am grateful to the staffs of the Guildhall Art Gallery, the London Picture Archive, the London Metropolitan Archives and the Surrey History Centre.

The pandemic lockdown has made it impossible for me to visit locations or consult original sources as much as I wished, and I am particularly grateful to Tricia Avery of St John's Church, Churchill, and John and Angus Murray of Churchill Court for supplying information and pictures. Likewise I am indebted to David Bromwich of the Somerset Record Society for his immense skill and industry in transcribing and editing the Giles *Diary and Memoirs*, an inspiration and essential source for this book. Edward Fenn of New Zealand (great nephew of Herbert Giles's first wife) kindly gave permission for the use of unique photographs which form part of his extensive family history website www.thekingscandlesticks.com.

I am grateful to the many friends who have taken an interest in this project: in particular Susan Jenkinson, Peter van de Bospoort, Brian Millo and Richard Edwards read all or some chapters in draft and suggested improvements. Brian Waters came to my aid when I was stuck on producing the Milk Street plans. My special thanks for constant encouragement go to my school-fellow, former colleague and old friend Lionel Knight, who read the whole text with an expert though tolerant historian's eye, and contributed the Foreword.

The Committee of the John Carpenter Club, led by the then President Richard Oblath, generously agreed to support the book's production, and the present Headmaster, Alan Bird, arranged for publicity and sales via the John Carpenter Bookshop at CLS. This has been organised by the CLS Alumni Relations team, ably supported by Karen Sage, Vagish Vela, Stephen Kelly, and Tim Osborne, to all of whom I give my thanks. I am especially grateful to Martin and Joanna Israel who have cheerfully given me the benefit of their business, artistic and publishing experience, without which I might well have floundered, and to Richard Barnes for his design and typesetting expertise.

It gives me great pleasure that any profits from sales of this book will go to supporting bursaries at CLS, thus helping to maintain the characteristic diversity of the school, which, as the reader will discover, has been there right from the start.

PICTURE ACKNOWLEDGEMENTS—The pictures on pages 49 Hale, 162, 163, and 177 Mortimer are copyright Guildhall Art Gallery, City of London; those on pages 16, 23, 50, 52 Blossom's Inn, 55 ground floor, 57, 91, 95 and 182 are copyright London Metropolitan Archives City of London; those on pages 165, 178 Windlesham are copyright Surrey History Centre. Permission to use other pictures has been received with thanks from City of London School Archive (pages 17, 22, 49 chair, 62, 74, 77, 151, 160, 161, 164, 195), Wellcome Collection (pages 33, 72), National Portrait Gallery (pages 21, 89), Edward Fenn of The King's Candlesticks, www.thekingscandlesticks.com (Frontispiece and pages 124, 170, 196), Tricia Avery of St John's Church Churchill (pages 179 tablet, 180), John and Angus Murray of Churchill Court (page 179 house and window), Daniel Crouch Rare Books, www.crouchrarebooks.com (page 51). The other pictures are believed to be in the public domain.

1

CLS before Giles

EDUCATION IN THE CITY

The old and good-for-nothing market in the city called Honey-lane Market is to be immediately removed, and substituted by a school, "for the religious and virtuous education of boys, and for instructing them in the higher branches of literature, and all other useful learning." The corporation have undertaken the task with a degree of zeal which does them great credit. John Carpenter,[1] formerly town clerk, amassed considerable wealth in that office, and testified, in a way not very likely to be imitated, his sense of obligation to those who appointed him, by bequeathing the rents and profits of his lands and tenements to the corporation, for the clothing and education of a few boys. Mr Richard Taylor[2] some time ago represented to the Court of Common Council the propriety of extending the benefits of the charity, which by being confined to so few was productive of mischief, for the youths selected as objects became entitled suddenly to the most expensive maintenance, and frequently contracted habits of extravagance not at all suited to their rank and future condition. The hint was adopted, and it is now determined to apply the profits of the Carpenter estate to the education of a considerable number of children. The building will be very large, and it is said will be made worthy of the city of London. The meaning of this, we apprehend, is, that it will vie with other large establishments in magnificence. Perhaps it would be more advisable to act upon Mr. Taylor's proposition, rather to dispense the blessings of education liberally, than to raise such a building as would, by its cost, put a check upon the power to carry the professed design of the corporation into effect. [...] Mr. Hall [recte Hale], the chairman of the City Lands' Committee, will move for a committee to carry the act which is to make this very remarkable improvement into effect on the next court-day.

This article appeared in *The Times* on 2 September 1834, soon after the City of London School Act[3] received King William IV's royal assent on 13 August 1834. The complicated history leading to this from John Carpenter's bequest of 1442 has been told elsewhere;[4] this account is of what happened next.

This private Act empowered the "Mayor, Aldermen, and Commons of the City of London in Common Council assembled" to abolish the redundant Honey Lane Market in Milk Street, off Cheapside, and to use its site to establish and "for ever thereafter maintain" the City of London School. This was to fulfil the City

Corporation's wish to make wider use of the income from the Carpenter bequest, which for nearly four centuries had been used to support just four boys. Each year £900 of this income was to be paid "towards the Maintenance and Repair of the said School" – that amount being then roughly the total income from the 119 properties which formed the Carpenter estate.

Clause XII permitted the Corporation "to appoint One or more Committee or Committees to manage and transact all or any of the Matters and Purposes which [the Corporation] are hereby required to do, execute or perform", the extent of the Committee's delegated powers to be decided by the Corporation. Two weeks after the Act gained royal assent, notice was given of a motion, proposed by the Chairman of the City Lands Committee, Warren Stormes Hale[5] (who had played a key role in

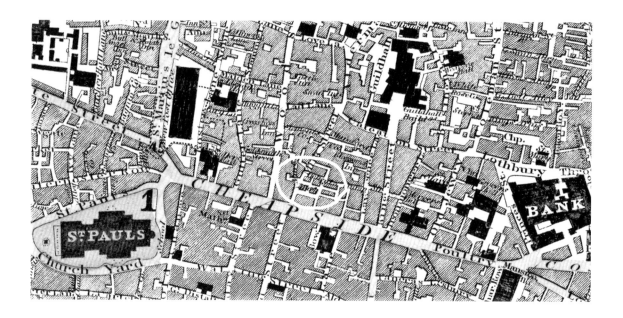

Honey Lane Market (apparently four houses and two other buildings), as shown on Charles and John Greenwood's 1830 map of London.

shaping the Act) to establish a Special Ward Committee for this purpose. This motion was passed on 9 September. This School Committee, as it was called, originally comprised the Lord Mayor, twelve Aldermen and one Commoner from each Ward, making an unmanageable total of 42. It was also resolved "That one fourth part of the Aldermen and one fourth part of the Commoners be removed annually, to commence from and after the expiration of the ensuing year, such removals to take place according to the least number of the attendances", a strange procedure that if carried out literally would have left the Lord Mayor on his own after twelve years. In practice the Lord Mayor was never present, and the normal committee attendance settled down to between ten and twenty.

The School Committee met for the first time on Tuesday 16 September 1834 with Alderman William Venables[6] temporarily in the chair. Two Aldermen and 23 Councilmen were present, though six were late. The Court of Common Council's orders of reference by which the committee had been created were read, and Warren Stormes Hale was unanimously elected Chairman, a position he continued to hold until 1868.[7] Immediate steps were taken to give notice to the tenants of the four houses which formed part of Honey Lane Market to vacate their premises by Christmas, to recommend that a current vacancy amongst the Carpenter Scholars at Tonbridge School (where they had been educated since 1827) should be left unfilled, and to direct the Clerk of the City's Works to draw up a plan of the whole site available for the School, with its adjoining streets, ways and passages. A Select Committee was formed (the Chairman plus nine members, including Venables, with a quorum of five) to recommend which of the various powers in the Act should be delegated to the Committee, and to consider making the Rules and Regulations for the management of the School.

The Select Committee met one week later, and "having attentively considered the Act of Parliament" recommended that all the "powers and authorities and discretions" given to the Corporation should be delegated to the School Committee, subject to the control of the Court of Common Council, with the sole exception of the strange and elaborate procedure for the appointment of the First and Second Masters, which should remain in the hands of the Court. These recommendations were approved by the Committee and, on 9 October, by the Court.

The Select Committee also asked the Town Clerk to arrange for a deputation to visit "the several Public Schools in and about the Metropolis" to see them at work, but unfortunately there is no list of which schools were contacted.

Education in England then was entirely in the hands of private or charitable institutions. There were two large groups of elementary schools, provided by the National Society for Promoting the Education of the Poor (closely linked to the Church of England) and by the British and Foreign School Society (with strong non-conformist connections). Both used versions of the monitorial system (with older pupils teaching younger pupils) to give a very limited basic education to large numbers at minimal cost. The first government involvement in education was in 1833 when £20,000 was voted for the erection of school-houses via these two charities; state funding and direction of elementary education then gradually increased, culminating in the Forster Education Act of 1870.

At a higher educational level were the endowed grammar schools, many of Tudor or earlier origin. By statute their curriculum was restricted to teaching Latin and Greek. This was unsuccessfully challenged in a notable court case brought by Leeds Grammar School in 1805, and not changed until 1840. Many grammar schools were in a state of neglect, with very few pupils.[8]

Unique to central London and better organised, but with a similarly restricted curriculum, were a number of schools run by city institutions: Charterhouse,

Mercers' School, St Paul's School (also run by the Mercers' Company), Merchant Taylors' School, Haberdashers' Aske's School, and Christ's Hospital. Most of these were of small or moderate size; Christ's Hospital was larger, but entry was restricted to those in financial need.

For the education of their sons most middle class families turned either to private tutorial establishments (often run by clergymen) or to proprietary schools. The latter were often set up as joint-stock companies by local groups to provide broad day schooling, taking account of the needs of commerce and the professions, at modest cost. London examples include Western Grammar School (see Chapter 10),

The Revd. Josiah Pratt engraved by Samuel William Reynolds after the painting by Henry Wyatt, mezzotint, published 1826.

Richard Taylor stippled engraving by Robert Hicks after the painting by Eden Upton Eddis, 1845.

Blackheath Proprietary School (1830-1907), Forest School (1834 onward) and Camberwell Collegiate School (see Chapter 2). Two important recent additions to the London school scene were the junior departments of London University (founded in 1826 as a secular alternative to Oxford and Cambridge, the school being established in 1830) and King's College London (founded 1829 as the Anglican response).

While comparisons with other schools were occupying the Select Committee, the rest of the autumn was taken up with clearing the site, including moving the water pump which stood at its centre, and dealing with the anxieties of the nearby residents and tenants. The Mercers' Company, which owned a number of shops in Cheapside, was concerned that the new school building might come too close to the backs of their properties, but agreed not to pursue the matter provided that a separation of 15 feet and their present Lights were maintained.

Four members of the Select Committee (now renamed the Sub Committee, and reduced to a total of six) met on 26 January 1835, and were attended, at their request, by the Revd Josiah Pratt (1768-1844) Vicar of St Stephen's Colebrook Street, Richard Taylor (1781–1858), and Thomas Pewtress (1785-1872). These three brought a variety of interests and experience. Pratt was an evangelical cleric, an acquaintance of William Wilberforce, who had played leading roles in the founding of the Church Missionary Society and the British and Foreign Bible Society, and in the education of missionaries; his numerous publications included a collection of 750 psalms and hymns which had sold more than 50,000 copies. Taylor and Pewtress were both Common Councilmen. Taylor, a printer and publisher, had been prominent in the Corporation discussions of the Carpenter bequest, always pressing for the income to be used to benefit more boys; he had strong scientific interests, was Secretary of the Linnaean Society, a founder member of the British Association, and had been closely involved in establishing London University. Pewtress was also a publisher, and ran a paper mill in Sussex; he was a prominent Baptist and a member of the main School Committee.

They did a good afternoon's work, by the end of which "after maturely considering the subject" they had drafted the following:

CITY OF LONDON SCHOOL

General Course of Instruction

To read well, with due modulation, and appropriate emphasis.

English Grammar and Composition

Latin Language (recommending the Eton Grammar)

French Language and Composition, with special regard to Conversation

Writing

Arithmetic and Bookkeeping

Elements of Geometry and Natural Philosophy

Ancient and Modern and English History

Geography

Instruction in the Scriptures to be given to all the Pupils, unless a written request to the contrary is made by the Parent or Guardian.

All to attend Courses of Lectures on Chemistry and other branches of Experimental Philosophy

Special Courses

In addition to the preceding General Course, applicable to the whole School, those Pupils whose Parents or Guardians might wish it, to be instructed in the Greek language, and, at a moderate extra charge, in the German, Spanish and Italian languages and Drawing.

Such of the Pupils as shall have distinguished themselves in the Elementary Course, and may desire to avail themselves of instruction in the higher branches of Literature and Science, to be formed into Superior Classes, and receive instruction, without any extra charge, in

The Study of the Poetry and Antiquities of Greece and Rome

The higher branches of Mathematical Science and the application of it to the Study of Physics

The Elements of Logic and of Ethics

All the Senior Pupils to be practised in Recitation and the *memoriter* delivery of their own Compositions

The Masters to have discretion in the application of these Courses of Instruction according to the aptness of the Pupils in learning.

No Book to be used in the School unless the same shall have been previously approved by the Committee.

This curriculum is as progressive as any in England at the time. It clearly aims to cater for the needs of commerce (writing, arithmetic, bookkeeping), while providing a broad general curriculum (English, Latin, French, history, geography, and science for all) and provision for higher academic study (Greek and three more modern languages, higher mathematics and physics, classical studies, logic and ethics). Particularly notable is the tolerance implied by the possibility of opting out of scripture lessons. None of the seven who produced this remarkable document was an educator by profession, but they knew what sort of education was called for at the centre of the capital.

Copies of this curriculum were sent to the Head Masters of King's College School and London University School (which became University College School in 1836) with a request to "favour the Committee with their opinions thereon at their earliest convenience". The Revd John Richardson Major[9] and Professor Henry Malden[10] obliged, and their responses were read to the full Committee at its meeting a week later (3 February), though sadly their detailed comments are lost.

Fourteen members were present (including Alderman Venables), and Richard Taylor also attended. The Course of Instruction was considered again, and a few changes made: the references to the Eton Grammar and *memoriter* delivery of Compositions disappeared, and two more subjects were added to the already long list, Natural History (coupled with Geography), and Elements of Choral Singing. This amended Course of Instruction was agreed by the Committee, but later in the meeting Venables had second thoughts about the scripture instruction section. He gave notice of a motion, which was passed at the next meeting (9 February), to change this to "The Authorised Version of the Holy Bible to be used and taught in the School, and on every Morning and Evening Prayers to be read therein." While it lessens the emphasis on tolerance, this replacement stops short of requiring all pupils to attend scripture lessons or prayers.

Having clarified what the school should offer, the Committee turned its mind to its accommodation. They decided to hold a public competition for the design, and agreed that the designs should be accompanied by testimonials confirming that they could be executed for the estimates provided and that the competitor was competent to superintend the works. Premiums of 60 and 35 guineas would be awarded for the second and third placed designs respectively.

One crucial question was how large the school should be. The Town Clerk's letter to the Heads of King's College School and the London University School suggested "upward of 200". The first draft of competition rules increased this, but was vague: "accommodation shall be provided for between 350 and 500 Scholars". Such uncertainty would clearly cause difficulties in designing the building and in judging competition entries; the final version agreed on 3 March was more precise:

Instructions to Architects desirous of preparing

Designs for The City of London School

It is required that accommodation shall be provided for not less than Four hundred Scholars, and that a portion of the Design shall provide the accommodation in one large Room to be appropriated for Prayers, Public Examinations, Lectures and other general purposes, together with a sufficient number of Rooms for Classes and other usual and necessary purposes.

15

A Residence to be provided for one of the Masters, sufficient for the accommodation of a Family, and Four boarders to reside with him.

All the Plans, Elevations and Sections to be drawn to a scale of 1/8th of an inch to a foot and are to be tinted in Indian Ink only, and any Design otherwise tinted, or drawn to a different scale, will not be inspected.

Not any Design is to have the name of the Artist marked thereon, but each is to be distinguished by a Letter, Number, or Motto, and to be accompanied with a sealed Paper, on the outside of which is to be a corresponding Letter, Number, or Motto, and within such sealed Paper the Artist is to specify his name and a place of abode. And as the Committee

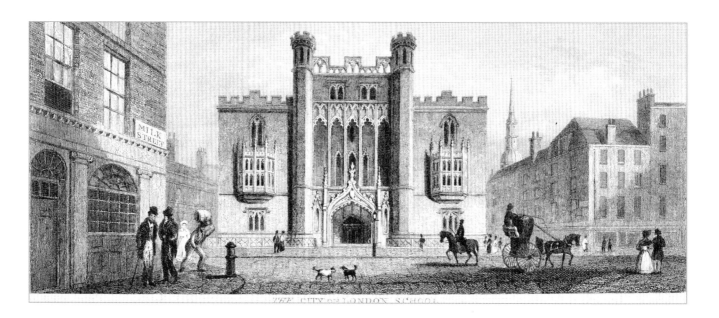

James Bunstone Bunning's *City of London School, Milk Street, west elevation*, wood engraving published 1838.

will only open the three sealed Papers of the three approved Designs, the other Designs and sealed Papers will be returned on application, and notice of the proper time for making the said application will be given by Public Advertizement.

The Designs &c are to be left, sealed up, at the Town Clerk's Office Guildhall on or before Thursday the 30th day of April next at Twelve o'Clock at noon, after which no Design will be received.

The Programme of Study and the Instructions to Architects both indicate that the Committee wanted the school to be a forward-looking institution on a large scale. The proposed size was considerably larger than many other London schools: Haberdashers' had 20 pupils, St Paul's 153, Charterhouse 128 in 1832 (a marked decline from its peak of 480 in 1825 under the highly regarded Headmaster Dr John

Russell – see Chapter 2). The more recent London University School and King's College School had grown to 249 (1833) and 350 (1834) respectively. The provision of separate classrooms was rare: most schools still had a single large school room, with separate classes conducted simultaneously in different areas under the overall control of the Master on his dais. A broad curriculum with classes in separate rooms were ideas favoured by non-conformist establishments (notably Mill Hill School, built in 1821), and perhaps their adoption was pressed by the several dissenters who were prominent members of the Committee.

John Leslie Thorp, Old Citizen and architectural model maker, created and presented this model as a Centenary gift. This view shows the boys' entrance (centre) and entrance to Head Master's house (left). Now displayed at CLS.

On Friday 1 May 24 members of the Committee met to inspect the competition entries. The Town Clerk had received a number of letters seeking an extension of the eight week period allowed for the preparation of designs, but this had not been allowed, and 42 entries had been received. The cost estimates ranged from £7,417 to £23,000, with an average of £12,392. One entry had no cost estimate and three others were not tinted in conformity with the instructions; these were immediately rejected. Of the remainder, 21 were chosen for further consideration. These were sent to the Council Chamber with an order to keep the door locked and admit nobody until the Committee had met again. All 24 members turned up again next day and made their final choices. The sealed papers accompanying the three approved designs were opened, revealing that the winner was Mr J.B.Bunning of Guilford Street, London; the estimate for his design (one of two he submitted) was £11,600.

The Morning Chronicle reported on 8 May: "Yesterday the approved model of the City of London School [...] was exhibited in Mr Woodthorpe's[11] office in the Guildhall. It has been adjudged the best of forty-two, and represents an extremely elegant and compact building. Indeed it is too handsome to be buried in so obscure a place as Milk-street, in which is intended the front should appear." This is the only mention of a model; no models had been asked for, but if Bunning had supplied one it may have been a smart move, helping the Committee (who did not feel the need for expert advice) to visualise his design. A.E.Douglas-Smith, writing in 1937, says that "A model of the Old School stood for some time in the Library of the New School, but fell into disrepair." The model now on display in the school was constructed in 1937 by J.L.Thorp (CLS 1912-15) for the Centenary celebration.

James Bunning, marble bust by Joseph Durham, formerly in the City of London School, but destroyed.

James Bunstone Bunning (1802–63) was then 32 years old. He had worked with Marc and Isambard Brunel as Surveyor of the Thames Tunnel, and was then Surveyor for the parish of Bethnal Green, and for the Foundling Hospital. Winning the competition gained him both recognition and "the usual allowance of 5% upon the amount that may be expended on the building" (about £580). His efficiency in carrying out this major commission led to his appointment in 1842 as Clerk of the City's Works (later renamed as City Architect), a post he held until his death. He was responsible for the building of Holloway Prison, the Coal Exchange in Lower Thames Street, and parts of Highgate Cemetery, where he is buried (as is Hale).

By the end of May the official set of eight plans, elevations and sections[12] had been signed by the Architect and the Chairman, and deposited in the Town Clerk's Office, with the instruction that they "be not allowed to be taken away therefrom, but that any copies or tracings that may be required by Mr Bunning be made at the said Office." Then, rather late in the day, the Committee turned to a directive from the Court of Common Council "to provide in the intended Building some suitable accommodation for the Pupils in the intervals between the hours of Study." Not surprisingly Bunning replied that he could not see how to do this without materially altering the arrangements of the Plan. A month later he reported that the only way to provide a Play Ground (by which he seems to mean an internal Play Room) of sufficient size would be to add another storey to the building. No more was heard of this idea, and the school was left to struggle on for the next fifty years without space for recreation.

June 1835 was spent preparing the working drawings and specifications needed for the building works to go to tender. While he was doing this Bunning suggested that "as the Eastern flank wall of that part of the Building that will front Milk Street will be seen by persons passing up Trump Street [the eastern continuation of Russia Row], the appearance would be improved by adding two Towers there to correspond with those intended to be placed on the West front." The Committee agreed, perhaps aware that they should make the most of any view of their fine new school which could be glimpsed between the surrounding buildings.

On 17th July the five tenders received were opened; the total costs ranged from £11,320 to £21,500. The builders submitting the three cheapest tenders were called in and asked to produce their scales of charges for various materials. After further discussion the contract was offered to Mr Samuel Grimsdell, who agreed to amend his tender (the cheapest) to include a completion date of 31 December 1836. Grimsdell, who was one of London's foremost contractors, provided two satisfactory sureties of £2,500 each, and work on the building proceeded.

Hale next convened the Committee on 10th September to consider the Laying the First Stone of the building. It was agreed to invite HRH The Duke of Sussex to perform this important ceremony. A deputation of seven, led by Hale, was formed to wait upon him and make this request. The Committee chose Lord Brougham and Vaux[13] as first reserve in case the Duke was not available, and agreed to dine together after the ceremony at the City of London Tavern (in Bishopsgate). A list of 28 guests was drawn up (in addition to numerous Corporation members and officials) "on account of the support publickly rendered by them to the cause of Education, or of their connexion with this City".

Prince Augustus Frederick, Duke of Sussex (1773-1843), the ninth child and sixth son of King George III and Queen Charlotte, has been described as "the most consistently Liberal-minded person of the first half of the nineteenth century".[14] He actively supported Roman Catholic Emancipation and the Reform Bill. He took a keen interest in biblical studies and Hebrew, at one time briefly considering being ordained in the Church of England, and collected a vast library which occupied ten rooms in Kensington Palace. From 1830 to 1838 he was President of the Royal Society, and advocated the compatibility of science and religion.

The deputation did not have the chance to make their request in person, as within a week the Remembrancer received a letter from the Duke's Secretary:

Prince Augustus Frederick, Duke of Sussex, by Emile Desmaisons, lithograph, 1841

Kensington Palace

14th September 1835

Sir

I am commanded by His Royal Highness the Duke of Sussex to beg that you will convey to the Committee of the Corporation of London, appointed to carry into execution the Act of Parliament for establishing a School on the site of Honey Lane Market, His Royal Highness's acknowledgment for the flattering distinction they have conferred upon him, by their request that His Royal Highness would lay the first Stone of the Building, which is proposed to be done about the third week in October. The present state of His Royal Highness's Eyes is such, however, as to lead to the expectation that, prior to the time named, he will have to submit to the operation of Couching[15], which will necessarily preclude His Royal Highness from quitting Home.

It is with great regret, therefore, that His Royal Highness is compelled to decline assisting at the intended Ceremony and [*sic*] which would have afforded to him the highest satisfaction, as well from the regard His Royal Highness bears towards the Corporation of London, as from the interest he feels for the success of the Institution they have so very liberally endowed.

I have the honour to be, Sir, Your most obedient humble Servant

William H. White

This letter was read to the Committee at a specially convened meeting on 16th September, as was a rather more testy communication from the Lord Mayor, Henry Winchester, to "Mr S. Hale":

The Lord Mayor having been informed by Mr Deputy Whitby that it is the intention of the Sub Chairman of the Corporation School to propose the laying of the first Stone of that Building upon an early day, and that the Duke of Sussex is mentioned as the party to perform that Ceremony, the Lord Mayor begs to know by what authority such an arrangement was made without his first being consulted to which he certainly cannot consent in the absence of all information on the matter which he ought to have, ere this, been in possession of.

The Committee swiftly replied that they were acting under the authority of the Act of Parliament establishing the School and the Order of the Court of Common Council of 9th October last delegating to them the powers and authorities of the said Act.

By 6th October Hale was able to report that Lord Brougham had consented to lay the first Stone, and the date for the ceremony was fixed for Wednesday 21st October. The Chairman, Town Clerk, Remembrancer and Mr Bunning suggested the wording for the inscription, which was approved, and various other details of the ceremony were agreed: Mr Bunning to supply "a silver trowel[16] and other necessary implements for the laying of the first Stone", the Royal Mint to be requested to supply a complete set of coins to be deposited with the Stone, members of the Committee to be furnished with Wands for the occasion,[17] application to be made to the Police Committee for the attendance of some Police Officers, "Wine and Biscuits to be provided for the refreshment of Ladies and other Visitors", and the Dinner following the Ceremony to "take place at Five O'clock precisely".

So all seemed to be going smoothly, but Henry Winchester (1777-1838), described as "an irascible and cantankerous man who carried the seeds of discontent into all his spheres of endeavour",[18] was not one to give up without a fight. He might have just tolerated having the King's brother lay the stone, but the prospect of the former Lord Chancellor Brougham, whom Winchester had strongly opposed in parliament over the Reform Bill, doing it instead was not to be borne. On Monday 19th October Winchester informed the Town Clerk of his intention to write to Brougham that evening "to prohibit his coming into the City on Wednesday next for the purpose of laying the first Stone of the School". Later in the day, when told that the Committee were then sitting, Winchester sent word that "His Lordship requested that the Committee would wait upon him at the Mansion House." A deputation of four was immediately appointed and went off to the Mansion House to see Winchester. The remaining members continued dealing with arrangements for Wednesday, until the deputation returned and reported that "in the interview which they had had His Lordship began by protesting against the Ceremony being conducted by any one but himself. Upon which the Deputation informed His Lordship that they did not attend him to discuss that point, but in consequence of the Committee having received through Mr Firth His Lordship's request that the Committee wait upon him. His Lordship thereupon positively denied that he had made any such request. The Deputation then informed His Lordship that they had therefore no business with him and being about to withdraw, His Lordship informed them that he should attend the occasion and if Lord Brougham should attempt to perform the Ceremony he would order him to be taken into Custody and that he should write to Lord Brougham on the subject this evening."

The Committee acted with resolve. On Tuesday morning the Chairman and Thomas Pewtress went to see Lord Brougham at his house in Berkeley Square. He had not yet returned to

Heny Brougham, 1st Baron Brougham and Vaux by John Samuel Templeton, after Sir William Charles Ross, lithograph, published 1840.

town, but his Secretary confirmed that a letter for him had arrived from the Lord Mayor. They intended to return to consult Lord Brougham that evening, and had meanwhile called the Committee to meet to decide what else should be done; twelve attended and five sent apologies for absence. It was resolved unanimously that "The Chairman of this Committee be authorised to direct the proceedings in the intended Ceremony [...], and that Mr James Bunstone Bunning, the Architect, and Mr Samuel Grimsdell, the Builder, and all persons acting under them be directed to take no orders on the occasion but from the Chairman of this Committee." The Chairman informed the Committee that he would convene a meeting "at an early hour tomorrow morning" if his interview with Lord Brougham that evening made this necessary. But Brougham honoured his commitment, and the next day the ceremony went ahead as planned.

The Evening Post of 22nd October described the scene:

> The ceremony of yesterday was a very imposing one. Around that part of the building on which the stone was to be laid seats were erected rising amphitheatrically, each over each, to which access was had by an archway handsomely decorated and hung with banners. The entrance was from Milk-street. On our arrival we found the place fully occupied. Half the audience being composed of elegantly dressed and handsome females the scene looked gay and animated in the extreme. In addition to those within the canopied inclosure, all the houses in the neighbourhood which overlooked the scene were thronged even to the roof with anxious gazers.

WINCHESTER *VERSUS* BROUGHAM, OR A RUMPUS OVER THE FIRST STONE OF THE CITY OF LONDON SCHOOL!

The Morning Advertiser's lengthy account (also 22nd October) starts by relating "a circumstance which afforded topic of much conversation in different knots of the company assembled." The spat between the Lord Mayor and the Committee is described in detail (who was the mole?), finishing with "Lord Mayor Winchester, it was said, had actually ordered out his coach yesterday, but he did not use it; and, consequently, the many speculations that were afloat on the subject fell to the ground, and the ceremonies of the day were minus the additional incident of Lord Brougham being marched to the station-house. We need not attempt to describe how the matter was treated by the public." The report continues:

Winchester vs. Brougham, or a rumpus over the first stone to the City of London School. A satirical print from the 'Political Drama' series of wood engravings by Charles Jameson Grant.

A little past two o'clock Lord Brougham was ushered in by the gentlemen of the Committee, bearing their wands of office. His Lordship, who had been much cheered outside, had a most cordial reception: he was cheered from all quarters of the place. Among the company present we noticed Mr. Grote, M. P.; Mr. Pattison, M. P.; Mr. Crawford, M. P.; Mr. Williams, M. P.; Sir James Shaw, the City Chamberlain; the City Recorder, the City Remembrancer, the City Solicitor, the City Clerk, Sheriffs Salomons[19] and Lainson, and the late Sheriff Ellidge; Under-Sheriff C. Pearson, Aldermen Wilson, Cowan, Thorpe, and Sir P. Laurie; Dr. Birkbeck[20], the Rev. Alexander Fletcher, the Rev. H. G. Watkins, the Rev. Mr. O'Brien, the Rev. Thos. Bennie, the Rev. W. C. Woodbridge, editor of the work entitled the "Annals of Education," from the city of Boston, in the United States; and nearly the whole Members of the Common Council.

The stone, which weighed about seven tons, was suspended from a practicable apparatus. A glass vase, hermetically sealed, contained a copy of the plan of the building, and other documents. A strong brass case, with glass on each side, contained one each of all the current coins of the realm, placed in positions so as to exhibit both sides of the coin. A large massive brass plate contained the inscription [as shown below].

The Chairman presented a splendid silver trowel, with inscription, to Lord Brougham. He said it had devolved upon him, as Chairman of the Committee, to present to his Lordship the trowel to be used in laying the foundation stone. In doing so he begged, on the part of the Committee, to express their sense of the honour done them by his Lordship in assisting at the laying of the first stone of Institution which would be a credit to the City of London.

Contemporary copy of the foundation stone inscription.

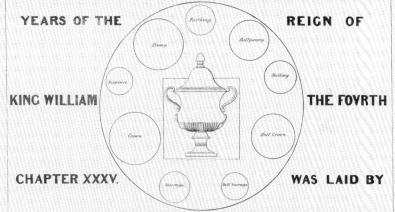

Lord Brougham said he had great satisfaction in receiving the trowel. He would always be happy to lend his assistance, and God knows the assistance he could give was but little; but he would always be happy to give his assistance to this or any other institution for the same purpose. He hoped the Institution would be as useful to the City as it was creditable in its origin.

The different articles above alluded to were deposited, and his Lordship used the trowel. Mr. Deputy Gorst remarked to his Lordship that he ought to have belonged to the Plasterers' Company. His Lordship applied the square and plumb, finishing in the usual manner by giving it three distinct knocks with the mallet. His Lordship was then about to take his departure without further notice, but Sir P. Laurie stopped him, and requested he should say few words.

Lord Brougham said, Gentleman, I can only repeat that which I stated to the Gentlemen of the Committee in private, on this occasion—that I feel great satisfaction in contributing to the foundation of this great, and I trust useful, establishment, which does infinite honour to this great City and to the Corporation; and I trust it will be as useful as it has been creditable in its object. His Lordship then retired, attended by the Committee. The company dispersed, but there appeared to be general feeling of disappointment prevailing that his Lordship had not treated them to a longer speech.

There was no cause for such disappointment at the celebratory dinner after the ceremony, "where about two hundred of the most distinguished friends of the education of the people assembled." Hale presided, with Brougham seated on his right. The meal concluded with *Non Nobis Domine* sung by a male voice trio, and then the toasts and speeches began. There were no fewer than sixteen toasts, the first five (The King, The Queen, Princess Victoria and the rest of the Royal Family, the Army and Navy, and his Majesty's Ministers) each followed by an appropriate song by the vocalists – two National Anthems, *When o'er the Hills* for the Princess, *Rule Britannia* for the armed forces, and *England, Europe's Glory* for the government.

Then Hale proposed Brougham's toast, referring not only to how "Lord Brougham directed all the powers of his mighty mind to the promotion of the people's happiness—(applause)—and they all knew that he especially sought their improvement through the means of education" but also to the crucial help he had given in overcoming difficulties the City of London School Act had encountered in parliament: "On every occasion Lord Brougham proved himself the friend of education, and on that occasion his powerful and successful exertions in their cause were well known to him (the Chairman) and those with whom he acted, in promoting the cause which was now so happily crowned with success.[21] The toast was drunk with immense applause, loud and long-continued. When the applause had in some degree subsided, Lord Brougham rose, and said he begged leave to return his grateful and respectful thanks for the very kind manner in which his health had been drunk."

This he did at very considerable length. He looked back to the foundation of London University ten years earlier, regretting that despite successful fundraising, "immense

Halls, Professors of the greatest talents and acquirement, and the most costly and beautiful apparatus for teaching every science" it was a failure: "general literature and science did not attract the numbers, that every man who knew the complaints which had been made for want of a University expected. —(Hear, hear.)" He offered two reasons for this: "one was, that he rather thought his fellow citizens of London were not in the habit of sending their sons to any University; and some of them preferred sending one son to Oxford or Cambridge at cost of 200*l*. or 300*l*. a-year, when for one-fourth of the sum they might educate four or five in London with the unspeakable advantage of having them brought up under their parents' roof, at the same time that they were receiving the best education. [...] The second cause of the partial failure of the London University he thought was its distance from the City.

He had reason to know that the citizens in that part of the metropolis where they then were would send their sons in greater numbers than those at the other end, but for the distance.

That brought him to the subject of the day - the new School. It stood on different grounds from the London University—there was rivalship; one gave a larger education, the other was more limited; but they had one common object—domestic tuition and public education; and he entertained the most sanguine expectations from the admirable institution founded that day.—(Hear, hear.) Both institutions stood on the same grand principle that they were open to all classes—to all religions. —(Great applause.) There were no tests.—(Applause.) Any man who in this country in the year 1835, would require a test as a qualification to receive education, would be considered much more fit for another institution of which this City possesses more than one. —(Applause and laughter.) To found a test to exclude from education—from office—from any secular advantage — because one person worships God in a manner differently from another, was not dreamt of in this institution.—(Hear, hear.) All the blessings of instruction were open to all—Dissenters of every shade—Protestant and Catholic —Jew and Gentile—all were admitted to the same advantages: religious instruction would be imparted under the eye of their parents—in the bosom of their families; and by the pastors approved by their parents. There were some things repeated often, and which it was necessary to repeat often: it had been said a thousand times, but it was forgotten a thousand and one times, that those who say there should be no creed taught - no exclusion on account of religion, so far from excluding religion from education, or holding it light, really held it in the highest reverence:— the proof of which was, that they would not allow it to be made matter of compromise: it was far too high in their estimation to be made a matter of bargain; and for that reason they held that no test should ever be admitted—that civil right should never be made to depend on religious creed.— (Great applause.) [Brougham then cited as examples of the rapid strides liberality had made in the last two years the appointments of Sheriffs who were Roman Catholic (Raphael) and Jewish (Salomons).] Before he sat down he would say one word more in respect of the school, the institution of which they had met that day to celebrate, and he hoped and trusted, nay, he felt confident, that the rules, established regarding the choice of professors and masters, vested as it was by the Act of Parliament in the

Professors of the London University, and of the King's College, were such as would be found equally beneficial and useful.—(Hear.) The regulations also by which the Institution was to be generally directed would, he was confident, be attended with success, not only as to the course of study to be adopted, and the manner in which it was to be applied, but also as to the terms upon which it was to be bestowed, which were neither so low as to give the teacher inadequate interest in keeping his class-room filled, [...] or so great, as to inconvenience the citizens of London, even in the more humble grade; and he (Lord Brougham) trusted that such medium, in that respect, had been struck as, keeping pace with the rules by which the schools were to be governed, would result in the prosperity of one of the most useful, and, as regarded the citizens of London, one of the most creditable institutions that had ever been founded. —(Loud cheers.) [...] He begged pardon for occupying their time so long—(" No, no,"); —but he was unwilling to waste it in the delivery of a complimentary speech, and he had therefore merely alluded to what occurred to him, which was of practical nature—and he would therefore conclude by drinking the healths of those present, thanking them for the honour they had conferred upon him.—(Loud cheers.)

The toasts continued: to Hale (proposed by Brougham), to "The Aldermen of the City of London who are present" (perhaps a dig at the Lord Mayor, whose absence was noted), to the four Members of Parliament returned by the City, to the Recorder of London, to Dr Birkbeck, to the Sheriffs, to the Professors of the London University, and of King's College. Each toast had its response (three in the case of the MPs, and both Sheriffs); two of these were of particular interest.

Dr George Birkbeck reminded the company that

Dr George Birkbeck, detail from oil painting by Samuel Lane *c*.1836.

The City, in former times, had not been wholly unmindful of the cause of education. The formation of a college in their immediate neighbourhood had been provided for[22]; it was established by mercantile munificence; but now its very existence was almost unknown. It was almost impossible to say in what remote or inaccessible corner it had existed. [...] To him the [day's] event was peculiarly consolatory, for when he had heretofore endeavoured to raise the humbler classes by means of education, it had been charged against him, that such a proceeding was dangerous to the class above them:- if, indeed, that were dangerous, how could that danger be better met than supplying the means to the next class of making corresponding advances? Here that class would have the opportunity of getting a step higher. There would now be afforded to the citizens of London means of procuring education, liberal education, at no great distance from their homes, for their sons—education at what he doubted not must become a flourishing institution—and education that would not merely embrace the languages, but the sciences, and in the hall of which he hoped the parents, as well as the pupils, would assemble to participate in the experimental instruction and lectures that would there take place.—(Hear.) There would, in fact, be hereby established a City College for the dissemination of the highest intellectual knowledge. He looked forward with confidence to the result, and he doubted not that sanguine expectations would be realized.— (Cheers.)

Mr Sheriff David Salomons struck a more personal note:

Sir David Salomons.

> The laws had proscribed him[23], but he was still worse proscribed by the prejudices of the community—prejudices confirmed, perhaps, by the education that had prevailed.—(Hear, hear.) Then how grateful must he feel for the peculiar occasion on which they had assembled—to celebrate the commencement of an establishment that would tend to remove unjust prejudices by advancing knowledge.— (Hear.) If within the last few years education had done so much in our own and other countries, what glorious results might not they expect from the further extension of that power and from the bringing of it to their own doors. Education had already produced the best of all possible results;— through it the middle classes had been enabled not only to ask for, but to obtain a share in the representation.—(Hear.) He believed that the noblest work in which man could be engaged, was the promotion of education. Its objects and triumph would appear in the drawing together of all mankind, and in the promotion of good works and general friendship. As education would have this effect, he was gratified in having shared in the glory of assembling on such an occasion.—(Hear, hear.)

Finally Hale drew the evening to a close. "He mentioned that the site of the ground had produced 300*l*. a year—that profit the Corporation had abandoned; then the property left by Carpenter produced 900*l*. year—that would be appropriated to the support of the School; and, beside all, the Corporation would defray the expenses of the building, the cost of which would be 13,000*l*. or 14,000*l*. over. He then proposed "Prosperity to the City of London School—(Cheers.)"

Lord Mayor Winchester had been firmly rebuffed. His term of office ended soon after, with the unique distinction that the motion proposing the customary vote of thanks was defeated, and a detailed vote of censure proposed by Richard Taylor passed instead. He left City life and died in 1838 in a lunatic asylum, one week after being declared bankrupt.[24]

Among the documents deposited under the foundation stone was a *Memoir of the Life and Times of John Carpenter* compiled by Thomas Brewer. A young clerk in the Town Clerk's office, Brewer had been selected by Hale to assist in the preparation of the parliamentary Bill, which had included a fruitless search for Carpenter's will.[25] The interest generated by this induced him to continue to collect information about Carpenter and write his memoir. Writing of this in 1856, in the Preface to a revised and expanded version, Brewer says "Brief and imperfect as was the account then given, its production was attended with many difficulties and much laborious research, partly from the object of inquiry being separated from our own times by the wide interval of four centuries, and partly from the peculiar character of the materials available for such a purpose."

27

Brewer continued to be Hale's assistant and was clerk to the Committee, writing lucid minutes in an elegant hand which it is a pleasure to read. His efforts were recognised by the Committee, who ordered that the *Memoir* should be printed and distributed to all Common Councilmen, and by the Court of Common Council who on 2nd November awarded him a gratuity of 100 guineas for "assiduous attendance" and "zeal and ability displayed by him in digesting the proceedings of the Committee and the very great pains and labour bestowed by him upon its business out of office-hours."

After the excitements of laying the first stone (the costs of which, excluding the dinner, amounted to £533) the building work proceeded quietly for the next six months. A subcommittee (Chairman plus eight members, four changing each month) was appointed to monitor and report on progress. The local inhabitants pressed for the speedy reinstatement of their water supply, but were told this could not be done before the hoarding around the site was removed. Bunning made minor additions to his design, and discovered that an inferior quality of lead was being used to form the roof. The subcommittee inspected the roof, and instructed Samuel Grimsdell (who professed ignorance of this defect) to replace it with the weight of lead specified in his contract.

A protracted problem arose with Mr J.A.Creaton who had agreed with the Town Clerk in 1835 to sell the building materials from the old Honey Lane Market. The City's Clerk of Works reported that he had not known of this arrangement, and that no monies had been received. The City Solicitor advised that Creaton's surety (the lease of a property in Lambeth belonging to his aunt) could not be used to recover this debt, and the matter was handed over to the Chamberlain, who called Creaton to account. In July Creaton wrote to say that he had sustained such heavy losses that the best he could offer was a settlement of five shillings in the pound, which on the City Solicitor's advice was accepted. A member of the Committee, Alderman Sir Chapman Marshall, clearly thought that the Committee had some responsibility to bear, and gave notice of this Motion:

> That in consequence of the Committee of the City of London School having neglected to make any demand upon Mr Creaton for the payment of the Old Materials sold by him, amounting to the net sum of £568.2.2, from the Month of June 1835 when then said sale took place until after the period of Mr Creaton being taken to Whitecross Street Prison in the Month of May last, - this Committee, desirous that no loss should accrue to the Corporation by such neglect, do each severally subscribe the Sum of Ten guineas to make good the loss occasioned thereby.

But as the Alderman was not present at the next meeting to propose his Motion this was ordered "to be expunged from the Minutes" (where of course it still remains). In June Grimsdell stated that he expected the building to be completed within the next three months. This prompted the Committee to turn its attention to writing the school's Rules and Regulations, which under Clause V of the Act should have been done within 12 months of the passing of the Act. Drafting these occupied the subcommittee for three meetings. They provide a more detailed framework for the way the School was to operate, summarised as follows.

Admission to be for sons of Freemen or City Householders, between the ages of 8 and 12 years, who must already have acquired some knowledge of Reading, Writing and Arithmetic. The four Scholars to be educated boarded and clothed at the expense of the Corporation should be selected from those Pupils in the School who are between 11 and 13 years of age and were under the age of 10 years on admission. There should be an annual public examination of the Pupils at which the first Boy in general proficiency and good conduct should be elected to the next vacancy on the Foundation, and other Prizes distributed according to merit.

The hours of attendance to be: in the morning throughout the year from 9 o'clock until 1, and in the afternoon from 3 to 5 from the 1st of March to the 1st of November and from 2 to 4 from the 1st of November to the 1st of March. The authorised version of the Holy Bible to be used and taught in the School and on every Morning and Evening Prayers to be read therein.

The School fee to be £8 per annum, excluding printed Books, Drawing Materials and Mathematical Instruments which are to be furnished at cost. Payments to be made quarterly in advance.

The Head Master should submit to the Committee for their approval the plan of Education, upon the principles already agreed upon, and from time to time confer with them as they may think necessary on all matters tending to the advantage of the Institution. He should keep a correct Register of the names of the Pupils, the dates of their entry and leaving the School, and of their attendance, progress in learning and conduct, in such manner as the Committee shall approve. The Head Master should be competent to suspend a Pupil for flagrant misconduct, such suspension to be reported to the Committee who, if they see fit, may expel the offending Pupil.

The Head Master should reside in the House provided for that purpose, and have the care and superintendence of the Scholars to be placed on the Foundation, but should not be allowed to take any other Boarders. The Scholars should be supplied with two Suits of Black Clothes annually, and other necessary articles to be provided from time to time under the direction of the Committee. The Head Master should be allowed a salary of £500 per annum, and a further allowance, for boarding the Scholars at a rate of £30 per annum each, to include washing and mending.

In addition to the First and Second Masters there should be not less than four assistant Masters, who should be subject to annual Election. No permanent Master of the School should take any private Pupils or give private tuition directly or indirectly to any of the Scholars of the Institution without the consent of the Committee, or perform any duty or undertake any occupation or employment which shall in any way interfere with their attendance and duties in the School.

A Clerk or Secretary should be appointed at a salary of £150 per annum. A comprehensive list of his duties is set out, running to four pages.

When the full Committee discussed the proposed Rules and Regulations on 26 July they made a few changes, the most important of which was that the Head Master's remuneration was to be £400 per annum with an allowance of £1 per annum for every Pupil in the School above the number of 200. These Rules and Regulations were approved by the Court of Common Council on 28 July.

On 7 September the Committee proceeded to the election of a person to fill the Office of Secretary. "The humble Petition of Thomas Brewer of the Town Clerk's Office praying to be appointed to that Situation was presented and read. And no other candidate appearing [hardly surprising, as the position had not been publicly advertised], it was Resolved unanimously that the said Thomas Brewer be and he is hereby appointed to the Office of Secretary during the pleasure of this Committee [...]." This just made official the *de facto* position of Brewer as Hale's principal assistant. Thomas Brewer occupied the post of Secretary (equivalent to Bursar in many schools) until his death 34 years later.

Last, and perhaps for some of them also least, in July 1836 the subcommittee had also resolved "that it be recommended to the Grand Committee to take the necessary steps for the election of a First Master." How this was done will be told in Chapter 3.

2

Giles before CLS

William Giles (1784-1853) married Sophia Allen (1787-1841) in January 1808. Both came from large families that were long-established in the area of North Somerset known as The Levels. They moved into Southwick House in the parish of Mark, about 3 miles from the coast at Burnham-on-Sea and 9 miles from the market town of Bridgwater.[1] The house, with its estate worth about £500 a year, had at various times in the previous century belonged to members of both their families, and now has a Grade II listing. Here on 26 October 1808 their first child John Allen Giles was born, in the same room as his father 24 years before. Although Allen was his mother's maiden name he was known in the family as Allen rather than John, perhaps to distinguish him from the many other Johns in their extended family. In this chapter we shall follow the same practice, and refer to him as Allen.

Allen was the first of sixteen children born to William and Sophia, the last in 1832, of whom four died in infancy. His memoirs[2] describe a happy country childhood, though even rural Somerset then had considerable worries that a French invasion was imminent, and caricatures of 'Buonaparte' decorated his nursery. When he was five a National School was built next to Mark church, and it was here that he learnt to read and write, tracing his letters in a sand tray. Then for two years he stayed with his grandmother in Bridgwater, attending Miss Millington's school (which seems to have left little impression). At the end of 1815 it was decided that Allen should board at Mr Crosswell's school in North Petherton, three miles south of Bridgwater. His entry there was delayed for three months by his recovery from a serious accident in which one foot and leg were badly scalded, but once he got to North Petherton he made rapid progress under "our dear old master Mr Crosswell". A letter to his parents, archly written when he had just turned eight, bears this out[3]:

Honoured Parents
Permit me to inform you that our vacation will commence on Thursday the 12th December, when I anticipate the happiness of seeing you and all friends well, particularly my uncle and aunt Allen, to whom be pleased to present my duty.

I now take the pleasure of informing you that the Miss Woodlands invited me to their house, about a fortnight since, where I spent three or four days very pleasantly, but as I was returning to school in a coach, with the glass down, I caught a cold and have consequently had a swollen neck.

Please to give my love to my brothers sisters and cousins. You will please to accept this letter as a specimen of my improvement in writing; when I have the pleasure of being with you at Christmas I trust my general progress in learning will merit your approbation. Mr and Mrs Crosswell desire their respectful compliments.

I am, Honoured Parents,
Your very dutiful son

J.A.Giles
North Petherton, 30th November 1816

At Petherton Allen also developed his love of reading and proficiency in arithmetic. He and his school fellows once paid tuppence each to see a company of strolling players perform *The Castle Spectre*[4] by M.G.Lewis, in a barn fitted up as a theatre. "From the moment that the curtain was raised I was in fairy land, and although I could have a very slight knowledge of the plot, no play since has ever interested me so much." The benign Mr Crosswell had his severe side too. Allen recounts that he was caned on nine occasions, and was once shocked when, on returning to school after a visit, "my ears were overwhelmed with shrieks of the most intense agony from one undergoing flagellation." The master in this case "wielded his weapon without regard to circular arcs or any other mathematical consideration, and aimed his blows wherever they were most telling, setting aside every thought of following Nature or of the place where she intended castigation to be applied." The victim's offence was to have designated his master as "Jemmy Longlegs!"

On returning home from school in December 1817 Allen saw waggons full of furniture being removed from Southwick. His father had decided to sell the house and estate, and to move the family to Frome, some 30 miles east of Mark over the Mendip hills, where he had spent some time in his youth. The town, with a population then of some 12000, had prospered since the 15th century as a centre for making woollen cloth. William Giles invested in what had hitherto been the profitable business of carrier[5] in the town, but knew little about it and so "ten thousand pounds was lost at the rate of £500 per year for 20 years",[6] and the family's comfortable circumstances were considerably diminished.

William had rented the Old Rectory from the Marquis of Bath (the lay rector). The house was at least two hundred years old; a garden, full of excellent fruit trees and commanding a beautiful view over the town and surrounding scenery, was the family's favourite spot. Shortly after William, Sophia and their five children moved in their elder daughter Maria died, aged four. Three years later their third son, eight year old Edmund, drowned in a skating accident, which was witnessed by Allen, who described him as "a hero from the cradle and too much so to admit of a long life". This tragedy was "looked upon as one of exceptional severity and months passed before our serenity was restored."[7]

During 1818 Allen attended a local school run by the Revd Mr Saunders, but learnt little, becoming bored and troublesome: "Marbles [...] were my chief occupation. I used to shirk all my lessons, made one last me a week, and if I had to write any thing, I copied it all out of another boy's book. When caned I laughed in the master's face, and when kept in took to my heels."[8] Towards the end of the year his worried parents must have welcomed a letter from the Revd Evan Davis (husband of one of Sophia's cousins) which offered a solution. Mr Davis explained that he had recently been appointed Master of the Grammar School in Dorchester,[9] and gave assurances that he would take great pains to promote Allen's educational welfare should this

Dorchester Grammar School.

task be entrusted to him. The result was that in January 1819 Allen was sent to Dorchester, where he was welcomed by the Master and his wife and placed to sleep in the long dormitory over the school room, where conditions were spartan. There were about sixteen other boys, including three of Allen's cousins whose parents had responded similarly to Mr Davis's invitation. The boys were often left unsupervised, with unsurprising consequences:

> Within a day or two of my arrival they asked whether I had ever been roasted. Of course I stated positively that such a thing had never happened to me. They replied that it was a process most necessary to my well-being, and they would see to it that very evening. They held me stretched out horizontally before the large fire in the school room, and pulling away my trowsers so as to leave a space between them and my body, they brought me still closer to the fire until the trowsers became most awfully hot, and then tightening them against my body, they almost burnt me alive, but as I had the good sense to take it all pleasantly and with good humour, I noticed that they did not put in force this unwritten law of education with all the severity of which the institution is capable.[10]

Although Allen enjoyed exploring the many delightful walks and objects of interest in the neighbourhood of Dorchester, the educational standards at the school were very poor. The Master was lazy and never made an appearance at the pre-breakfast lessons, leaving these in the incapable hands of the Usher, Mr Yealden, who "knew nothing of Greek and little of Latin". After six months Allen returned home for the mid-year break. His parents were uneasy about his lack of progress, and about three months later came to spend a couple of days with Mr and Mrs Davis to see the school for themselves. Then in November Allen had an acute attack of rheumatic fever. After a visit from the doctor he was carried from the dormitory to a private bedroom, where he lay for six weeks unable to move hand or foot. His friend Stephen Bryer "not more remarkable for benevolence than the rest of us" often sat by his bedside, read to him and gave him food when he had no strength to do anything for himself. When he began to improve his father arranged for him to be brought home to Frome, where he continued his recovery. His parents used his illness as a reason for not sending him back to Dorchester, but then had to face the question of what to do with him.

Luckily there was an obvious solution close by. Mr William M. H. Williams, a graduate of Trinity College Dublin, had recently moved to Frome and had been appointed Master of King Edward VI's Grammar School there. This sounded grander than it was. The school, founded in the 1550s and built next to the vicarage, had been closed for some years since the departure of its eccentric former Master,[11] and its endowment was only £5 a year. So Mr Williams depended on his scholars' fees, which were 10 guineas a year for day pupils.

Allen started at Frome Grammar School in January 1820, following his younger brother William who had already been there for six months. There were then only five pupils in total, so Allen got plenty of attention. Mr Williams proved to be a skilful and energetic teacher. "I learnt as much as I could have learnt at the best schools in the world, and more than I should have learnt at nine tenths of all the other schools."[12] The school day started at 6 a.m., with lessons until 9 when there was an hour's breakfast break, followed by further lessons until the boys dispersed for dinner at 1 p.m. They continued their studies from 3 to 5. "Thus eight hours having been occupied in learning, it might be supposed that the evening might be our own: but No! *non progredi est regredi* was the message of our master. We had to prepare our lesson for the next day, and on Wednesday and Saturday afternoons, being half-holidays, we had an increase of work to do."[13]

Mr Williams was successful in building up the school numbers, which during Allen's four years there grew to seventy. But as the school grew so did the strain on the Master, and his impatience: he made himself both dreaded and at the same time ridiculous to the boys.

> Mr Williams was one day very angry with every one, and at last coming on John Fussell he remembered some flagrant deed with which he accused him, and said he should cane him. For this purpose he took up his cane, which had been lying *in terrorem* on the desk, and smote the culprit a smart blow across the shoulders: the boy was as big as the man, and he seized the cane in his left hand and the master's collar in his right: a struggle ensued, and the two rolled over one another on the floor. "Boys! boys!" cried Mr W. "will you suffer your master to be treated thus?" Of course every boy in the school stood up: two only left their seats, of whom I was not one, but the brother Ernest Fussell was the other. "You shall pay for this, Sir!" said the master. "I live too near the wood to be frightened by the owl," said the rebellious pupil. At last order was restored, but the school surged and swelled like the sea after a storm, until the hour of dismissal came.[14]

Writing over 60 years later Allen recalled the effect of various national events on his schoolboy life. The military spirit caused by the Napoleonic threat was not yet extinct, and it was thought that boys at school should be drilled in order to make them perfect members of society. "A drill serjeant was appointed, a thorough disciplinarian, but more of a tactician than a grammarian. When an erroneous movement was effected, the word of command was uttered "As you are!" which of course fixed the whole line in the erroneous position which they had taken up. An explanation was necessary: "When I says As you are, I mean its you was!" caused less explanation than laughter."[15]

Frome was not exempt from the Luddite riots, protesting against the introduction of machinery and the consequent loss of jobs, which had started in Nottingham in 1811 and spread to other manufacturing districts. In Frome the weaving mills were the target. Allen's father, who had the reputation of being impartial and just, was often asked to support the cause of order. On one occasion it was known that a sizeable mob was planning to attack the mills, carry away the new looms and burn them in the market place. William Giles arranged for 40 to 50 well-disposed and able-bodied men to be sworn as special constables, and supplied some with fire-arms. They hid themselves in the inner courtyard of the Wheatsheaf Inn, which was at the narrowest part of the road leading to the market place. The rioters passed in a long train in the middle of which were about twenty men carrying five looms. When they reached the inn Mr Giles's constables rushed out, cutting them off from those ahead and behind, and forcing them into the inn yard. Here muskets were presented through the windows of the upper storey and the Riot Act was read. The rioters gave in and the looms were saved, though months passed before good feeling was restored.[16]

Rather more surprising were the disturbances caused by the trial of Queen Caroline, the estranged wife of George IV, which took eleven weeks in the autumn of 1820. This was not actually a trial, but parliamentary proceedings aimed at passing a Bill of Pains and Penalties which would have deprived Caroline of the title of Queen and dissolved her marriage without the necessity of proof as required in a court of law. Many felt that the Queen had been badly treated, but William Giles, influenced by the Tory view that "the King can do no wrong", "took the side of tyranny against – I will not say innocence, but mercy and good feeling, or whatever other sentiment a man might have who disapproved of the shameful oppression exercised by George IV against his unhappy wife."[17]

The Queen's case was ably put by Henry Brougham, who became famous as a result. The Bill was passed by the Lords, but with such a small majority that the Prime Minister Lord Liverpool withdrew it rather than face defeat in the Commons. There was national satisfaction at what was seen as the Queen's acquittal, taking the form of illumination of houses. At first William refused to join in, acquiring a dozen sabres from the yeomanry cavalry depot and engaging twelve men to guard his unlit house. A deputation of principal inhabitants then persuaded him to give way a little to pacify the mob, and two farthing candles were placed in each window. The grudging scale of William's rejoicing was noted and commented on, but at least there was no violence, and Allen enjoyed himself "swaggering about with a cudgel almost as big as myself."[18]

In his memoirs Allen pays tribute to his father for "the anxiety which he showed that his children should know what was going on in the world around us". He took them to see every exhibition that was brought to the town: these included Esquimaux Indians, whose technique of throwing javelins the local boys then imitated, a Mermaid (perceived to be "a forgery by the notorious Barnum" made by sewing the head of a monkey to the body of a fish[19] and a collection of automata. A memorable excursion was to William Beckford's extraordinary Fonthill Abbey about 30 miles away in Wiltshire.[20] This Gothic fantasy, "the most interesting place it has ever been my lot to see", had a great central tower whose height of 90 m was exceeded by only St Paul's, Salisbury and Norwich Cathedrals. "After five ascents I knew pretty well the construction of this tower, and was surprised to see that its exterior wall, rising to such a height, was only 7 or 8 inches thick". Allen's concern was justified, for on 21 December 1825 the tower collapsed.

Feejee mermaid, as exhibited in London in 1822.

As Allen progressed in his studies his father formed the idea that he should go to Oxford, but it was generally agreed by his friends that the increasingly irascible Master of Frome Grammar School was not the person to provide the necessary final tuition. The Charterhouse[21] school in London had gained a good reputation since Dr John Russell[22] had become headmaster in 1810, and it was decided Allen should study there. In June 1824, after a thirteen hour journey, Allen and his father arrived in London by the Frome coach, and lodged at the Castle and Falcon Inn in Aldersgate Street – Allen remembered that for supper the first evening they had

Fonthill Abbey, Wiltshire, view to the west and north fronts from John Rutter's *Delineations of Fonthill*, 1823, engraved by T. Higham.

cold meat and lobster. After two days to see the sights and begin to get accustomed to London life (this was his first visit), Allen was deposited by his father at the Charterhouse.

> On the day after my arrival, at 7 o'clock in the morning, I followed the other boys into the Lower School, which was used as a place for assembling on all public occasions. Four hundred and seventy five boys were here met together under the command of eight majestic dignitaries in their caps and gowns, forming to my eyes a most imposing spectacle. The first thing done was to call the roll of the boys' names, and each as called answered *Adsum*! [...] When the roll was ended, all the newcomers were summoned before the masters who were seated behind a long high desk, like a pulpit, under a canopy in the middle of one side of the room. We were asked our ages, names in full, whether we had had meazles, Whooping cough &c. and whether we had been vaccinated or not. I was then placed at the bottom of the 12th form, which was the lowest in the school, and was told that I must work my way up. I was therefore quite satisfied, when evening came, to find myself already in the fifth form.[23]

Charterhouse school room, wood engraving.

In Allen's time the Lower School had nine forms, and the Upper School three. Each of the nine lower forms was divided into two, and all eighteen classes were taken simultaneously in the Lower School hall. Within a week Allen was at the top of the Lower School, the fourth form. To gain further promotion he had first to spend three weeks as monitor to one of the three lowest forms, and then compete with all the others in the fourth form in writing Latin verse, without the use of a dictionary or any other book. The thorough grounding Allen had received in Frome led to promotion to the Upper School, where after a further three weeks as a lower school monitor he came under the eye of Dr Russell. When Russell found that Allen's classical reading went far beyond that of his classmates he placed him in the highest class, the first form. All this was achieved in the two months before the school broke up for the August holiday, for which Allen returned home to Frome.

During this holiday his father noticed in a newspaper advertisement that a Somersetshire scholarship at Corpus Christi College, Oxford, would be filled in November. When the new Charterhouse term started in September Dr Russell agreed that Allen should compete for this scholarship, and gave him personal tuition, alongside William Lloyd Birkbeck,

> son of the well known Dr Birkbeck, who had as great a desire to become a good classical scholar as I had. He used to come to the room where I slept, and call me up before 5 o'clock in the morning, until the other boys who slept there shied their boots at him for disturbing them so early. He then came no more, and I woke

as well as I was able. It would be difficult for anyone to work harder than I did at this time, and the consequence was that when I went to Oxford, I had read so large a quantity of Latin, Greek and History, that my progress towards obtaining a degree with honours was very much accelerated.[24]

Allen joined his father in Oxford on Friday 19th November, staying in the Angel Inn in the High Street. The next day he presented himself at Corpus Christi College

Corpus Christi College, Oxford, drawing by Vernon Howe Bailey, 1902.

as a candidate for the scholarship. On the following Monday the examination began in the college hall, where a thesis was given out by one of the five or six examiners, about which the candidates[25] wrote without any help from books. Each candidate left off whenever he pleased, and could go out of the hall, but without the right of returning. Each sitting lasted three hours in the morning and three in the afternoon, with *viva voce* examinations in Latin, Greek and History in the evening. This continued throughout the week.

> On Friday morning, not Saturday as I expected, we were all standing in the Quadrangle when the President's servant came out of the chapel, where the Fellows were assembled, having in his hand a paper on which my name was inscribed. I went into the chapel and was informed that I was the successful candidate. My father was of course much pleased; and in the afternoon the Rev. Edward Greswell, Tutor of the College, took me, dressed in cap and gown, to undergo the usual process of matriculation before Dr Jenkins, Master of Balliol, the Vice-chancellor. On my way Mr Greswell said to me "Mr Giles, it is very excusable because you are not aware of it: you have put on your cap with the back side in front!". The next morning I returned to the Charterhouse, and my father to Frome, both well satisfied with our week's campaign.[26]

After a well-deserved Christmas break Allen started his Oxford studies in January 1825, aged sixteen. He was pleased to have rooms of his own in College, a sitting room and a small bedroom where "I could lie in bed and touch both the side walls", and soon settled into a daily routine.

At half-past seven his scout or bedmaker Taylor ("an old man between 60 and 70 years of age") woke him, swept his sitting room, lit the fire and placed the kettle on it, laid a cloth with bread and butter, then moved on to do likewise for his other men. At nine Allen went to the chapel, wearing a gown or, on Sundays and Saints days, a surplice. After chapel came breakfast and the distribution of any letters received, followed by one or two lectures, each lasting an hour. Lectures were given by Fellows of the college, either in the Hall or in their own rooms. "At 1 o'clock we might have lunch brought to us from the buttery, but I never indulged in lunch, but read on with my private studies until 2 o'clock, after which hour I took a walk of 2 or 3 miles into the country, a practice which I always kept up, in company generally with a friend who was also studying for his examination."[27] Dinner at Corpus was at 5 o'clock, when the junior scholar (for two years this was Allen) read the graces before and after dinner. After dinner at 7 p.m. was chapel again (one attendance per day was obligatory, with two on Sundays). There was a common room where Scholars and Exhibitioners assembled after dinner, but Allen preferred to return to his own domain to resume his reading. He says "As I intended still to be a 'sweater', as I had been at Charterhouse, I could not afford to lose so much time, and perhaps disqualify myself by drinking too much wine from continuing my studies until a reasonable hour at night." But sometimes he studied in the company of a like-minded friend, "winding up with a tern (pint and a half) of Magdalen College beer", so perhaps life was not quite as austere as his account suggests.

Allen's 'sweating' at school had given him a head start in Latin and Greek, and he clearly did not think that Mr Greswell's tutorials added much to that: "we sometimes picked up a grain or two in the chaff, but sometimes the grain was of the smallest size." The mathematical tuition was even worse:

Diagram from Robertson's *Properties of the Conic Sections.*

The only other mathematical student besides myself was Nowell, the son of old Admiral Nowell of Iffley. Mr Greswell signified his intention to teach us Conic Sections, and by his command we procured copies of a work on that subject by Robertson, a volume of 4 or 5 hundred pages arranged in the shape of geometrical problems, like those of Euclid, and some of these problems extended to four or five pages. The manner of dealing with this volume was as follows. We meet, Nowell, the tutor, and myself. [...] I read the first problem out of the strange volume. The statement of the thesis [problem] is intelligible, but the argument [solution], read without a pause, is soon lost in obscurity: I read to the end without a word of remark. "Mr Nowell, will you please to read the next problem!" This too is done, and at the end of an hour we break up the sitting without having more than one clear idea

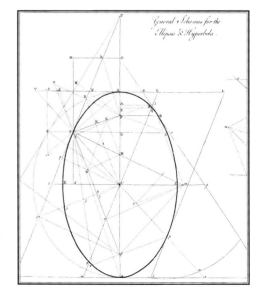

on the subject of mathematics; and that single idea was that I must not look to the college tutors for any assistance in mathematics, as I had already come to the conclusion that they would afford me none in classics.[28]

Fortunately in summer 1827 Allen was able to spend several weeks at Blakeney Rectory near Cley in Norfolk, where the Rector, Joseph Cotterill, whose first wife had been Allen's godmother, helped him with his mathematics. Allen in return helped Joseph Cotterill's son Henry[29] with his classics. "Mr Cotterill gave me every day a lesson in Fluxions and Differential Calculus, which I had previously looked at in utter despair of knowing the meaning of the words, much less the drift of those sciences."

With the mathematical blockage removed Allen's studies proceeded smoothly, and in April 1828 his final examinations began. First came five days of classics, including a *viva voce* day in public ("they kept me from ten o'clock to a quarter to six with only half an hour's interval"), attended by Dr Bridges, President of Corpus, the two college tutors, five or six other Masters of Arts, and about thirty fellow students. "The gallery was crowded to excess, so that many Queen's men, who were my friends, were unable to get in." Fifteen days later came a similar quantity of mathematics examinations. On 24 May he heard, rather to his and his father's surprise, that he had been placed in the First Class for mathematics; he took his B.A. degree that day, though the classics result was not announced until the start of June, when as expected he was again in the First Class. So Allen gained his double first and his B.A. four months before his twentieth birthday.

After relaxing in Somerset for the Long Vacation Allen returned to Oxford in October. Initially he spent his time in reading plus a little private coaching. The Corpus dons, in particular Benjamin Thorpe, urged him enter his name at the Temple and to read for the bar. For this payments had to be made: his father and two uncles responded to requests, his father giving £10 and each uncle loaning £15, and Thorpe put into his hands a £50 note, telling him to repay it when he could. Thus funded, on 21 November Allen went to the Middle Temple and entered his name. In London he stayed at first with family friends, Mr and Mrs William Middleton, in Doughty Street, and later at the Grecian Coffee House in Devereux Court near the Temple.[30] This pattern of studying law and coaching half a dozen pupils in Oxford with periodic visits to take the necessary dinners in the Temple continued until the end of the academic year. Then in June Allen and two friends went to Boulogne, where Allen stayed until the Oxford term started in October.

On 26 October 1829 Allen held a supper party in his rooms to mark his 21st birthday: "Some of my guests came without invitation. They made a tremendous row, and I got through it as well as I could." Celebrations were cut short by news from Frome of the death that day of his uncle Robert Giles, father of Allen's younger cousin Douglas who was then an Exhibitioner at Corpus. Douglas went home at once, and Allen obeyed his father's instruction to "put on Black Clothes immediately." Before Christmas Allen completed his first book, *Scriptores Graeci Romanes*, Vol 1, and gained permission to dedicate it to Professor Thomas Gaisford, later Dean of Christ

Church; this was published in 1831. Over the next 50 years 178 more books were to follow!

In December Allen wrote to the Secretary of the newly founded King's College, London:

> I take the liberty of writing to enquire when and to whom applications should be made for Tutorships or Professorships in King's College. From the public journals I learn that the building is in progress, and that, within a reasonable time, the Institution will be opened. I would be obliged if you would honour me with any information on the subject, and in particular should be glad to know what Tutorships or Professorships are to be disposed of, who has the disposal of them, what qualifications and testimonials will be required, and whether any fixed emoluments will be attached to each office.[31]

He also decided to compete for the Vinerian Scholarship[32] which would fall vacant in February. This was to be filled by an election in which all Oxford Masters of Arts were entitled to vote, so after Christmas serious canvassing started. After some others had withdrawn there were three candidates, Giles, Watley of Queen's and Ormerod of Brasenose. Allen was disappointed that, except for the President and Edward Greswell, his college did little to support him; various friends at other colleges did what they could but, as Allen wrote to his father afterwards "As is usual in such cases, my best friend was myself, and if I had not canvassed with the utmost diligence I should not have got so many votes by twenty or thirty."[33] A late influx of Watley's supporters called for further exertions, and a little gamesmanship: by sending in one of his voters every five minutes Allen twice caused the deadline for voting to be extended, giving more time to round up more backers. These tactics worked, and he was elected with a majority of 18 (Giles 94, Watley 76, Ormerod 36). Although the Vinerian was worth only £30 a year, to hold it was considered a great advantage to any one going to the Bar.

During the 1830 Long Vacation Allen again went to Boulogne, but this time carried on to Paris, Dijon, Mont Blanc, Geneva and Lausanne (where news reached them of the overthrow of Charles X in Paris), eventually returning to Dover on 19 September. The account of this three-month trip occupies 16 entertaining pages of the printed *Diary and Memoirs.*

While continuing his law studies and dinners at the Temple Allen had not forgotten King's College, London, sending a reminder in February and going to London at the end of March to enquire in person. In his letter to his father of 26 May Allen says "If Mr Astell[34] will help me, I have a good chance of becoming Professor of Classical Literature at King's College."[35] On 10 November he received a letter from Mr Smith, Secretary to King's College, giving him the greatest hope that he would receive this appointment.

But he was not to be either a barrister or a professor. Over the Christmas holidays there were serious discussions with his father and mother, and a drastic decision was made, as set out in this letter of 2 January 1831 to John Middleton of Canonbury Square (brother of William Middleton):

> You will probably be surprized to hear what I have to communicate. I gave up residence in Oxford the last term and meant to go to London for the purpose of pursuing my studies for the Bar; but on coming into the country I found my father and mother so unwilling for me to do so, that I have at last acceded to their wish that I should give up the Law and enter the Church. I have determined to take a house at Bridgewater among my friends and keep a Grammar School for the present. So my father went down with me, and bought a very nice house on King's [*recte* King] Square, where I shall take up my residence on the 14th of this month. Will you kindly get back my testimonials from King's College, as I do not now wish to be appointed to that Institution. [...]

It is difficult to see why Mr and Mrs Giles took such a strong line on this: Allen's Vinerian scholarship clearly indicated his legal potential, and the King's College appointment seemed at last to be within his reach too. Ordination was "a calling for which he had no inclination and for which he was little suited."[36] His own religious views were distinctly sceptical: in 1835 he wrote "I would always read prayers rather than preach. To read prayers is to say something on the authority of those who wrote them, but when you preach, you speak your own ideas, and mine have always been very obscure on all religious subjects."[37] His friends and Oxford colleagues seem to have been equally puzzled. One wrote: "I was little prepared to hear that a plan of life deliberately formed, founded on early predilections and consciousness of requisite qualifications, would be hastily abandoned."[38] Perhaps William Giles, whose finances were by then straitened, reckoned that a Fellowship at Corpus (almost certain to follow Allen's ordination in view of his academic successes) was a better financial bet than the uncertainties of the bar. But his immediate outlay in purchasing one of the grand Georgian houses of King Square must have been considerable.

Allen refers to having a few private pupils in King Square, but apart from that nothing much seems to have come of the idea of a Grammar School. He took his M.A. degree in 1831 and also had to prepare for holy orders; he was ordained as deacon on 12 December 1832 by Dr George Murray, Bishop of Rochester, acting for the Bishop of Oxford, though neither this nor his later ordination as priest is mentioned in his *Diary and Memoirs*. On 16 November 1832, anticipating his ordination, he was appointed a Probationary Fellow of Corpus Christi College Oxford; the probationary period at Corpus Christi was two years, so he was never admitted as a full Fellow.[39]

At a party early in 1833 he met Mr and Mrs John Dalley[40] and Mrs Dalley's sister Miss Anna Dickinson[41] "with whom I fraternized, and very soon made up my mind that she would make a much more satisfactory housekeeper than Mrs Aldrit, although the last named lady is very good, amiable and respectable. I did not let many days pass before I rode on my good old horse Silver-tail to Huntworth Cottage [where the Dalleys and Anna lived] in the parish of Petherton about two miles from Bridgewater on the Taunton Road. One visit led to another, and in about a fortnight we were engaged to be married."[42] Allen and Anna were married in Bridgwater Church on Tuesday 17 December 1833, and then set off for Oxford. On Christmas Day they dined with Dr Bridges, President of Corpus. But at that time Fellows had to be unmarried, and so although Allen's relationship with the College remained cordial he had to surrender his Fellowship.

At the start of 1834 Allen began looking for "some public appointment, either literary or scholastic". He soon saw an advertisement in *The Times* that a Headmaster was wanted for the Camberwell Collegiate School, with annual salary £500. He applied, sending the various testimonials he had assembled for King's College, and on 22 March received notification that the Committee of Management had, without seeing him, elected him to the post, with the vague enquiry "Have you any idea of being in London before entering upon the duties?"[43] He immediately set out for London to meet the Committee. It was agreed that his duties would start at Michaelmas (29 September), with the new Institution housed in a house in Camberwell Grove while the purpose-built school house was being erected.

The Camberwell Collegiate School was being established under the patronage of the Bishop of Winchester by a group of locals led by the Rev. John Storie, Vicar of Camberwell, and mainly financed by 150 shareholders who contributed £20 each. It was to be a "school in union with King's College, London" under a system devised in 1829 to promote establishments with shared Anglican beliefs and educational tenets; pupils from such schools were given preference if they wished to proceed to King's College. The building under construction on the east side of Camberwell Grove was designed for 200 boys by Henry Roberts, the architect of Fishmongers' Hall, and cost £3,600. It was built in white brick with stone dressings, with a collegiate-style cloister at the front and an entrance hall, a library, three classrooms, a large hall (60 feet by 33 feet) and accommodation for a master.

After his appointment Allen and Anna set about disposing of the King Square house and auctioning most of its contents ("every thing was sold infinitely below its value"). In mid-June Allen moved to London, staying with a friend in Newington, and began looking for a suitable house. Anna joined him at the end of the month, and on 1 July they took 17 Chatham Place, Camberwell Grove (exactly opposite the school site) at a rent of £50 a year.[44]

On 10 September 1834 their first son, William Arthur (known as Arthur or Arté) was born[45], though this event does not get mentioned in the *Diary*. The autumn was spent as planned, getting the school started in its nearby temporary premises.

> We very soon got together between one and two hundred boys from the neighbourhood, which was beginning to be very populous. The third master was the Rev. Joseph Sumner Brockhurst, a contemporary of myself at Charterhouse, where he gained the prize for English verse: the second master was the Rev. Myers, who turned out a methodist, a hypocrite and a sneak[46] : he was dismissed at the end of the first year for trying to undermine me and bring me into contempt with the boys and disfavour with the members of the Committee.[47]

Mr Sumner Brockhurst became a friend, and the two families dined together quite often; for example on 24 February 1835 "I dined at the house of the Rev J. Sumner Brockhurst [...]. Mr Jephson, master of the old Grammar School[48] , and a jolly man over his wine, also the Rev. Myers, our second master but less jolly anywhere, [and others] dined with us. Anna and some other ladies drank tea with us." In January 1840 Sumner Brockhurst succeeded as Head Master of the Camberwell Collegiate School, but had to leave in strange circumstances in 1843.[49]

26 January 1835 was a busy day: in the morning Arthur was christened by Allen in the parish church, then at 2 pm "the Collegiate School, having been completed, was

Camberwell Collegiate School, lithograph by Frederick Mackenzie, 1834.

opened in grand form, and I delivered an address on the plan of education which was to be adopted. In the evening a large party dined at the Grove House Inn, and Mr Storie the Vicar took the Chair." The school's progress was assessed at the end of the summer term when on 19 June Dr Russell, Allen's former schoolmaster at Charterhouse, came to examine the boys and award prizes. This was the school's first big public occasion. The Bishop of Winchester, Dr Charles Sumner (was he related to J. Sumner Brockhurst?), Patron of the School, presided, with "probably 700 persons present". As usual there was a dinner to follow, this time at the Vicarage. At some time during 1835 Dr Sumner ordained Allen priest.

In 1836 few happenings of note are recorded. On 20 February "One of the great plaster ventilators in the large school-room fell and struck off my cap from my head in its fall. If it had fallen three inches further towards me, I should have been killed on the spot, as the ventilator weighed nearly 100 pounds." Anna produced their second son, Henry Douglas, on 21 March. On 16 June he was baptised by his father in the parish church of St Giles. It seems strange, given the high infant mortality of those times, that the christening had been delayed for nearly three months, and even stranger that it should be held on the most important day of the school year, when Dr Russell again examined the school – and all this in the morning, as this time there was a lunch for about 60 people in the Giles's house. Their hospitality sometimes extended to the boys too:

> Saturday, Sep.10. This afternoon twenty of the boys who attended the Collegiate School came to spend their holiday afternoon in our house and garden. There was a small mulberry tree in one corner of the garden, and this was a point of great attraction to the boys, who climbed up into it, much to the amusement of little William Arthur. Children about the age of three or four always pay great attention to what bigger boys do.[50]

Despite the success of the school, which had grown to nearly 150 boys (still 50 below the planned maximum), Allen began to doubt its long-term viability. The costs of the land and building had been great, and the 150 shareholders expected to get an income from their investment. He was right in thinking that numbers would decline (in 1840 there were 80 boys), though in fact the school survived until 1863 when it succumbed to competition, mainly from Dulwich College. But Allen (or Giles as we shall now call him) began to look around:

> About this time there was much talk of a new school that was to be established in the midst of London by the Lord Mayor and the Common Council. I was told that the building was in fact almost completed, on the site of Honey Lane Market, and I went one day to see it. [...] I was advised to offer myself as a candidate for the Head-Mastership of the City of London School, and I readily consented to do so.[51]

3

Appointments and Arrangements

In mid-August 1836 this advertisement appeared twice in each of seven London newspapers.[1]

CITY OF LONDON SCHOOL

The Committee of the Corporation of London appointed to carry into execution the Act of Parliament for establishing a School on the site of Honey Lane Market Cheapside "for the religious and virtuous education of Boys and for instructing them in the higher branches of Literature and all other useful Learning" do hereby give Notice that they will MEET at the Guildhall of the said City on Wednesday the 7th day of September next, at Twelve of the Clock at noon precisely, to receive Applications and Testimonials from Gentlemen who are desirous of becoming CANDIDATES for the OFFICE of FIRST or HEAD MASTER of the SCHOOL. By the Provisions of the Act of Parliament no person can be appointed to the said Office unless he shall have been examined by the Professors for the time being of Divinity, and of Classical Literature[2], and of Mathematics, at King's College, London, and the Professors for the time being of the Greek Language, Literature and Antiquities, and of Mathematics, and of Natural Philosophy and Astronomy, at the University of London; and unless such person shall obtain a certificate signed by the majority in number of such Six Professors that he is a fit and proper person, and qualified to perform the duties of such Master, or by the majority in number of such of the said Six Professors as shall be willing to undertake such examination. And if upon the examination more than three Candidates shall be found to be duly qualified, such Professors are to certify which three are in their opinion best qualified, from whom one is to be appointed by the Lord Mayor, Aldermen, and Commons of the City in Common Council assembled. Notice of the time and place at which the Professors will meet for the examination of Candidates will be given in a future advertisement. – Further particulars relating to the School may be obtained at the Town Clerk's Office, Guildhall, every day (Sundays excepted) between the hours of ten and four, where all applications and testimonials must be left at least one day previous to the meeting of the Committee.

WOODTHORPE

This elaborate procedure is set out in detail in Clause VII of the Act, and was also to apply to the appointment of the Second Master. The Act uses the title "First Master" throughout, but the alternative "Head Master" was used alongside this in the June 1836 Rules and Regulations, and then became the accepted designation, later contracting to "Headmaster". The description "Second Master" survived much longer, continuously until the present author's retirement in 1997, and then again from 2000 to 2007. The current titles are "Head" and "Senior Deputy Head". This appointments procedure for the two posts remained unchanged until 1968.

Thomas Brewer had already written to each of the six professors on 9 August, informing them of the duties imposed on them (apparently without consultation) by the Act, and conveying the Committee's "earnest hope that, in a matter of so much importance to the future welfare of the School as the choice of a Head Master, they shall be favoured with your valuable co-operation, and that of the other Professors, agreeably to the intentions of the Legislature and the wishes of the Corporation of London." The initial responses were not too helpful: Dr William Otter, Principal and Professor of Divinity at King's, had recently been appointed Bishop of Chichester and was unable to help, and news was received that the Professor of Mathematics at the University of London, G.J.P White, had "by a fatal accident lost his life at sea off Guernsey." So the six were reduced to four, who were not available to meet together until November.

On 19 October another newspaper advertisement appeared, inviting candidates for the posts of First or Second Master "to deliver their testimonials, sealed up and addressed to the Professors, to Thomas Brewer [...] on or before Tuesday 1st November. The package should indicate which post is being applied for, but with no name on the outside." Next to this advertisement was this first call for pupils:

> CITY OF LONDON SCHOOL, Milk-street, Cheapside. – the above School having been founded and endowed by the Corporation of London, with a view to provide, at a moderate expense, for the sons of respectable parents connected with the City, an education of liberal and useful character adapted both to professional and commercial pursuits, the Committee have the pleasure to announce that the same will be opened early in the ensuing year. The course of instruction includes English, French, and other modern European languages, Classics, Mathematics, Writing, Arithmetic and Bookkeeping, Geography, History, Natural Philosophy, &c. The boys who are eligible for admission are the sons of persons who are free of the City wherever they may reside, and also the sons of persons who are householders in the City, but are not free thereof. The payment to be made for each pupil at £2 per quarter. Detailed prospectuses and forms of application for the admission of pupils, and any other information that may be desired, may be obtained of the Secretary, at the Town Clerk's office, Guildhall, any day (Sundays excepted) between the hours of ten and four.
>
> THOS. BREWER, Secretary.

On 1 November the testimonials were delivered, unopened, to the Professors, and by 18 November they had made their selections (in alphabetical order, they were careful to note):

First Master: John Sherran Brewer[3] Esq M.A. of Queen's College Oxford

> Revd John Allen Giles M.A. late Fellow of Corpus Christi College Oxford, & now Head Master of the Camberwell Collegiate School

> Revd Richard Wilson M.A. late Fellow of St John's College Cambridge, & now Head Master of Wigan Free Grammar School, Lancashire

Second Master: Revd T. Oswald Cockayne M.A. of St John's College Cambridge (Keynsham Bristol)

> Robert Pitt Edkins Esq M.A. of Trinity College Cambridge, Second Master of Kensington Proprietary School (31 Kensington Square)

> Revd William Webster B.A. of Queens' College Cambridge

The shortlisted candidates were informed that the Court of Common Council would meet to make the appointments six days later, on Thursday 24 November. Giles immediately went into action, using the experience he had gained when he applied for the Vinerian Scholarship:

> I was told by every body that I should fail unless I canvas[s]ed, and I had no objection to the process. I went into the City, sent round a circular to every member of the Common Council, telling them that I should call and have a personal interview within a day or two, and adopted every device I could think of to insure success. Nor did I hesitate in one case at least to adopt tactics of doubtful morality, but *Fas est et ab hoste doceri*[4] and I took a leaf out of the Common Councilman's own book. At the time this election was going on, Mr Moon[5], later Sir Francis Graham Moon, was a rising citizen and was engaged in procuring subscribers to his famous engraving from the more famous picture of John Knox preaching. I called at his shop: "Good morning Mr Moon: I am come to solicit your vote for the headmastership of the new school." – "Good morning," said he, "I don't know much about it: we shall of course choose the best man" – "Of course" said I, "but I wish you to vote for me" – Here I pretended to be startled at the number of beautiful engravings contained in the shop, and the following dialogue, after the style of Boswell in his Life of Johnson, takes place – G. What beautiful engravings! – M. Ha, do you admire engravings, Mr Giles? – G. Certainly, such ones as yours Mr Moon. – M. I shall be pleased to show you them. – G. I thank you: I am canvas[s]ing this morning, but can spare a few minutes. – M. Have you seen my John Knox? – G. No, but I have heard of it. – M. I will show you a proof

Warren Stormes Hale, oil painting by J.W
Allen, first CLS Drawing Master.

Gothic Revival Chairman's
Chair, as seen in the Allen
portrait, the only surviving
piece of furniture from the
Milk Street school.

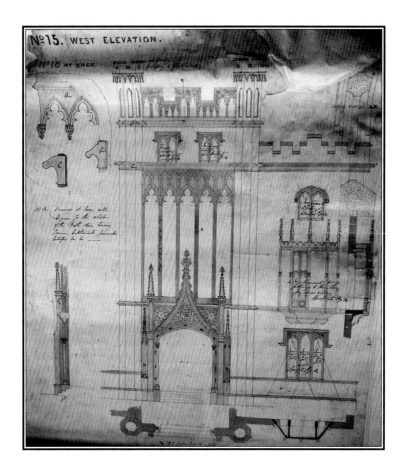

Bunning's elevation of
the West Front

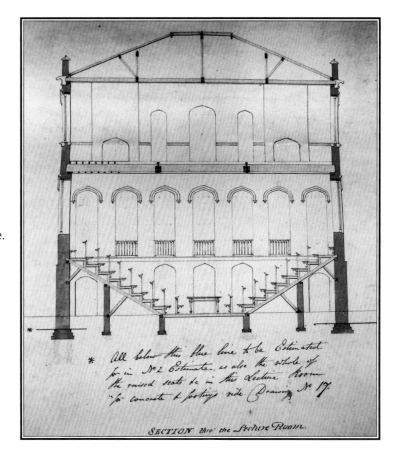

Bunning's section of
the Theatre with
Writing Rooom above.

Lithograph from an idealised drawing
by James Bunstone Bunning, the
architect. The school could never be
seen like this because of surrounding
buildings.

THREE WATERCOLOURS BY THOMAS HOSMER SHEPHERD SHOWING THE SCHOOL'S SURROUNDINGS.

Cheapside looking West. Honey Lane, leading to the boys' entrance, almost opposite St Mary-le-Bow. Engraved by W. Albutt after T.H Shepherd, published 1837.

Moon's Print Shop on corner of Threadneedle Street and Finch Lane, 1854.

Blossom's Inn, off Lawrence Street, just north of the then school, 1850.

before the letters. – G. I should like to buy a common print, but can not afford a proof before the letters. – M. Oh, they are dirt cheap, only fifteen guineas. – G. And what is the price of a common print? – M. Only two guineas, not worth your notice: there, see the beautiful touch the engraver has given to those lines. – G. Very true, but I must really attend to my own business; and I dare say I shall come back. If I get the election, I should certainly prefer the proof before the letters, and it would look well in the great dining room. – M. My dear sir, here is a form for ordering copies. – G. Well, I see: I write "Please to put down my name for a copy of your John Knox" – (I hesitate, for I must think of my own business). – M. I am sure you will succeed in this canvas[s]; and I believe it is the general opinion. – G. Well, Mr Moon, the picture is too beautiful to be neglected: I will on your own recommendation write "a proof before the letters." Of course Mr Moon voted for me as a free and independent Councillor, and one day, at the end of 3 or 4 months, whilst we were dining at the City of London School, in came a roll of paper 4 or 5 feet long, containing the picture of John Knox preaching, for which I gave the bearer a cheque for fifteen guineas.[6]

Giles thought his canvassing was succeeding, but at a late stage there was a problem[7]: he discovered that Hale, whose support he had reason to expect, had switched to backing Wilson. "The reasons which I heard whispered about were that I had not good health, that I was too lenient in managing boys, and that I was not so religious a character as I ought to be. The first plea was an absolute fiction; the second was equivalent to saying that I treated school-boys like gentlemen; and the third that I was not a Puritan like Mr Hale." That evening, 21 November, Giles went to see Henry Melvill, incumbent of the Camden Chapel, Camberwell, and one of the Committee of Management of the Collegiate School, who was known and admired by thousands for his popular preaching. Melvill at once wrote a letter which Giles had printed and sent to every member of the Common Council next morning. This concludes "Besides Scholarship of the highest order, he has displayed unremitted zeal and attention, sparing no pains that he might advance the interests of the Institution over which he presides. I am bound also to add that his moral and religious character will bear the very closest examination. Under these circumstances, I feel that you would do yourselves credit and secure an admirable Head for your new Establishment by electing Mr GILES to the office which he seeks."[8]

This did the trick, and on 24 November the 211 participating members of Common Council cast 99 votes for Giles, 91 for Wilson and 21 for Brewer. At the same meeting Edkins was elected Second Master (107 votes, with Webster 93 and Cockayne 11). So by his energetic and astute campaigning Giles had achieved what he wanted, but at the cost of souring the crucial relationship with the Chairman of the Committee.

Things now had to move rapidly if the School was to open early in 1837 as had been advertised. The Committee met on the following Monday (28 November). Bunning reported that the School would be fit to be opened safely in the middle of January, but not before, but that the Head Master's residence would not be ready then as it was the last part of the building to be finished. Giles and Edkins were present at this meeting, and Giles outlined his plan for organising the school, based on the decisions already taken by the Committee, which had been sent to all the candidates. He was asked to present these in writing.

Two days later the Committee met again. By then Giles could submit an outline in writing of his plan for subdividing and classifying the pupils. The Committee adjourned and all moved to the building in order to view the classrooms and consider the plan *in situ*.

The front of the building faced Milk Street which runs north from Cheapside to what was then Cateaton Street, where Hale lived at No. 21.[9] The main axis of the site ran east from Milk Street, and was bordered to the north by Russia Row running into Trump Street, and to the south and west by alleys forming the remnant of Honey Lane Market. The Milk Street frontage contained the impressive Lord Mayor's Entrance in gothic style, with an arched doorway above which was an open gallery of five lofty trefoil arches and then two mullioned windows and an embattled parapet. This central section was flanked by buttress turrets and side wings one storey lower. The whole building, measuring a maximum of about 200 feet by 100 feet, would have fitted twice into the playground of the present school.

Inside[10] was an entrance hall with the Head Master's living accommodation (to be described later) to the south, and what in the plans was labelled the Professors Room to the north. It was decided that a smaller classroom would be adequate for the occasional needs of the Gresham Professors[11], so this rather grand room became available for other uses. The main East-West corridor had one classroom on each side (labelled on the plans Class Room 1 on the north side and 3 on the south) before reaching the central crossing. Here on the north side was the Grand Staircase going up in a single central flight to a landing before dividing into two flanking flights, and down in a single flight reached by corridors on either side of the main stairs. Opposite the central flight of stairs was the corridor to the boys' entrance in the centre of the south side, opposite Honey Lane which led south to Cheapside. This corridor was bordered on the west by the Secretary's room, and on the east by the Porter's lodge, each of these being south of a separate small closet room (used as a cloakroom) near the central crossing.[12] East of the Porter's lodge was the room allocated to the Professors (Room 2) and, opposite this, was another classroom (Room 8) which had two doors and could be divided into two by a movable partition. Perhaps the rooms were numbered like this out of sequence to allow for flexibility in the use of Room 8.

At the East end the main corridor was the lobby of the Theatre, the most impressive room in the school, separated from this lobby by a colonnade of six square pillars. The Theatre had 400 seats arranged in raked horseshoe formation like those of the well-known lecture theatre of the Royal Institution (built 1799-1801), though without a separate gallery. In front of each seat was a writing ledge. Near the centre of the lobby two sets of stairs led down to the Theatre's central Arena at basement level, while at the north and south ends of the lobby was access to the semi-circular walkway that went round behind the top tier of seats.

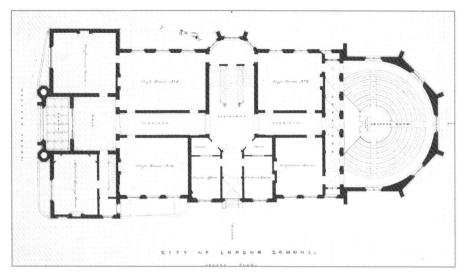

The ground floor plan that was deposited with the foundation stone and recovered in 1882 when the school moved. The original Professors' Room (N. of the entrance hall) had already moved to the former Class Room 2, next to the lecture theatre. The room labelled Class Room 2 here is Class Room 8 in the original plans, and was soon divided into two with the eastern half becoming the Masters' Room. The Secretary is here described as Clerk.

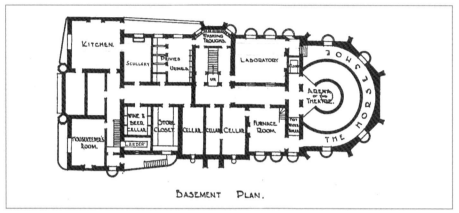

Basement Plan.

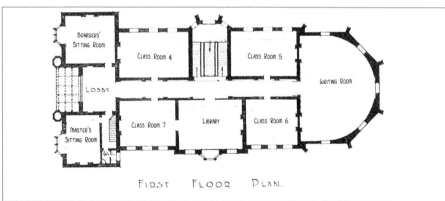

First Floor Plan

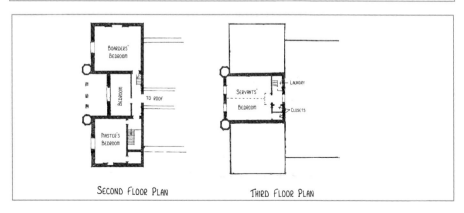

Second And Third Floor Plans

On the first floor opposite the top of the stairs was the Library. To the right (West) the upper corridor led between two large classrooms, Room 4 on the North and Room 7 on the South, to a lobby giving access to the living accommodation and to the loggia behind the five trefoil arches. The corridor to the east from the top of the stairs led between Class Rooms 5 on the north and 6 on the south, to the large Writing Room occupying the whole space above the Theatre.

> The Committee [...] considered the plan suggested by Mr Giles for fitting up the same, by which it appeared that accommodation could be provided for 400 Pupils in the Rooms on the Upper Stor[e]y alone, viz.
>
> On the North side of the Corridor
> In the Room Eastward of the Staircase
>   13 Desks, 6 Boys to each –   78
> In the Room Westward of D° [ditto] –   (the same) 78
>
> On the South side of the Corridor
> In the Room Eastward of the Library
> 11 Desks, 6 Boys to each –   66
> In the Room Westward of D° –   (the same) 66
>   288
>
> In the large Room at the East end of the Corridor
> and over the Theatre ---   about 112
>   400
>
> It also appeared that the two Rooms on the Ground floor fitted up with Raised Seats would accommodate about 180, viz.
> That Eastward of the Staircase,   about 80
> & that Westward of D°   about 100
>   180
>
> And that there would then be left for future appropriation (besides the Room on the South side, adjoining to the Theatre, which has been offered for the use of the Gresham Professors) another Class Room on the South side, adjoining to the Head Master's Residence, of the same size as the Room over it Westward of the Library.[13]

The Committee approved, and instructed Bunning to fit out the rooms as directed by Giles. Strangely there is no mention of a room for the Head Master's use, though he must have needed somewhere in the school to use as an office and for teaching. Room 3 on the ground floor had been left spare, and was conveniently situated between his house and the Secretary's office. So this is the obvious candidate for "appropriation" as Giles's library, study, and sixth form teaching room.

The Committee next explored the basement. Here they clearly thought it advisable to make a clear separation between the areas which were for storage or part of the Head Master's residence and those to which the boys needed access. They ordered an iron gate and railings to be fitted so that at the foot of the stairs the boys could only take a passage on either side of the stairs leading to the washing troughs and the entrance to the boys' privies and urinals on the west, and to a large room on the East.

The original purpose of this room is obscure. In the plans it is clearly labelled "Laboratory", though in Douglas-Smith this is misread as "Lavatory", which must be impossible as there is no provision for drainage. Neither could it have been a laboratory in the current sense. Although the published curriculum included "Courses of Lectures on Chemistry and other branches of Experimental Philosophy" these did not happen until 1838 when some lecture demonstrations were given in the Theatre. Proper teaching of science started in March 1847, when Thomas Hall, who was appointed that month, started teaching chemistry, involving the boys in practical science for the first time in an English school. But this was done in a narrow laboratory made from the basement corridor leading to the Theatre. By then the room labelled "Laboratory" had another use (see p. 68). So perhaps this description just has its original meaning of "Workshop".

Bunning's Basement Plan, including 'laboratory'.

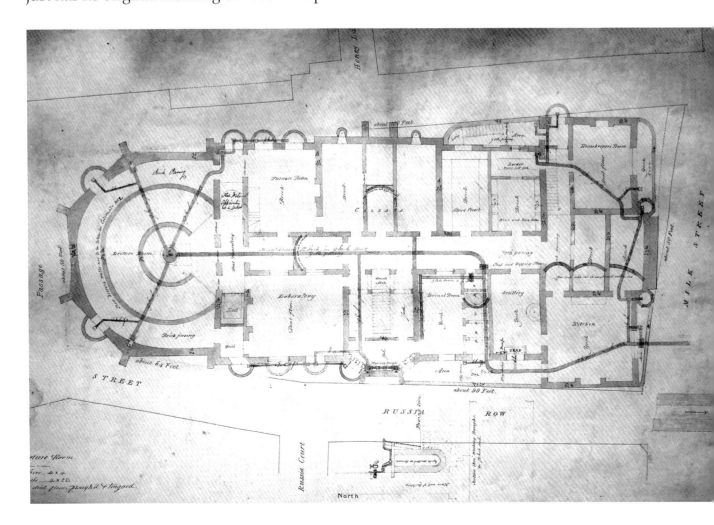

On the far (East) side of the "Laboratory" a door led to a small landing area (later known as "The Fort") from which a few steps descended to a wide semi-circular corridor running under the tiered seating of the Theatre and paved in brick. The door at the other end of this led to the furnace room, and so was kept locked. This dead-end area was the only space the boys had for recreation. It soon became known as the "Horseshoe", and was to be the scene of many energetic games and much hard-fought combat, later recalled with affection.[14]

Such was the basement territory available to the boys. Beyond the iron gate at the foot of the stairs a corridor led into the arena area of the Theatre to the east; it was this that later became Thomas Hall's laboratory. On the south side of this corridor were two cellar rooms and the furnace room. The rest of the basement, to the west of the stairs, was blocked off to form part of the Head Master's residence, as is described in Chapter 4.

In his *Memoirs* Giles recalled another use of the corridor:

> Not many months ago (I am writing in 1878) a great fuss was made because a schoolboy was shut in a dark room by way of punishment. [...] Now whilst I was head-master of the City of London School, hardly a day passed without one or two imprisonments of this kind. In the long passage under the school and my private house they made two partitions parallel to one another and only about 2 feet apart. Into this narrow place an unruly boy was immediately conveyed, and expiated his crimes by standing one – two – or three hours, as the case might be.[15]

The delay in completing the Head Master's residence caused problems for the Giles family. On 6 December Anna and the two little boys left the house in Camberwell Grove and went to Frome to stay with William Giles. "We packed up our furniture, and sent it to be placed in one of the empty rooms at the City of London School, and I knocked about the best way I could during the remainder of the year."[16] Giles was now fully occupied in preparing for the opening of the City school, so presumably had delegated his Camberwell Collegiate School duties to his friend Sumner Brockhurst, but this is not documented. It seems that he stayed for a while with an Oxford friend, Arthur Bryer, at 6 Canterbury Row, Newington, and later at Blossom's Inn in Lawrence Lane off Cheapside, very close to the school building.

A Special Committee of eight set up to confer with Giles on his plans met on 7 December, when Abraham Sumner (always known to the boys as "Tom") was appointed Porter, a post he was to hold until his retirement in 1873. One week later William Webster, the close runner-up for the Second Mastership, was appointed Third Master. This seems to have been a personal title (it does not appear in the Act), and did not survive beyond Webster's departure in 1847[17]; his successor was called Second Classical Master.

With the subdivision of the school into classes now decided, it was possible at last to specify what other assistant masters would be needed. The Special Committee did this on 14 December:

2 Junior or Assistant Classical and Mathematical Masters at a Salary of £150 p.a. each
1 Principal Master of the Junior Department at a Salary of £200 p.a.
2 Assistants to D° at £100 p.a. each
1 Writing Master at £150 p.a.
1 French Master at £150 p.a.
1 German & Hebrew Master at £100 p.a.
1 Drawing Master to be remunerated according to the number of Pupils who may learn that Art, out of the extra payments to be made by such Pupils.

These posts were advertised in the London newspapers on 17 and 20 December, with applications and testimonials to reach Brewer by 31 December.

One week later it was reported to the Special Committee that there were already 255 boys approved for admission, with another 97 referred for further information. On 27 December (no long Christmas break in those days!) Giles and Edkins were asked "to verify the Testimonials and consider the qualifications of the Candidates for vacant Masterships and choose (if possible) the best three for Election to each Situation." At the same meeting the Committee agreed, after consulting Bunning, to replace the skylights above the Grand Staircase with "a Lantern of an appropriate nature which shall be more in accordance with the general character and style of the Building", at an additional cost of £160.

Giles and Edkins must have worked hard over the New Year sifting the applications. Giles met the Special Committee on Monday and Tuesday, 2 and 3 January 1837, to confirm their selection of the most eligible candidates, who were then summoned to appear before the Committee on 11 January. Then he escaped: "At 4 o'clock I got into the night coach for Bath, and stopped to sup at Newbury." The coach reached Melksham in Wiltshire at 5 a.m., where Giles changed and went "in a sort of van" to Trowbridge; there he caught the mail coach to Frome, where Anna and his sons were awaiting him.

While he was away the Committee met on 11 January as planned, and elected the following assistant masters:

Revd William Bailey BA & Thomas Astley Cock BA, both of Trinity College
    Cambridge, as Assistant Classical & Mathematical Masters
Thomas St Clair MacDougal, as First Master of Junior Department
Charles Nathaniel Woodroffe, as Assistant Master of Junior Class
Charles Jean Delille, as French Master
Henry Manley, as Writing Master
Revd Dr Christoph Heinrich Friedrich Bialloblotzky, as German & Hebrew Master
Joseph William Allen, as Drawing Master[18]

The process was not without controversy, as was reported in the *Morning Chronicle* on 12 January: "Yesterday a vast deal of interest was excited at Guildhall in the Committee of the City of London School in consequence of the expected election of the Rev. Mr D. Davison, as first master of the junior class, that gentleman having been known to favour Socinian[19] doctrines." With "a very full attendance of members" many vigorous opinions were expressed and reported. Those against Davison feared that his unorthodox views would not be acceptable to parents of the boys. Those for him argued that his religious opinions were not relevant to the post in question, for which he was otherwise fully qualified. They had more general concerns too, as put by Alderman Wood, who had "travelled to town post-haste to be present at the election".

> He was surprised to perceive that the spirit of intolerance had crept into the infant institution, notwithstanding all that had been said about flinging overboard all religious distinctions.[20] The circumstance was all the more to be deplored, as the spirit had made its appearance at the very opening of a great establishment for the education of youth. The principle but ill corresponded with the general sentiment of the present day, and he regretted to find some of those, who on other occasions were in the habit of advocating the liberal side, were aiding the friends of intolerance on the present occasion.[21]

When the vote was taken MacDougal defeated Davison by 20 votes to 15. But Davison did not let the matter rest there. Two days later a letter appeared in the *Morning Chronicle*[22]:

> Gentlemen
>
> Allow me to return to you my best thanks for the honour of your support in the late Election for the office of FIRST MASTER of the JUNIOR CLASS in the London School. I estimate the value of that support the more highly, in consequence of the peculiar disadvantages to which I was exposed.
>
> Undoubtedly I regret that my exertions, and the kind support which I received, did not lead to a more favourable result, and readily acknowledge that a serious injury has been inflicted on me. There can be no reasonable doubt that my interests in this case have been sacrificed to a spirit of intolerance and religious persecution; and that no principle of integrity, no intellectual acquirements, no measure of experience would have been sufficient to sustain me against the attacks of insinuation, calumny, and falsehood, which some members of the committee privately made, and shrunk from publicly avowing.
>
> I shall consider it a duty to myself and the public, in such manner as I shall be advised, to expose the means which have been taken by individuals to defeat my election, in the formation of a school founded by Act of Parliament on the most extended principles of religious liberty.
>
> I have the honour to be, &c.,
>
> D. DAVISON.
>
> To the Members of the Committee of the City of London School who honoured me with their support.
>
> Islington, January 12, 1837

David Davison then went on to write a 39 page pamphlet entitled *A Letter to Mr. Warren Stormes Hale, Chairman of the Committee of the City of London School* which was published by Smallfield & Son in 1837, and went to a second edition. In this he alleged that religious discrimination had prejudiced his candidature for the post of Second Master [*sic*] at the school. No response from Hale is recorded, but the incident rankled in liberal quarters (see page 66).

There was one other hiccup in the appointments: William Frost was elected Writing Master, but then declined the post because of the hours of attendance required (which presumably he could have found out about earlier). So Henry Manley got the job instead, which was fortunate for him as he had walked about 140 miles from Clewer near Cheddar in Somerset to obtain an interview.[23]

Giles left Frome by the night mail on 15 January "having, contrary to custom, taken an inside place, as I had been ill of a bilious attack three days. On the way a man, who sat behind the coachman, fell off, but was not much hurt. Being unfit for travelling, I slept at Devizes."[24] He reached London on Monday 16 January, and slept at Blossom's Inn. On Wednesday that week, though still lodging at Blossom's, he began to fit up his library at the school, a task he completed ten days later. On 31 January he went with two friends to view a plot of land for sale in Windlesham near Bagshot, Surrey. On his return early next day he moved into his school accommodation, where Anna, their two sons and Anna's brother Henry Dickinson soon joined him.

The date of the school's opening had been fixed for Tuesday 2 February (which happened to be Hale's birthday), so there was still much to do. Giles began to receive nominations of pupils personally on 24 January, when he registered 78. This presumably took place at Guildhall, since the school building was not yet finished. He did likewise on 28 January, when the total registered reached 350, and was still registering pupils on the day before the school opened.

Meanwhile he had consulted the other masters and drawn up a list of books to be used in the school. The Special Committee considered his recommendations on 27 January. Apart from *Reading Lessons in Prose and Verse* published by James Bohn, these were all by Giles himself (Latin, Greek and English Grammars, and Arithmetic) or assistant masters (*Elements of Geography* by MacDougal and *Introductory Lessons in French* by Delille). These were agreed, but with a cautionary motion proposed for, and in due course passed by, the Grand Committee:

> That this Committee knowing that Masters of Schools are in the habit of composing various works for the use of their respective Schools are of opinion that it is desirable that the Books to be used in the City of London School should be confined to works of acknowledged utility, and that none be introduced solely or principally for the benefit of their Authors, nor without the previous sanction of the Committee.

On the same day tickets were sent to those attending the opening ceremony ("Members of the Court are requested to appear at the School in their violet Gowns"), and members of the Committee were told that they would dine afterwards in the London Coffee House, Ludgate Hill, where they could if they wished introduce a friend, who would need a ticket costing one guinea. Giles was asked to ensure that the masters wore suitable academic dress at the opening ceremony.

On 1 February the Special Committee made further provision for the Public Opening of the School the next day, ordering 600 Buns for distribution amongst the Pupils, 1 dozen of Sherry and 4 dozen of Marsala, 6 dozen Rout Chairs[25], and 10 dozen wine glasses, and asking for six Police Officers to be in attendance at the entrance to the school.

The Lord Mayor's entrance in Milk Street, engraving by J.Woods after a sketch by Robert Garland, 1838.

On the morning of the opening day there was a crowd of boys waiting at the front door when Abraham Sumner unlocked it at 9.25. Fifty years later at least seven middle aged gentlemen claimed to have been the first boy to enter, but apparently that honour went to Hale's son Josiah, who had been smuggled in by his father half an hour earlier.[26] Both Douglas-Smith and Hinde[27] say that there were 200 boys present on the first day, but the registration numbers reported above, the newspaper report below, and the school account ledgers all suggest that the figure of 441, given in the proceedings of the 1839 Inquiry[28] is more likely to be right – and is certainly more in line with the number of buns ordered. So the school was immediately the largest in London except for Christ's Hospital.

Once the boys were inside there was chaos. Giles ordered the French master Delille to "Sort those boys!" Perhaps he intended this to be done by attainment, though it is difficult to see how that could have been judged when the boys had been registered apparently with no assessment. Delille adopted a simpler method: he assembled the boys in the long first floor corridor, arranged them in order of height, and divided them into classes on that basis. This was a start, and William Huggins recalled 55 years later "The occasion is distinctly photographed on my mind – it occurred either on the same day or a day or two afterwards – when the Headmaster, Dr Giles, called up the new boys in batches of about twenty and asked them simple questions for the purpose of a rough examination; and I still remember my delight at going at once to the top of the batch of boys with whom I stood for putting correctly into Latin the very simple sentence 'I love my mother'."[29] But it took several weeks for short clever boys to ascend to the right classes while tall duller ones moved in the opposite direction.

So who were the boys in this first cohort, and where did they come from? The City of London School Register[30] gives their names, addresses, whether they had a brother at the school, date of leaving, the parent's name - almost always the father, with just eight entries in the mother's name – and, usually, occupation.[31] The City of London in 1837 was very different from what it is today. There were then about 127,000 residents in the City, 6.7% of an approximate total of 1.9 million in Greater London. Now there are less than 9000 out of just under 9 million (about 0.1%).

Three-quarters of these 441 boys lived in the City's square mile itself, so had less than a mile's walk to school. Nearly all the rest were just outside the City boundary, mostly in Islington (21), Holborn (13), to the east in Aldgate, Whitechapel or Hackney (16), or just south of the river in Southwark (24) or Lambeth (9). There are a few strange outliers, living in places from which it would have been very difficult or impossible to travel daily, including East Ham, Walthamstow, Croydon, Aylesbury, Maidstone, and Hastings; presumably these boys lodged closer to the school during the week. The most extreme were George and Morton Sparke, whose father John Guyse Sparke, M.D., M.R.C.S., a naval surgeon, gave his home address as Huyton Park, Huyton, Liverpool. A surprisingly large proportion of the initial intake, more than 40%, had (or would in future have) brothers in the school.

The occupations listed give a vivid impression of how all-encompassing life in the City was then. As intended, the school had attracted support from all sections of the community. There were professionals such as accountants, solicitors, company secretaries, medical men (doctor, surgeon, optician, dentist), and the organist of St Paul's Cathedral. Their commercial needs were met by printers, engravers, bookbinders, booksellers and stationers. Food and drink were catered for by butchers (eleven of them), bakers, grocers, fishmongers, tea dealers, wine or ale and porter merchants and, for continental delicacies, oil and Italian warehousemen. For an evening out you could visit a hairdresser and then patronise one of six coffee house or dining room proprietors or ten publicans. You could be clothed by seven tailors or a breeches maker, furriers, hosiers, hat makers (including a "chip [straw] and fancy hat manufacturer"), seven boot or shoe makers, and, if required, a staymaker [corset maker], serviced by a whalebone cutter. For the home there were carpet makers, linen drapers supplied by three "Manchester warehousemen" [dealing in cotton goods from the north], a cutler, a brushmaker, ironmongers, painters and decorators, plumbers, bricklayers, builders and six coal merchants. Craftsmen included gold, silver and copper smiths, two gun makers, an instrument maker and Mr Nicholas Rolfe of 112 Cheapside who was a "patent self-acting pianoforte manufacturer". Perhaps strangest to us today was Mr John Harslett of St Andrew's Hill (just across Queen Victoria Street from the present school), who was a cowkeeper.

Rabbi David
Aaron de Sola.

Fifteen months earlier, after laying the foundation stone, Lord Brougham had stressed that "All the blessings of instruction are open to all—Dissenters of every shade—Protestant and Catholic —Jew and Gentile—all are admitted to the same advantages." Since religious affiliations are not recorded in the Register it is impossible to know to what extent that noble aim had been met. But for a small group of boys we can be more certain. Abraham and Isaac De Sola were sons of David Aaron De Sola, who from 1818 had been a rabbi at the Bevis Marks synagogue,[32] and was noted for his scholarly publications and musical compositions; John De Pass, son of Daniel, belonged to a prominent Sephardic Jewish family, other members of which founded the first synagogue in South Africa; and Raphael Lindo's father, Elias Haim Lindo, was several times warden of the Bevis Marks synagogue. So there were certainly Jewish boys in the school right from the start.[33]

There is not much information about the later careers of this first intake, but some did achieve distinction. At least five went on to study at Oxford or Cambridge, including Henry Judge Hose (1826–83) who in 1848 while at Cambridge formed "The Carpenter Club", which became the John Carpenter Club (JCC, the school's old boys' association) in 1851, with Hose as its first President. Nine of his contemporaries later served as President of the JCC. In civic life five boys would be members of the Court of Common Council, one becoming a Sheriff, two of them later chairing the School Committee, and one being responsible for the lighting of City streets by electricity. Another was the City Solicitor and acting Remembrancer. Edward Stanford (1827–1904) became a bookseller, with the contract for supplying the school, and later founded Edward Stanford Ltd, map engravers and printers.

George Smith (1824–1901) also followed his father's trade of bookseller, then moved into publishing. He was agent and friend of many celebrated authors including Ruskin, D.G Rossetti, Charlotte and Anne Brontë, George Eliot and Thackeray. He founded the *Dictionary of National Biography* and the *Cornhill Magazine*. Most celebrated was Sir William Huggins (1824–1910), known as the founder of astrophysics for his pioneering work on astronomical spectroscopy. He was President of the Royal Society, KCB, and an initial member of the Order of Merit.

After their hectic first morning the boys were packed into the Theatre with the guests for the opening ceremony. The *Morning Chronicle* of 3 February 1837 reported:

> Yesterday the ceremony of the opening of the City of London School was performed by the civic authorities, the right honourable the Lord Mayor in the chair.
>
> At three o'clock his lordship, attended by the sheriffs, the aldermen, the chairman of the school committee, and several members of the Court of Common Council, &c. &c., entered the building. After having visited the numerous smaller apartments of the institution, they, together with Doctor Ritchie, the professor of the London University, Doctor Birkbeck, and the several lately elected masters, entered the theatre, in which were assembled as many ladies and gentlemen as could be accommodated.[34] The scholars were stationed in the upper tiers of seats, and the passages leading from these seats to the arena.
>
> The spectacle was one of the most animating imaginable, the number of boys present being upwards of 400, and the most intense delight was manifested by all present during the whole of the proceedings.

The Lord Mayor Thomas Kelly, renowned for his piety and certainly more amenable than his predecessor Henry Winchester, started his address by outlining the story of how the John Carpenter bequest led to the founding of what he (uniquely and wrongly) called the City of London Classical School. He soon concluded: "For myself I may hope that with the divine blessing upon the assiduous attention of the distinguished scholars who have been elected to the several masterships, the City of London School will in due time produce men eminent in every branch of literature and science [loud cheering]", and then introduced Prof Ritchie[35], deputising for Dr Birkbeck who though present was not well enough to give the main speech.

> Dr. RITCHIE then addressed the assembly in an admirable manner upon the advantages with which such an institution would abound. [He spoke at length on the advantages of a scientific education, contrasting it with traditional school course in Latin and Greek] and showed how infinitely superior was the union of classical literature with the sciences, and how the study of the latter could in persons of the most tender years be adopted as a most effective and captivating means of improving and expediting that of the former.
>
> Dr BIRKBECK then proposed the thanks of the assembly to Doctor Ritchie [...] and hoped that the school would by and by add to its other great advantages

those which could be made to result from the bequest of Sir Thomas Gresham[36] [loud cheers].

Thanks having then been unanimously voted to Doctor Birkbeck, the Lord Mayor, and the professors of the institution, the assembly separated.

At half past six o'clock the committee and several other gentlemen dined at the London Coffee-house, in celebration of the day of the opening of the school. The Lord Mayor took the chair on the occasion.

This time the newspapers did not give a detailed account of the dinner, "where civic gastronomy, enlivened and enlightened by civic eloquence, displayed itself in every imaginable form".[37] To make up for this Hale wrote to the papers next day:

Sir, – In the account which has appeared in your columns of the proceedings of yesterday, on the opening of the City of London School, there is a circumstance omitted which added greatly to the interest of the occasion, and which I feel persuaded will, when known, afford a high degree of satisfaction to the public, who have, in a most striking manner, exhibited the deep interest they feel in the prosperity of this important establishment.

At the dinner, with which the proceedings of the day were concluded, the Lord Mayor, who was in the chair, proposed the healths of the sheriffs of London and Middlesex, who were both present on the occasion; upon which Mr Sheriff Duke, after acknowledging the compliment in a highly appropriate speech, generously offered to place at the disposal of the committee the sum of ten guineas, as a reward to the first boy at the annual examination of the pupils.

Immediately after this gratifying announcement, Dr Conquest,[38] in proposing the health of the Rev. Mr Giles and the other masters of the school, stated that he should be happy to present a gold medal of the same value every year during his life to such boy in the school as at the annual examination shall be thought most worthy of that distinction.

I am, Sir, your obedient servant,

W.S HALE,

Chairman of the Committee
Cateaton Street,

Feb. 3, 1837.

The acerbic editorial response in *The Constitutional* of 4 February showed that such "civic eloquence" had its critics:

Reflections on the ill treatment experienced by the Rev. Mr. Davidson [*sic*], at the hands of Mr. Hale and his narrow-minded coadjutor, will always diminish our gratification in giving publicity to the affairs of the City of London School. Mr. Hale will always be more notorious with us as the persecutor of Mr. Davidson, than honourable as Chairman to the School Committee.

4

Settling In

Although there was still work to be done on the Head Master's residence, the Giles family soon settled in, and by 13 February 1837 were already entertaining guests there.

Their accommodation was at the west end of the building, behind the impressive Milk Street frontage, on five levels. At the west end of the south side, steps led down to a sunken area from which the tradesmen's door led into the basement entrance lobby. From this a corridor ran northward, past a staircase leading to the ground floor, to the kitchen which connected with the scullery and a store room. To the west of this corridor were the housekeeper's room and another store room. To the east were the larder and a corridor with, on the south side, the wine and beer cellar, a store closet with stone shelving and another cellar, and on the north side another entrance to the scullery and a W.C. for the servants.

The plumbing at basement level caused recurrent problems. Giles later "complained of an annoyance in the lower part of his House occasioned by the smell of the Water Closets on the Basement Stor[e]y and suggested that the inconvenience would be remedied by bricking up the Window between the Boys Urinal place & the Passage leading from his Kitchen."[1] Apparently smells were acceptable if confined to the boys' side of the wall.

Above the tradesmen's door, with access from the pavement via a platform that acted as a porch for the door below, was the private entrance to the Head Master's house. Inside was a small lobby and then a corridor leading past the staircase to the lobby inside the Lord Mayor's Entrance. West of this corridor was the dining room. On the first floor at the top of the stairs was a W.C. and the Head Master's sitting room. A corridor past this led to the first floor lobby leading to the loggia behind the trefoil arches. On the opposite (north) side of the lobby was the boarders' sitting room. On the next floor, level with the roof of the main part of the school, were the Head Master's bedroom in the south and the boarders' bedroom in the north, with another bedroom in between. At this level there was access to the roofs over most of the school. Finally the staircase led up to the servants' bedroom in the central tower, with two closets and a laundry area.

Though the dining and sitting rooms were spacious (about 25 feet by 16 feet) it was not a grand house. The Head Master had only two bedrooms at his disposal, and the servants only one (though pencil markings on the plan suggest that this may have been partitioned).[2] Presumably the two small boys slept with their parents, and Henry Dickinson had the central bedroom. In 1839 the Head Master was instructed "That the Scholars on the Foundation should have a Sleeping Room appropriated and preserved to their sole and exclusive use,"[3] which suggests that the family may sometimes have used the boarders' bedroom for overspill.

The school started to settle to its routine. The hours of attendance were from 9 to 12 in the morning, and from 2 until 5 (March to October) or 4 (November to February) in the afternoon. There was a half-holiday each Saturday, and the vacations were three weeks at Christmas, five weeks in the summer commencing on the Saturday preceding Midsummer day (24 June), and from Good Friday to the Tuesday following at Easter.

No catering was provided, as it was assumed that all boys would live within walking distance of the school and would go home for lunch. Giles soon told the Committee of "the inconvenience that was sustained, and the injury that was likely to be occasioned to the Building by the Boys being allowed to stay on the premises in the interval between morning and afternoon school", and from Easter onward no boys were allowed in the building between 12 and 2. This policy lasted for only one quarter, as in August it was agreed that the "Laboratory" in the basement should be "appropriated when not required for other purposes for the accommodation of those Boys who reside at too great a distance from the School to be able to return home for Dinner between the hours of 12 & 2, and that a Table and Forms be provided for the same."[4]

Immediately after the opening Giles told the Committee that because more boys had been admitted than had been planned for, he had to recommend the appointment, as soon as possible, of two additional Assistant Classical and Mathematical Masters. On 8 February they agreed to do this, at £150 p.a. each. The Secretary contacted those who had been unsuccessful applicants in January, and ten days later two of these, Frederick Hathaway and Abraham Newland, were appointed, though, as will appear, neither stayed beyond August.

Giles soon brought other requirements to the Committee's attention. These included improving the ventilation and heating of the class rooms, providing the Masters with chairs, providing accommodation for the pupils' hats, cloaks and umbrellas, remedying the smell arising from the urinals,[5] and appropriating a room for the accommodation of the Masters in the interval between school hours. The last need was met in March by giving the Masters half of the subdivided classroom 8 next to the theatre. This was to be provided with a table and half a dozen chairs (not even one between two!), and a W.C. for their use was installed nearby at the north end of the theatre lobby. The Committee also decided to meet at the school instead of Guildhall; they chose the Library as a suitable room to use (though later they met in the former Professors' room), and asked Mr Robert Herring,[6] upholsterer, to supply two oak tables covered in blue cloth and three dozen chairs "of a suitable pattern to correspond with the character of the Room."

The daily arrival and departure of over four hundred schoolboys clearly had an effect on the neighbours, and on Cheapside, the City's prime shopping area. To guard the reputation of his fledgling school Giles advised all parents in a printed circular of 28 February that "It is necessary that parents should impress upon their sons the propriety of their walking to and from the School without loitering on the way."[7]

An indication of how Giles communicated within the school is given by a surviving set of three handwritten notices pasted onto card, undated, which presumably the Porter would take round for all the masters to read: [8]

> It is requested that the Masters will be very careful not to omit sending the usual note to enquire into the absence of any of the boys, as one of them in the Junior Class has been detected playing truant upwards of a week.
>
> Further: the Porters have orders not to detain any of the boys after school hours, unless under the eye of one of the masters, great inconvenience having arisen from the practice.
>
> The practice of sending boys who behave ill out of the class must be modified in some way or other, as I sometimes find 10 or 12 such boys, playing in the passages, apparently heedless of the disgrace, and causing every kind of annoyance and interruption to the business of the School.
>
> J.A.Giles

On 9 March Brewer wrote to the fathers of the two Carpenter scholars still at Tonbridge School:

> The Reverend Mr Giles the Head Master of this School having, with his family, now taken up his residence here and being fully prepared to receive into his care the Boys who have been placed by the Corporation at Tonbridge School on Carpenter's Charity, I am directed by the Committee to request that you will acquaint me for their information at your earliest convenience whether it will be agreeable to you that your son should be removed from Tonbridge and placed under the care of Mr Giles at Easter next.
>
> In pursuance of the Act of Parliament establishing the School and the Rules and Regulations made by the Court of Common Council (a copy of which is enclosed herewith for your information) four Foundation Scholarships have been established to be occupied by the Boys educated under the Will of John Carpenter and the expenses of their education maintenance and clothing and the other

advantages to be allowed them will henceforth be defrayed out of the sum with which the School is endowed. One of the Boys who have been sent to Tonbridge will at the request of his Parents be immediately transferred to this School and the appointment to the Scholarship which has been for some time vacant will be made from the Pupils who are already here, and it is considered desirable that the other two Boys who are chargeable to the School should also enter it with as little delay as possible.

The boy who transferred immediately was Samuel Roberts, and the other two, who moved at Easter, were W.D.Were and Alfred Ledger. Their homes were all within 10 minutes' walk of the school, so the boarding requirement no longer made much sense. But the Committee stuck to the rules and refused the request of Mr George Ledger, who lived about 100 yards east of the school in Ironmonger Lane, to allow his son to live at home.

It seemed that the school had got off to a good start, and the numbers of pupils increased to 477 in the second quarter. But already there were tensions: in his memoirs Giles writes

> I have no memoranda of events which happened in March and April of this year. My days were employed in organizing and managing the various classes of the City of London School, but I found the Committee appointed by the Court of Common Council very unwilling to let me have my own way, or indeed to exercise any independent authority at all. All this was aggravated no doubt by the strong opposition that was made to me at the time of the election by the friends of Mr Wilson, one of whom was Mr Warren Stormes Hale, a tallow-chandler near Basinghall Street and a Common Council man. Notwithstanding their suspicious and meddling conduct, I felt satisfied with my position and the time passed away agreeably enough.[9]

As part of this agreeable routine Giles went to Camberwell every Sunday to preach the evening lecture "although there was no pay attached to the office", entertained the members of the Philological Society[10] every fortnight, and "every Wednesday evening we received at our dinner table every one who chose to partake of it."[11] But life in the household was soon to be tragically disrupted:

> *May 6, Saturday.* As I was going down stairs about half past 8 in the evening, Anna, who had been sitting with our little boy Henry Douglas laid up with meazles [*sic*] and Whooping Cough, shrieked out to me to come back. I hastened up again and found the dear little fellow in a dreadful fit of epilepsy.

> *May 9, Tuesday.* For the last three days our poor little boy has had but little rest, and this day at 3 o'clock in the morning he breathed his last. [...] Anna, Henry Dickinson and myself had sat by him all the last three nights, obtaining only a little sleep at intervals. [...] Mr Jackson, our medical man, was most attentive, but evidently all aid was fruitless. [...] It was my turn to rest until 3, but 10 minutes before that hour I was called on to assist the poor baby who was again in a fit. It

was his last! As I held him on the pillow into a sitting posture, he died. We both witnessed the departure of life from his little body, and our dear little "Dicky", as we used to call him, was no more. Anna had never before seen death, nor had I ever witnessed it so plainly. [...]

May 10, Wednesday. The whole household felt the loss of our poor baby. In the course of the day, a lady artist called Miss Daniel came at my request and made a pencil drawing of little Henry Douglas, as he lay on the bed in our spare[12] bedroom.

On the following Saturday the 13 month old baby was buried in the vault of Bow Church "a most remarkable place [...] of immense antiquity. Hundreds of coffins piled in rows along the path-way up to the ceiling formed an awful sight." On their return home their elder son, William Arthur ("Arté"), who had also caught measles and whooping cough, became seriously ill. Over the next ten days, despite the efforts of Mr Jackson and Dr Davis ("famous for his knowledge of the diseases of children"), he gradually weakened. Arté died at 7 o'clock in the morning of Wednesday 24 May.

St Mary-le-Bow crypt, where Henry and Arté were buried.

The room was still covered with his playthings, the box of tools which Smith the baker had given him only a week before, and the box of bricks which had so often furnished him amusement. His third birthday, if he had lived so long, would have been the 10th of September. He had endeared himself to all the family in a thousand ways: no doubt the case is the same with other persons in the case of their first two or three children, and now we felt that our house was left desolate. [...] It was not 2 months ago that I found him in the long passage of the City of London School running up and down among 300 of the boys, all of whom seemed as delighted as he was. [...] The boys of the City of London School had a holiday this day, being the 18th birthday of the Princess Victoria, and the day on which she came of age.[13]

Family and friends rallied to help the grieving couple. William Giles and Allen's brother Frank came from Frome. Since the boy's body was in the only spare bedroom, they had to sleep at the Castle and Falcon, as did Giles's old friend John Middleton. Mrs Aldrit, the former Bridgewater housekeeper, paid an unexpected visit, and Mrs Thurlby came several times from Camberwell to comfort Anna.

May 29, Monday. On this day which we used in Somersetshire to celebrate with much fun as oak-apple day, we conveyed the body of our dear little William Arthur to Bow Church. My father, my brother Frank, and Henry Dickinson followed the coffin: the same awful vault was opened, and the same sad ceremony gone through. The coffin of the younger child again lay before us, and the sexton promised to place them one on the other. [...] And so we saw the last of our dear little boy. His death took place on the birthday of the princess Victoria (now Queen of England) and his funeral on that of the King [William IV]; and so two days of public rejoicing were to us days of mourning![14]

Dr John Tricker Conquest, lithograph by M.Gauci after R.W Warren.

Of course school life continued despite these personal tragedies. There were two weeks left before the end of the second quarter and start of the summer holiday, which was seen as the end of the scholastic year.[15] The regulations required an annual public examination of the pupils and distribution of prizes, the first of which was held on Friday 16 June. With the school less than five months old, the examination was low-key, conducted "by their respective Masters in the presence of the several Members of the Committee",[16] with prizes distributed by Hale. All this took place in the Theatre "the VI. V. IV. Classes, from 10 till half-past 11; III. II. I. Classes, from half-past 11 till 1; Junior Class from 1 till 2. The Distribution of Prizes will commence at 2 o'clock, when all the Pupils of the School will be present in the Theatre."[17] This must have all been a bit of a scramble, as can be seen from the prize lists: each class (or division of a class) has a separate list, apparently hastily written by its Master. A note on the list for Class VI says that the examiners awarded the prize as 1st Boy, which was presumably the gold medal offered by Dr Conquest, to Henry Judge Hose.

Instead having a peaceful start to the holidays the now childless couple spent the whole of the following Monday packing up their furniture, so that the painting of the school and other remaining work could be completed. The next day, 20 June, they began their travels. On the journey they heard that the King was dead, and the Princess Victoria was now Queen. "This news did not prevent our having a very pleasant journey down to Windlesham" where, in the company of Henry Shaw[18] the distinguished architectural draughtsman and Mr Mann the builder, they speedily chose the site for the house they planned to build on their recently purchased land. Shaw, who had been a friend since the Camberwell days, designed the house; his architect's fee was £70.[19] Next month Giles's brother Charles was to join Shaw's office to study architecture.[20] After spending the night in Bagshot they set off for Cornwall, reaching Exeter on Wednesday and Falmouth on Thursday. For the next month they enjoyed touring in Cornwall, Devon and Dorset.[21] They were therefore not present at the School on 5 July when

> The Committee viewed the several parts of the Building and inspected the progress making in Painting, Colouring, and otherwise completing the same, and finding that a Drawing Room Stove had by some mistake been fixed in the Room at the North West Corner of the first floor, they directed that it should be forthwith removed to the Room on the same floor at the South West Corner, the first mentioned Room being considered by the Committee to belong to the School department (in accordance with the original Plans[22]) and not to form part of the Head Master's House. The Walls were therefore directed to be painted, similar to those of the Library or Committee Room, instead of being papered.

Mr and Mrs Giles started their return journey from Charmouth on 18 July, going via Southampton and Windlesham ("the walls of the new house are now about 2 feet from the ground") and reaching London in the afternoon of Thursday 20 July. They found that the work at the school was not yet finished, so slept at Blossom's Inn and went next day to temporary lodgings in Camberwell. On the same day Brewer had to write to all the parents:

> City of London School 21st July 1837
>
> Sir,
>
> I am directed to acquaint you that, in order to prevent the possibility of any injury to the health of the Pupils by their assembling at School too early after the completion of the Painting and other works which have been carrying on during the vacation, the Committee have deemed it advisable to postpone the reopening of the School for one week, viz. until Monday the 31st day of July Instant, by which time the Building will be completely fit for the reception of the Pupils.

Strangely the *Diary* entry for Tuesday 1 August says "our apartments at the City School being now ready, we returned to them and spent the whole day in arranging the furniture,"[23] which suggests the Head Master had nothing better to do on the second day of term. He does not mention the Committee's thwarting of his attempted territorial expansion, but no doubt this rankled.

In fact he was busy finishing a large-scale "Report of the state of the City of London School. June 1 1837"[24] which he delivered for the Committee on 3 August. This refers to "The Scheme, which is drawn out for the whole School on one large sheet of paper, which will be easily understood with the help of the following explanations." This one large sheet of paper (i.e. the school timetable) has not survived, but the explanations give details of the curriculum for each class, including homework. For example, for Class IV:

> Bible & Sacred History – 4 Lessons besides Scripture Questions on Saturdays
> History, Chronology & Geography (reading aloud) – 2½ hours
> Geography – 2 Lessons besides one evening
> Writing – 4 hours in the week
> Mathematics & Arithmetic – 5 hours in the week
> Latin – 5 hours in the week & two evenings
> French – two lessons of 1½ hours each & one evening
> Greek – 4 hours in the week
> English Grammar & Poetry – one lesson of 1½ hour & one evening

It is interesting to see that English Grammar & Poetry lessons are timetabled for every class. The City of London School has long been recognised as a pioneer of the teaching of English, but this has previously been dated to the Beaufoy Shakespeare prizes (1850) and the enlightened Headmastership of Edwin Abbott which started in 1865. It seems that Giles deserves some credit too.

The Report includes the arrangements for teaching Hebrew and German, French, Drawing and Writing, and concludes with the Head Master's routine:

> Superintends the whole & visits each class once a day.
> Takes the exercises of each class in turn throughout the School, one class every day.
> Has three smaller classes every day:
> > One – in Greek selected from the higher pupils
> > A second – in Latin ditto
> > A third – in History, Geography & Chronology or any other subject according to circumstances, selected from the 4 lowest Classes in the School, 3 boys from each.

Benjamin Wyon's
Commemorative medal

The Committee had decided to commemorate the successful start of the school by issuing a medal, and had approved a design commissioned from the distinguished engraver Benjamin Wyon.[25] This showed the Milk Street facade of the school on one side, with on the reverse a seated figure of Knowledge instructing a youth who leans on a tablet inscribed "John Carpenter 1447"[26] surmounted by the City badge. On 3 June the Committee ordered 60 of these in silver at 21 shillings and 300 in bronze at 7 shillings. One was sent to Dr Conquest, who replied to Brewer:

> Finsbury Square
> August 21st 1837
>
> Dear Sir
> I beg to acknowledge the receipt of your letter with the silver medal which accompanied it. Have the goodness to tender my thanks to the committee and assure them that I feel the liveliest interest in the prosperity of the City of London School, & shall have much pleasure in fulfilling my engagement to present a gold medal of the value of ten guineas every year, as long as it may please God to

prolong my life, to the boy who may be selected by the proper judges as deserving of such an expression of their approbation.
I remain
Yours faithfully
J.T.Conquest

On 5 August 1837 the Head Master and Mrs Giles marked the start of the new academic year by having all the masters dine with them in their newly papered house. But despite this show of harmony there were staff problems brewing.

At the end of the previous term Abraham Newland had been absent for several days, and had written to Giles to say there might be further absences because of "urgent family business". This Giles conveyed to the Committee, with the result that the Secretary wrote to Newland on 2 August to say that the Committee "have directed me to acquaint you that they cannot allow your absence to be protracted beyond the end of the present week, and that unless you resume your duties on Monday morning next they will be under the necessity of considering your Situation in this Establishment as vacant." It is not known whether Newland complied, or what else was going on, but the result was that on 23 August

> The Committee were attended by The Revd J.A.Giles, Head Master, who presented a Letter that had been addressed to him by Mr Abraham Newland, one of the Assistant Masters, stating that hearing that some suspicions are in circulation which have called his character in question, and as such reports will have the effect of preventing the efficient discharge of his duties with comfort to himself, he thought it better at once to vacate his Situation at the School.

The Committee accepted Newland's resignation, but complied with his request for a Testimonial stating that the Secretary was "authorized by the Committee to bear their testimony to the very efficient and satisfactory manner in which you acquitted yourself in your several duties."

At the same meeting:

> Mr Giles stated that he had to call the attention of the Committee to the circumstance of Mr Fredk. Hathaway, one of the Assistant Masters, having struck a Boy named Stephen Blackburn a blow on the head with a knobbed stick, so as to cause blood to flow and render him unfit to attend the School, and that this was the third instance in which the severity of the punishment adopted by Mr Hathaway had occasioned Boys in his Class to be kept at home.

> Mr Hathaway being sent for was heard in explanation of the circumstance, and Abraham Sumner, the Porter, and Mr Robert Pitt Edkins, the Second Master, were also heard.

> A Motion was made and question proposed:

"That Mr Frederick Hathaway be dismissed from his Situation of one of the Assistant Masters of the School."

To which an amendment was proposed [and agreed]

"That the further consideration of the subject be adjourned to an early day, and that the Boy Blackburn and one of his Parents be requested to attend this Committee thereon."

The adjourned meeting resumed on Friday 25 August, when Mrs Blackburn and her son Stephen attended and gave their accounts. But by then Hathaway had offered his resignation, and the Committee "Resolved that the resignation of Mr Hathaway be accepted, the practice of severe corporal punishment, which appears, upon enquiry, to have been repeatedly resorted to by him, being incompatible with the Spirit of the Regulations of the School."

At the same meeting Giles first mentioned to the Committee his concerns about Dr Bialloblotzky, the German and Hebrew teacher. This is the start of a long saga which will be the subject of Chapter 7.

On 6 September Charles Woodroffe was promoted to fill Newland's position. He was to serve the school with distinction for forty years; in 1937 the former Prime Minister Lord Asquith (CLS 1864-70) recalled[27] that "he had never the least difficulty in maintaining order, or in securing not only the attention but the interest of the boys". A week later three new masters were elected: Thomas Ward as Assistant Master in the Junior Class to replace Woodroffe, Thomas Hellyer to replace Hathaway, and Thomas Hall to the additional post of Assistant Writing Master which had been created to ease the pressure on the Writing Master (who had classes of up to 80 to deal with) and allow more time for teaching Bookkeeping.

A carefully composed letter to the Committee, written in a clear bold hand and dated 16 August,[28] is the earliest surviving pupil document, and is perhaps the first instance of the independent initiative that is characteristic of CLS boys:

Gentlemen

We beg leave to inform you that we have established a circulating library consisting of above 100 members, have chosen a committee, and purchased books to the amount £12.

Under these circumstances we would respectfully request a room to keep our books and for the transaction of the business incident to our society. We further hope that your Committee will approve of the books we have selected, of the regulations by which we purpose to conduct ourselves, and our desire to cooperate with you in the advancement of sound and polite learning. If this be the case we assure you Gentlemen we shall receive with the greatest gratitude any further assistance you may think proper to give to our infant association.

In the name of our body we beg leave to sign ourselves most respectfully

J.H.Wright (Secretary), C.W.C.Hutton (Treasurer)

The first
boys' letter.
16 August 1837.

The Committee agreed that, subject to their receiving further details of the regulations by which the library was run, the names of those involved, and lists of books already purchased and proposed, the books should be kept in the Boarders Sitting Room, and that they would provide a suitable bookcase and a grant of £20 for buying more books.

Less commendable was the behaviour of the first boy to be suspended from the school. Giles wrote to the Committee on 29 September:

> I have to inform you that a boy by the name of Sumerfield [*sic*] has very much insulted Mr Edkins by drawing figures on the large slate in the 6th Class room. The matter having been reported to me, I have suspended the boy from attending the School with the intention of expelling him altogether. In the mean time his parents have entreated me to restore him, but I have thought proper not to accede to the request. I now leave the affair in the hands of the Committee, and hope that they will deal with the case in the way that seems to them best, on consulting with Mr Edkins. I have no wish to inflict so serious disgrace on the boy as final expulsion, if he can be brought to see the impropriety of his conduct.[29]

The Committee tempered justice with mercy on this occasion, and Alfred Summerfield, whose father was a pocket-book maker of Noble Street, Cheapside, remained a pupil until summer 1838.

The Sub Committee held an important meeting on 20 September. Having made various recommendations relating to the German class (see Chapter 7) they then considered the Report and Scheme of Studies which Giles had submitted seven weeks earlier. They wanted "Mapping and Planning to be taught by the Writing Master at the same time and in the same room as Drawing is taught by the Drawing Master" (the Report had stated that the Writing Master did this "in a private room with a few select pupils") and recommended that boys should be provided with exercise books rather than loose sheets of paper. Their main conclusion was that "it would tend greatly to promote the interests of the School if the Head Master were in future to have charge of a separate and distinct Class, in the same manner that other Masters have, for the study of the higher departments of knowledge."

They then addressed a domestic matter:

> The Sub Committee having ascertained that a large number of Slates on the Roof have been broken, and the Lead flats and gutters exposed to serious injury, in consequence of the Boys who reside with the Head Master, and his Servants, having access thereto and of the Slop Pails etc from his House being emptied there

> Resolved that the Architect do forthwith cause the damage to be made good, and that the Head Master be informed that the Committee expect he will take care to prevent a repetition of such practices, and preclude the Boys and Servants from all access to the Roofs by keeping the Key of the Door exclusively in his own possession, otherwise the Committee will be under the necessity of either requiring the Key to be returned to them or directing the communication from the House to be stopped up.

The Grand Committee agreed to these resolutions on 4 October (by which time the roof had been repaired), and on 10 October Giles wrote in response. On the establishment of a separate Head Master's Class he says "a distinct class is already under my own tuition and has been so during the whole half-year, except such times as I was engaged in discharging the duties of the Masters who have lately left us". Regarding the roof, he confirms that he has complied with their wishes, but adds that "the two boys on the Foundation are exceedingly well behaved and have never done any mischief to the roof" and notes that "The Committee probably do not consider the number of carpenters and plasterers who worked upon the roof in making the ventilators to the class-rooms, and of the quantity of timber which was then carried out upon the leads and which probably caused the damage to the slates."[30]

The Committee's response the next day was to point out that what Giles stated in this letter was at odds with what he said in his Report about having only an occasional or temporary class, and to repeat that they wanted him to form a Seventh Class under his charge. Compromise was reached after joint discussion on 25 October when Giles, Edkins and Webster all agreed that "the Fifth Class be left entirely to the care of the Third Master, and that the Sixth Class be divided into two Classes or Divisions to be alternately taught Classics by the Head Master and Mathematics by the Second Master".

The enterprising pupil Joseph Henry Wright attended the 11 October meeting to thank the Committee on behalf of the School Library's managing committee for the assistance they had been given. He did not miss the opportunity of requesting on behalf of the whole school that "the Committee would, if possible, provide some accommodation for the Boys to witness the visit of Her Majesty to the City on Lord Mayor's day next [Thursday 9 November]." This was referred to the Court of Common Council, who within a week agreed that a vacant site between Newgate Street and Paternoster Row at the west end of Cheapside could be used, at a cost not exceeding £250.

By 16 October Bunning had produced designs for a stand to accommodate 520 boys (allowing 18 inches each), at an estimated cost of £166 excluding decorations, and these were put out to tender. The Sub Committee sought permission for a boy to deliver a Congratulatory Address to Her Majesty, but the Home Department replied that there would not be time (though a boy from Christ's Hospital was allowed to do exactly this at Temple Bar). Final arrangements were made on 6 November. The boys, Masters and visitors were to assemble at the School by 11.30 and proceed in a body to the Platform and Seats erected for them. Each boy and visitor was requested to provide himself with and wear a white rosette not exceeding three inches in diameter. The visitors (members of the Committee and of the Committee of City Lands) would sit at the north end of the stand in numbered seats which would be allocated by lot. The Chairman assumed responsibility for providing the pupils and visitors with sandwiches and two 36 Gallon barrels of ale (1.1 pints each).

The great day started cold and foggy, though the sun broke through in the afternoon. Queen Victoria's visit to the City of London drew enormous crowds, as this was the first opportunity that many had had to see their new young monarch. The extensive newspaper coverage includes the following:

> In the course of yesterday the inhabitants of Cheapside and the east side of St Paul's decorated their houses with evergreens, and in numerous instances Union Jacks and ornaments, consisting of flowers, &c., were extended from one side of

the street to the other. The road on each side was lined with Household Troops and police constables to keep a clear passage for the procession. Every street and avenue was completely blocked up by the crowd.

At an early hour of the morning masses of people were seen flocking in every direction, and ladies and gentlemen by daybreak proceeded eagerly to take possession of their seats, and by seven and eight o'clock the shop fronts and every room in the various houses were filled with beauty and fashion. The tops of the houses were also lined by spectators, who remained during the day with the most anxious suspense until the arrival of the procession. The belfries of the various churches and every situation commanding a view of the road were also fitted up for the accommodation of the public; and, by the hour of nine o'clock, the spectacle exhibited was splendid and highly interesting. The erection for the pupils, &c. of the City of London School was crowded to excess by the boys and their tutors; and the spacious building, being covered with drapery and evergreens, had a most beautiful effect.[31]

The costs of providing the School's accommodation (with decorations) and refreshment were slightly over budget at £266.19.11.[32]

On 6 December "A Member of the Committee having brought under their notice a case of general insubordination manifested by the Boys of the 6th Class on Monday the 27th Ultimo, the Committee were at their request attended by Mr Edkins, the Master of the Class, and also by the Head Master, who explained to the Committee the steps that were taken on the occasion to suppress the insubordination and that the result was that the Class had since been reduced to a proper state of discipline." The brilliant but eccentric[33] Edkins, though esteemed by his star pupils, was renowned for making unreasonable demands on most; perhaps this time the worms had turned.

Just before Christmas came the unwelcome resignation of the Revd William Bailey, Master of the Fourth Class, in consequence of his having been appointed Chaplain to the Ionian Islands. In accepting this the Committee were "desirous of testifying to that Gentleman their cordial approbation of the manner in which he has performed the duties of his Office and the esteem they have been led to entertain for his character."[34] His successor, the Revd William Cook, M.A. of Trinity College, Cambridge, was elected on 10 January 1838.

The fourth quarter ended on Friday 22 December, by which time there were 481 boys in the school. The next day Giles and Anna set off to visit her old Aunt Ann at Ware.[35] Her sister and brother-in-law had recently died, and so she "being now lonely and also more independent, turned her thoughts to her nephews and nieces, and so invited us to come and spend Christmas every year at her house. Henry Dickinson went with us, as also my brother Charles and [Anna's niece] Lucy Dalley, all three of whom were living at our house."[36] Christmas Day was Dickensian *avant la lettre:*[37] "a gigantic turkey, an immense piece of boiled beef, and a plumb [sic] pudding, to match them, formed our dinner, at 5 o'clock."

5

Gresham College

Sir Thomas Gresham (1519-1579), prosperous merchant and founder of the Royal Exchange, left his house in Bishopsgate[1] and income from the Royal Exchange jointly to the Corporation of the City of London and to the Mercers' Company to establish and support the institution which became known as Gresham College. The College was to have seven Professors who were to reside in the house and to receive £50 annually (then more than the stipends of Regius Professors at Oxford and Cambridge) to give public lectures. The Corporation had the nomination of the Professors in Divinity, Astronomy, Geometry and Music, while the Mercers had Law, Physic and Rhetoric. These provisions could not be put into effect until the death of Gresham's widow in 1597, by which time many of those who had known him had also died, and clear sight had been lost of his intentions. These seem, at least in part, to have been to make available to the merchants and mariners who thronged the City free instruction on useful topics in geography and navigation. To balance these practical aims with scholarship, and to cater for the large number of foreigners in London, each lecture was given twice, in Latin and then in English. The Joint Grand Gresham Committee (JGGC), with representatives from the 'City side' and the 'Mercers side', was set up to govern the College and be its Trustees.

The Professors were appointed, moved into the Bishopsgate house (renamed Gresham College), and began to lecture from October 1597. Notable early incumbents included the musician John Bull, and the mathematician Henry Briggs, who had turned Napier's invention of logarithms into a practicable system of enormous value to science. Although Gresham's aim for useful popular education seems to have been met only partially, and some of the professors were notably negligent, Gresham College did come to play an important role as a meeting place for scholars, particularly scientists. Christopher Wren, appointed Professor of Astronomy in 1657 at the age of 25, was one of the leaders of the group of scientists who in 1660 formed the Royal Society,[2] which was housed at Gresham College until 1711. Robert Hooke was appointed Curator of Experiments in 1663, and became Gresham Professor of Geometry the following year, retaining this post until his death in 1704 – he was the last professor to live in the College.

Gresham's Bishopsgate house occupied a very valuable site, which in the early part of the 18th century the JGGC were keen to redevelop. Various plans were challenged and defeated before the Gresham College Bill passed in 1768 and the Professors were ousted from their quarters. They were awarded an additional annuity of £50 each for the loss of their accommodation (the eldest objected, but settled for £100), and "as their Collegiate life would be at an end" they were allowed to marry, despite this being prohibited in the Founder's will. These changes were later seen to be disastrous:

> "Gresham College was levelled to the ground and all trace of its beauty and grandeur obliterated by an Act of the Legislature. I believe that this act of wanton and ruthless barbarism to be without parallel in the history of civilised man. [...] All that is now known of Gresham College is the periodical announcement in the newspapers that lectures are to be delivered in the Royal Exchange in an obscure corner and at an inconvenient hour."[3]

The "obscure corner" was a room provided for the lectures in the Royal Exchange, tucked away above various offices and counting houses and difficult to find.[4] By the 1820s the average attendance at lectures in English was ten per lecture, while for Latin lectures it was thirteen per *year*. Mr Deputy Gorst "recollected years ago having gone to the lecture room some five minutes before the hour appointed for the lecture, and the door was closed, the porter[5] stating that the lecturer had not come. He went there again ten minutes afterwards, and was told that the lecturer had gone away as there were no persons present to hear the lecture,"[6] and even the Town Clerk (Woodthorpe) confessed that "I am not aware what accommodation there is in the lecture room for the public. I have never been at a lecture. I have tried many times but found the door locked."[7]

In December 1829 a determined effort was made to improve matters. The JGGC first sought legal advice from the Attorney General and the Solicitor General as to whether the Committee had powers to alter the subject, language of delivery, location, and timing of the lectures. Counsel's opinion was no to the first and yes to the rest, provided that the lectures remained in the City of London. The JGGC then proposed moving the lectures to the London Institution[8], and holding them in the evening and in English only[9]. The Gresham Professors resisted strongly, and after a year's discussion the plan was dropped. Various other locations were suggested, including the Guildhall Library and St Paul's School, but nothing happened.

The first hint of a link with the City of London School came in February 1834 when Royal Commissioners,[10] sitting in Guildhall to gather evidence on the Corporation of London, enquired about the Gresham College Estates. The Clerk of the Mercers' Gresham Committee wrote, saying he was directed by the Joint Committee not to attend, but referring the commissioners instead to the report of the Charity Commission (printed ten years earlier)[11] "which I believe will be found to contain all the information required by the Commissioners of Inquiry into the state of Municipal Corporations." So all the evidence the commissioners heard came from the City representatives.

There was much discussion of the fact that the Gresham Trust was heavily in debt to the Corporation, due originally to loans for rebuilding the Royal Exchange after its destruction in the Great Fire of 1666. Richard Taylor, later a prominent member of the School Committee, was very critical of the division of responsibilities between the Corporation and the Mercers: "The Gresham Committee expended money just as they pleased, and were not accountable to any body. The union of the City with the Mercers' Company had destroyed the control over the expenditure of the Gresham Committee."[12]

In acknowledging that the whole situation was far from satisfactory Woodthorpe informed the committee that the Court of Common Council had determined to petition Parliament to get rid of Honey Lane Market, and appropriate it to the purpose of what he called the London Corporation School, the whole management to be in the hands of the Common Council. The City Lands Committee had been instructed to confer with the Committee of the Gresham estate about introducing some clauses in the proposed Bill, authorising the Gresham lectures to be delivered in some part of the City of London not connected with the Gresham property, and at other times. In the event these clauses were discussed, but according to Hale[13] the committee "were assured by the lecturers that if they persevered they (the lecturers) would do all they could to defeat the bill", so they were dropped.

However, connecting Gresham College with the City of London School remained a live issue, as can be seen from the May 1835 plans of Bunning's winning design. These clearly include a capacious Professors' Room, though no such accommodation was mentioned in the Instructions to Architects. By November 1836 – perhaps in response to the attitude of the Gresham lecturers – their grand room had been taken for other purposes, and they had been given Classroom 2 (on the ground floor near the Theatre). Later there was a proposal to subdivide the room immediately above, Classroom 6, giving two thirds to the Professors and the rest to storage, but this did not happen. By May 1838 it seems that the Professors had no room allocated to them (see p.93).

On 5 November 1836 a sub committee of the Gresham Trustees viewed the "spacious lecture-room within the school-house" and resolved that "it appeared a more eligible place for the delivery of the lectures than that now occupied for the purpose". Two days later the Gresham Lecturers were formally informed that the Gresham and City School Committees proposed moving the Gresham lectures to the new City of London School. All the Professors except the Professor of Astronomy, Joseph Pullen, met on 17 November to consider this. Pullen, who had been appointed in 1833 on more flexible terms than the rest, was tractable, but the other six were entrenched. Two had been appointed recently, Henry Southey (Astronomy) in October 1834 and William Palmer (Law) in February 1836. The rest averaged over 30 years of service each and had no wish for their undemanding routine to be disturbed. As the City Solicitor put it: "[A] vacancy seldom if ever occurs until the death of a lecturer, and that energy and thirst for popularity, which would naturally stimulate a young man looking to preferment in later life, fails to operate upon those of more advanced age."[14]

The six Professors present summarised their opposition by unanimously agreeing nine resolutions, including

> 5. That Sir Thomas Gresham designed to establish a college for the cultivation of science in its higher departments; and, without any disparagement of the new foundation, or any pretensions on the part of the lecturers, the Gresham lectures would be rather degraded in being delivered in the lecture-room of a school.

This obduracy, when communicated to the School and Gresham committees, brought matters to a head at a lively meeting of Common Council on 8 December 1836, reported extensively in *The Times*[15] :

> THE CITY OF LONDON SCHOOL AND THE GRESHAM LECTURES.
>
> The report of the proceedings adopted on the subject of transferring the Gresham lectures from the small incommodious room at the Royal Exchange to the City of London School was introduced, and caused a good deal of observation. There are seven lecturers under the will of Sir Thomas Gresham each of whom is paid a liberal salary for occasionally lecturing upon scientific and other topics, in an obscure apartment in the Royal Exchange, and the very spacious and commodious school endowed by the corporation being almost finished, a committee was appointed to consider and report the best means of deriving some public advantage from the employment of the lecturers. The corporation have been for some time endeavouring to obtain the consent of the gentlemen who derive the pecuniary emolument from these appointments to transfer their exertions to some more enlarged sphere of action within the city; but hitherto all attempts to induce them to leave the old station, whose walls have so long witnessed their abortive labours, have been ineffectual. Within the last month a more than usually strong effort has been made to prevail upon the lecturers to accept the accommodation afforded by the new City of London School, upon the suggestion of Mr. Baylis[16], a member of the Court of Common Council, and yesterday the result of the application was stated.
>
> The lecturers replied to the application of the corporation, who together with the Mercers' Company are trustees to the Gresham estate, by several objections, all of which were persisted in by six of the lecturers, Dr. Pullen's, the lecturer on astronomy, being the only name not signed to the refusal to acquiesce in the proposition of the Court. They were, they said, most anxious to promote the public utility of the lectures, but they would not acknowledge any authority upon the part of the trustees of the Gresham estate to interfere with them in accomplishing that object. They regretted to be obliged to state their conviction that the removal of the lectures to the City of London School would not be advantageous to the public, but on the contrary would be injurious to the foundation of the Gresham institution, by attaching it to the school and destroying its independence; that by the act of Parliament the lecturers were to have the undivided, undisturbed possession of the

place in which the lectures were to be delivered - a condition which could not be conceded in the City of London School, a connexion with which would be rather a degradation than anything desirable to the lecturers; that the Gresham funds were quite adequate to the carrying on of the existing system, and that, as a proof of the popular nature of the exertions of the lecturers, 1,900 persons had attended during the last year. The lecturers added some less material objections, and concluded by expressing a hope that the corporation would, if they entertained the intention of making any alteration, effect it by improving the lecture-room of the Royal Exchange, or by erecting an independent building for the lectures on another part of the Gresham estate. The committee appointed to negotiate reported to the Court that, for the reasons expressed above, they found it impracticable to carry into effect the resolution of the corporation.

Mr. BAYLIS said, that having brought forward the subject some time ago, and expressed a sanguine opinion that the lecturers, as men of literature and science, would have gladly acquiesced in the proposition to render the Gresham will more available than it had been for so long a period, he felt that he was in a painful position. If he was surprised at their disinclination to render the service he had requested of them, he was still more surprised at the reasons which they had advanced, and which appeared to him to be an insult to the Court, and a disgrace to themselves and to the institutions and to the memory of the founder. (Hear, hear.[17]) The lecturers, it would appear, thought that they could do as they pleased; but he would pledge himself to the Court that he should persevere in bringing forward the question in different shapes until the object he sought should be accomplished. From one thing their conduct had effectually relieved him at all events - the obligation to treat them with any extraordinary delicacy or forbearance. (A laugh.) The lecturers exercised, it was evident, a power completely despotic. Notwithstanding the opinions of Lord Abinger and Sir Edward Sugden, in 1830, that it was competent to the trustees to remove the lectures to any part within the city of London, they asserted their authority, and showed an utter disregard of the rules either of law or of honour. The London School Committee had offered them the undisturbed possession of an apartment in every way calculated for the office which, as lecturers, they would have to perform; but it occurred to them, amongst other grounds of opposition, that they would be degraded by the association. (A laugh.) Degradation implied a falling down to something lower than the former position; but how was that definition borne out by the change from an obscure closet to a lecturing theatre, equal in size to any in the universities, and where, provided the lecturers were competent to the task they undertook, a crowded audience would be sure to attend? (Hear, hear.) It had been said that 1,900 persons had attended the lectures during the last year. By the calculations of themselves, it appeared that Mr. Pullen, the popular astronomical lecturer, had had 600 of those, and that there were 78 lecture days, so that taking into account the labours of the seven professors, the average of the six must have amounted to a very beggarly exhibition. Mr. Baylis then argued upon the intention of the founder, which he said was not confined to the greater improvement of the learned, but to the diffusion of intelligence through all ranks of the citizens of London, to whom, as Sir Thomas Gresham had gained much from them, he was determined to leave something. (Cheers.) Now the question would be asked; what they were to do ? He should answer that question by asking another. Were they prepared, as trustees of the estate, to allow the will of the lecturers to be the law by which they were to be guided? Were they to suffer themselves to be trodden under foot by the dependents upon the institution which they were bound to see answer the purposes for which it was framed ? (Hear, hear.) No. The Court must show those who set their authority at defiance, the nature and quality of the power they possessed, and if it should turn out that the lecturers were omnipotent, why then a remedy might be sought for at the hands of the Legislature. (Cheers.) Mr. Baylis concluded by moving "That the communication of the clerk to the Mercers' Company to the Town-clerk be referred to the City of London School Committee, and that it be an instruction to such committee to consider the relative rights of the corporation and the Mercers' Company, as co-trustees of the Gresham estate, and of the professors, and whether any and what steps should be taken more fully to carry out the intentions of Sir Thomas Gresham's will, by making the lectures more beneficial to the public."

Mr. HALE (Chairman of the City of London School Committee), seconded the motion. He stated that the school committee had shown the warmest disposition to meet the wishes of the lecturers; but could not think of acceding to the demand as a speculative condition of removal of the exclusive use of the theatre of the school. (Laughter.) The committee offered an apartment, however, of which they should have unbounded control; and he little thought, after the high encomiums they had passed upon the building, and the commodiousness of its arrangements, that they would have preferred the miserable hole in which they hid themselves from the public eye. But he understood now that it was their intention to make a stir about erecting an exclusive building, although contrary to their own assertion, the estate was considerably in debt to the corporation, he believed 20,000*l*.

Mr. R. L. JONES stated, that he was afraid the present reference would meet the fate of all past references on this subject. He, as a member of the London Institution, had used his utmost efforts to remove the lectures thither, but the excuse was, that the building was not within the limits of the ancient city, and upon that ground the attempt failed. He believed that as long as the present lecturers existed the evil would be without remedy, and he feared that no power of compulsion upon them was to be exercised.

Mr. STEVENS thought that a very good way to effect the object the corporation had in view would be to endeavour to prevail upon the public press to send reporters to the closet in the Royal Exchange, to give accounts of the lectures delivered there. He apprehended that the real objections of the lecturers would then be shown to be, that they were sensible of their own total incompetency to the offices they pretended to fill. (Laughter.) He had reason to think, that with the exception of the astronomical lecturer, they were a miserable set of sticks. But their tendency to lazyness was quite inexcusable. They might surely read from a paper copied from a book, their only source of intelligence, a lecture, of the originality of which the public were no judges; but even that they would not do, and he had been frequently doomed to hear in this place of obscurity where the professors flourished as great trash as ever issued from the mouth of a fellow creature. (Laughter.) The Court was bound not to suffer the matter to rest, but to prosecute it with vigour, now that they had a splendid establishment ready, to which the Gresham institution might be made infinitely serviceable. (Cheers.) [...]

Undersheriff WIRE [...] regarded the whole of the objections as a system of mere special pleading, wholly unworthy of men of literature and honour. As for the removal, the original place was the site on which the Excise-office stood at that moment, from whence a removal took place to the Royal Exchange, and, as a matter of course, it would be as reasonable to remove from the present situation to one which was also within the well-ascertained boundaries of the city. (Hear, hear.) [...] For himself he could say, that frequently, upon going to the closet three minutes after the exact time, the door had been shut in his face. (Laughter.) And why was this? Because it was easier to pocket the salary for doing nothing than to earn it by the performance of duties, however obligatory and with whatever facility discharged. (Hear, hear.) How did those lecturers manifest their disposition to promote the public utility? By stowing themselves into a room 12 feet by 10 feet, and slapping the door in the faces of those who attempted to enter three minutes after their own hour. [...]

Mr. GALLOWAY [...] highly commended the exertions of Mr. Baylis on the subject, and hoped that the unanimous support of the Court would be rendered to that gentleman's labours. The motion was then agreed to.

The Gresham Professors quickly respond to these aspersions by means of a letter dated 9 December and published in *The Times* on 13 December. This was signed "One of the Lecturers" but their spokesman seems to have been Samuel Birch, Rector of St Mary Woolnoth, chaplain to two Lord Mayors and son of an Alderman, who had been Professor of Geometry since 1808. One of his lectures (on air resistance and friction) was described by Birkbeck as "not very original and rather drowsy". The letter included all nine resolutions, with footnotes, in order to "better enable you [...] to judge fairly concerning the present question." The reaction was swift: two days later at the Court of Common Council Mr Baylis presented the following petition, signed by 120 citizens of London, headed by Dr Birkbeck and some of the most opulent of the bankers, traders, and merchants in the city.[18]

To the Right Hon. the Lord Mayor, Aldermen, and Commons of the City of London, in Common Council assembled, the petition of the undersigned citizens of London, humbly sheweth:-

That your petitioners are anxious to claim the renewed attention of your honourable Court in the subject of the lectures founded by Sir Thomas Gresham. That your petitioners belong to that class of the community for whose benefit these lectures were especially intended, namely the citizens of London. That as it is notorious that the Gresham professorships have been, for a long time, (with one exception) little better than useless sinecures, it was with much satisfaction we learned that a proposition was sanctioned by your honourable Court, having for its object an alteration in the time for delivering the lectures, and their removal to the Theatre of the City of London School, an institution in which the citizens of London feel a deep interest, and where the public might derive that benefit which the munificent bequest is calculated to yield if the real intentions of Sir Thomas Gresham's will were carried into effect. That your petitioners have heard, with mingled surprise and indignation, that the only obstruction to the arrangement has arisen from the obstinacy of the Gresham lecturers, whose objections they conceive to be of the most frivolous and vexatious character, and calculated to induce in the minds of your petitioners a suspicion of their incapacity to perform the duties of the offices they hold. That this conduct is so decidedly opposed to the interests of literature and science, and to the enlightened spirit of the present age, that your petitioners have thought it their duty respectfully to urge your honourable Court as trustees of the Gresham Estate to take such decisive measures as the nature of the case may demand for making the lectures really useful to the citizens of London and creditable to the memory of the founder.[19]

The Lord Mayor having asked the petitioners whether they wished to add anything, Dr Birkbeck then spoke at length, adding a personal touch to the familiar arguments. He recalled that he had

directed public attention to this subject in the year 1819, in a lecture delivered soon after the opening of the London Institution, and subsequently took a part [...] in the negotiations actively, and to a certain extent successfully, carried forward by the Gresham Committee. (Hear, hear.) Had not the opposition of the professors prevailed, the lectures would then have been transferred to that splendid and prosperous establishment. (Cheers.) Those gentlemen, to the great astonishment of all who were concerned in this negotiation, resisted most obstinately every idea of change as illegal, forgetting how much change in the original plan and purposes of the Gresham College had already occurred [...]. The power which can legalize this deterioration can certainly legalize improvement; and the authority by which professors are appointed can, it is hoped, be exercised for the purpose of rendering them efficient dispensers of the literary and scientific bounty of the illustrious founder.

He was scornful of the Professors' meagre attendance figures, pointing out that a recent set of six lectures elsewhere by an eminent professor of chemistry[20] had drawn a total audience exceeding 4000, more than double the whole Gresham year, and also of their high remuneration: £700 per year, when "for five guineas per lecture, the services of men possessing the most extensive acquaintance with ancient and modern science, may be procured". After repeating the familiar arguments Birkbeck concluded "considering how little has been accomplished by the grossly misapplied liberality of Sir Thomas Gresham we may apprehend, unless we succeed in the great purpose in which we are now engaged, some future poet, pointing to the Royal Exchange, may declare it to be, like the towers of Julius, 'London's lasting shame.'[21] (Loud cheers.)

It was unanimously agreed that the petition be referred to the City of London School Committee, who in turn passed it to the Special Committee who were ordered to meet Dr Birkbeck to speak on behalf of the Petitioners.[22] The Special Committee then sought further discussions with the JGGC, which proved difficult to arrange, and the matter was shelved while the more pressing issue of opening the school took priority. The 1837 lectures were given in the Royal Exchange as usual.

In September 1837 the Professor of Music, Richard Stevens, died after 36 years in post. The Corporation side, still led by Baylis, seized their chance and on 5 October persuaded the Court of Common Council to instruct the Gresham Committee that before being elected as Professor of Music the candidates should give probationary lectures at the school, and that it be a condition of appointment that "the professor do deliver his lectures in the theatre of the City of London School, commencing at the ensuing Michaelmas term, at such hours as may be appointed by the Gresham Committee on the City side, with the concurrence of the City of London School Committee." Furthermore, the Gresham Committee was instructed "to take the opportunity of respectfully intimating to Mr Joseph Pullen, the Professor of Astronomy," that he should also deliver his lectures at the school.[23]

On Friday 13 October William Horsley[24] and Edward Taylor[25] (the only two candidates in attendance) appeared before the JGGC and "expressed their desire of being allowed to bring some professional Friends on the occasion of their delivering their probationary lecture for the purpose of better illustrating the Subject." The Committee agreed that "A Grand Piano Forte from Messrs Collard & Co of Cheapside[26] be provided by this Committee for the use of the Candidates: the said instrument to be tuned afresh previous to the delivery of each Lecture" and that each candidate would be allowed the assistance of his "professional Friends, not exceeding 10 in number." The Gresham Lecture Room Keeper Uriah Yarrow and the two Royal Exchange constables would attend each lecture at half past 6 o'clock precisely, as would the members of the Committee, and admission tickets would be issued.[27]

Giles noted in his diary for 17 October that

Mr Horsley delivered his probationary lecture for the Gresham professorship of Music in the Theatre of the City of London School, and Mr E. Taylor is to deliver his tomorrow. There can be no doubt which of the two will be preferred. The city people mostly decide such questions by favouritism, and they not only acknowledge it but try to a certain point to remedy it. They appoint some one of known impartiality to reduce the number of candidates to 2 or 3, and then going on the supposition that those few are equally qualified, they refer the decision to a vote, and each supports the candidate he likes best, and if all the candidates are strangers alike to a voter, he makes a bargain with another voter to support the candidate whom that voter supports on condition of receiving a return of the favour at some other election.[28]

Edward Taylor by Henry Edward Dawe, after Robert Scott Tait, mezzotint, *c.* 1840–48.

The report in *The Times* the following day in some ways contradicts Giles's customary critical view on City practice:

> The first of the probationary lectures by the candidates for the vacant lectureship at Gresham College was delivered last night in the theatre of the City of London School, by Mr. Horsley, Mus.Bac. The lecturer took a survey of the history of English music, and illustrated his observations with a variety of madrigals and glees from the various ages and masters. [...] The illustrations [...] were sung by [eight gentlemen and two ladies, all named], accompanied on the piano by Mr Horsley himself.[29] There are five candidates for the vacant lectureship – Mr. Horsley, Mr. E. Taylor, Mr. Bishop, Mr Phillips, and Mr Gauntlett; each of these gentlemen will lecture in his turn, and the appointment will be made by the Gresham Committee of him whom they consider best entitled to it.[30]

But the result was as Giles expected:

> Yesterday the election of a musical professor took place. The probationary lectures delivered in the theatre of the City of London School in the course of the past week have been crowded to overflowing. The candidates in the course of their several lectures all recognized the principle that the intentions of Sir Thomas Gresham were to make these lectures of the utmost utility to the public. Mr. Edward Taylor was the successful candidate, the numbers being, for Taylor, 8; Horsley, 2; and Phillips, 1.[31]

Baylis and his colleagues may have thought that this was the way forward: wait for each lectureship to fall vacant, and insist that the terms of the successor allowed for the lectures to be given in the School (or elsewhere). But an unexpected calamity brought swifter change. In his diary for Wednesday 10 January 1838 Giles notes "The Royal Exchange caught fire about 11 o'clock [p.m.]", and, for the next day, "The fire not yet out, and the whole building reduced to a skeleton." Valiant efforts to save the building had been hampered by the extreme cold of the night, which caused the water to freeze. The Professors' "small incommodious room" and its valuable library were destroyed with the rest. *The Globe* for 11 January noted "It is melancholy fact that in the papers which detail the destruction of this fine building appears the usual advertisement, announcing the Gresham lectures for the present term [...] Many of the Professors objected [to previous attempts to move the lectures], and the thing was allowed to proceed in its useless course. Under the present circumstances, however, this advantage will not, of course, be lost sight of, and these lectures will become, what their founder no doubt intended them to be, of some utility to the children of his fellow citizens." The newspaper's assumption that in the school the lectures would be targeted at children supports the Professors' fear of "degradation".

For once there was speedy action. On 11 January the JGGC met to consider what steps it would be necessary to take in consequence of "the great public Calamity which had occurred last Night". Hale attended and, on his own initiative, offered the use of the Lecturing Theatre *pro tempore* for the delivery of the Gresham Lectures,

CONFLAGRATION of the ROYAL EXCHANGE, LONDON.

10ᵗʰ JANUARY, 1838.

Taken upon the Spot during the time the Chimes were playing _____ " There is nae luck about the Hous

adding that he had no doubt that the School Committee would concur in this offer when they met the following morning. The JGGC unanimously accepted Hale's offer, with any necessary expenses to be defrayed by the Gresham Committee. Uriah Yarrow was told to perform his duties as Keeper at the City of London School.[32]

The following notice was issued from Mercers' Hall on 12 January, and the Professors were told of this the next day.

The burning of the Royal Exchange, engraving by Nathaniel Whittock, lithograph 1838.

> BY ORDER of the GRESHAM COMMITTEE— Notice is hereby given, that in consequence of the destruction of The Royal Exchange by Fire, the LECTURES founded by Sir THOMAS GRESHAM will be read to the Public gratis in the Theatre of the City of London School, Milk-street, Cheapside at Twelve o'Clock at Noon precisely, in Latin, and at One o'Clock in the Afternoon, precisely, in English, during the present Hilary Term which commenced on THURSDAY, the 11th of January, instant.
>
> N.B. The Lectures will be read by the several Professors on the days undermentioned, viz. :
> Jan. I5, 16, and 17— Rev. Joseph Pullen, M.A. F.R.A.S., on Astronomy.
> Jan. I8, 19, and 20— Rev. Henry John Parker, M. A., on Divinity

Jan. 22, 23, and 24 — William Palmer, Esq., M. A., on Law.
Jan. 25, 26, and 27— Rev. Samuel Birch, D.D., on Geometry
Jan. 29 and 31— Rev. Edward Owen, M.A., on Rhetoric.
Jan 29 and 31— Edward Taylor, Esq., on Music, at Seven o'Clock in the Evening precisely.[33]

By the following Thursday, when the Court of Common Council meeting was largely concerned with how to deal with the results of the fire, it was reported that three of the Professors had consented, and one (Mr Owen) had been excused because all his lecture material had been lost in the fire, but that Dr Birch had written to the Secretary of the Mercers' Company:

Dear Sir,
Late on Saturday evening I received your communication relative to the offer of the theatre of the City of London School to the Gresham Committee, and the printed circular as to the delivery of the lectures there during the present term. In reply, I must beg you, with all deference, to refer the Gresham Committee to the resolutions which my colleagues and myself agreed to, and communicated to them about a twelve-month since in regard to the said school, as containing ample reason why I am under the necessity of not acceding to their wishes that I should deliver my lectures there on the 25th, 26th, and 27th instant. Even as a temporary measure to lecture there would be a recognition of the fitness and propriety of the place, which I do not admit, and would be the first step on my part towards rendering the Gresham foundation a mere appendage to the City of London School. It would amount also to a tacit admission, that, contrary to all precedent, the committee should fix up a place for the delivery of the lectures, without consulting in any way, or obtaining the consent of the Gresham Lecturers.

At the same time I am quite willing on the present emergency to deliver my lectures on the forementioned days in any part of the City of London where the Gresham Committee can provide and appropriate rooms to the distinct use of the Gresham Lecturers during the remainder of this term; and I am prepared to render them every facility by assenting to their selection before the next term of any eligible place within the city, which may be assigned to the free use and enjoyment of the said lecturers, and may be considered distinctly as Gresham College, until such time as the re-building of the Royal Exchange will afford to the Gresham Committee the favourable opportunity of constructing a lecture room upon the Gresham estate for the Gresham professors worthy of Sir Thomas Gresham, and not within the mark even of the most fastidious objection.
[...]
I am, dear Sir, your faithful servant,

SAMUEL BIRCH.

Such dogged inflexibility did not meet with sympathy in the Court, who ordered the Chamberlain to withhold the payment of the salary to any professor who should refuse to lecture in the theatre of the City of London School. This did the trick: "Dr Birch consented to lecture in the theatre of the City of London School on divinity.

He at first refused, but was brought to his senses by a threat that his salary should be stopped unless he complied with the directions of the Gresham Committee."[34] However, Birch's lectures were reported (in several newspapers) to be on divinity rather than geometry. Perhaps this was just an error, as he was a well-known cleric, or perhaps he was making a point by delivering lectures, but not on the subject advertised.

After this things settled to a routine, with the lectures given in the school's theatre at 12 noon (Latin) and 1 p.m. (English), except for Edward Taylor's music lectures which were at 7 p.m. Luckily the school's lunch break from 12 to 2 made this possible without too much disruption. At first the boys were allowed to attend, but they proved restless (not surprisingly, if the lectures were still intended for adult audiences and were as poor as has been described), and were later excluded. Although most of the boys went home for lunch, some stayed, and made their presence felt. On 2 May

> The Committee were attended by The Revd Edward Owen M.A. the Gresham Lecturer on Rhetoric, who stated that yesterday and today he had experienced much inconvenience while delivering his Lecture in the Theatre of the School from the noise made by the Boys in various parts of the Building contiguous to the Theatre, and that several persons who attended to hear the Lectures complained of the same thing. He also represented that he found the Desk placed in the Theatre for the use of the Lecturer was much too low and required to be raised a little, and that the Lecturers generally would feel much obliged if the Committee could accommodate them with the use of a separate Room to themselves.

> Ordered that the Porter do take care that all the Boys who are allowed to remain in the Building in the interval between School hours are entirely kept from the Eastern end of the Building and confined to the Western end during the time that the Gresham Lectures are being delivered.[35]

By the end of the month the School Committee had given further thought to the arrangements for the lectures, and made a series of proposals to the Court of Common Council. In summary:

> 1. The lectures should in future be delivered in the theatre of the City of London School, at seven o'clock in the evening, and in English only.

> 2. There should be better publicity by means of printed circulars distributed in advance and notices of the lectures placed previous to and during each Term outside the theatre of the City of London School, at the Guildhall, the Mansion House, and the Royal Exchange.

> 3. The lecturers should be requested to furnish a syllabus of their respective lectures, and printed copies of these should be provided at the expense of the trust, and distributed in the theatre before the commencement of each lecture.

> 4. Appropriate apparatus and illustrations should be furnished at the expense of the trust for all those lectures which are susceptible of illustrations.

These were unanimously accepted and referred to the Gresham Committee for implementation.[36] But the lectures remained at 12 and 1, at least until 1848, and the lecturers (predictably) declined to provide the requested syllabuses. Furthermore the indefatigable Mr Baylis, pointing out the depleted state of the Gresham funds, proposed that the City cash instead should pay for illustrating the lectures. He said that "The experiment which had been made with regard to the music lecture, which was illustrated and delivered in the evening had been most successful, both as to the number and the respectability of the audiences, and their gratification. (Hear, hear.)" He claimed that upwards of 8000 had attended that lecture in the past year (in fact Edward Taylor's total for 1838 was 7490), and embarked on a high-flown but dubious argument that Gresham had intended the lectures to be illustrated. "The corporation had now an opportunity of discharging part of the debt due to the memory of Sir T. Gresham and to the public, [...] thus making commerce tributary to the improvement of the minds of his fellow-citizens and their descendants, conferr[ing] an almost unparalleled lustre on the memory of that eminent man. (Hear, hear.) Proportionate would be the disgrace attaching to the City should such an institution be suffered to fall into utter uselessness or sinecurism. (Cheers.)"[37] The Court agreed unanimously, and Mr Baylis was added specially to the Royal Exchange and Gresham Committee.

The main "illustrations" were the piano and singers used by Edward Taylor. He was at pains to point out that these were essential to the educational aims of his lectures, and not to be thought of as providing a mere concert for his audience. While accepting this, the Gresham Committee did feel obliged to keep him in check: they agreed to pay his bill of £41-2-0 for 1838, but resolved "That the expence [sic] to be incurred by the Lecturer on Music for illustrating his lectures during the present year do not exceed twenty one pounds."[38]

The enforced change of venue certainly had the desired effect of attracting greater audiences. The attendance registers[39] for 1838 and 1839 give interesting details. A note states:

> In consequence of the destruction of the Royal Exchange (including the Gresham Lecture Room and valuable library of books), by fire on the night of the 10th of January 1838, the Lectures were read for a time, from the 15th of January 1838 to the end of Trinity Term 1843, in the Lecturing Theatre of the City of London School.

Although all the 12 noon lectures in Latin are recorded, the attendance at them was zero throughout this period. Joseph Pullen gave the first English lecture in the school (apart from the probationary music lectures) on 15 January, but there are no attendance figures recorded until 25 January when Samuel Birch lectured (on geometry or divinity) to an audience of 26, which had dropped to 10 by his third lecture. Thereafter most of the lectures attracted audiences in the twenties or thirties, with a few in single figures including some zeros. There were two unsurprising exceptions. Joseph Pullen retained his popularity, with audiences close to or on two occasions above one hundred. And Edward Taylor's evening music lectures were overwhelmingly popular, never attracting fewer than 250, and on two occasions reaching 940. It is difficult to imagine how an audience of that size could be squeezed into the theatre, which was designed to accommodate 400 – Uriah Yarrow must have been under pressure on those evenings.

A report one year later confirms this:

> The Professor of Music concluded the lectures of the present term on Monday
> evening [25 November 1839]. The subject this and the previous evenings was the
> dramatic music of England to the commencement of the reign of Charles the
> Second, in the course of which some curious specimens of the masque music of
> the reign of James the First, and one of the original songs in Shakespeare's plays
> (the only one known to exist) were introduced. Crowded and attentive audiences
> filled the theatre of the City of London School every night, and many hundreds
> went away unable obtain admission. More than 3,000 persons attended the
> Gresham lectures during the late term.[40]

The ambition of the Gresham Professors to have their own premises was still alive.

> It is to be hoped that the Gresham rustics will avail themselves of the present state
> of their affairs to restore to its original independence and usefulness the princely
> endowment of Sir Thomas Gresham; for this, as the administrators of his will, is
> their primary duty. We hear that they have in contemplation to purchase Crosby
> Hall[41] for this purpose; and it would be impossible to find, or even to erect, a building
> more completely adapted for the accommodation of the public, and better fitted to
> carry out the enlarged and liberal views of the founder of Gresham College.[42]

Inspection of Crosby Hall showed that, on the contrary, it was unsuitable in many
ways, noisy and in very poor repair, so nothing came of this plan. Eventually it was
agreed to build a separate Gresham College for the Professors, containing a lecture
room and a library, on the corner of Basinghall Street and Cateaton (now Gresham)
Street, at a cost of £7000. This was opened with great festivity on 2 November 1843.
From then on the lectures were delivered there,[43] and the direct connection with the
City of London School ceased.[44]

The New Gresham College,
wood engraving by Barrow
in the *Illustrated London
News*, 1843.

6

1838

After Christmas with old Aunt Ann in Ware, Giles spent about a week with his family in Somerset, but was back home in time to witness the burning of the Royal Exchange on 10 January. Anna was nearing the end of her third pregnancy and therefore in no condition to travel; a Miss Roberts was engaged to act as midwife and nurse, and on 31 January their first daughter was born (an event not noted in his diary). On 19 February Giles wrote to his mother:

> I have nothing very particular to tell you, and the only object I have in writing to you at present is to try a curious machine which I have just purchased, and by which I write two letters at once.[1] Anna and the little baby are going on very well: they talk of giving her the name of Anna Isabella. [...] There never was a time when our house was so crowded. We are obliged to put two or three in a room, and at this moment Mr Wm. J. Coope[2] is in town, and we have fitted up a bed for him in the Library. Miss Roberts has been of the utmost service to us during Anna's confinement; and I cannot conceive what we should have done without her. [...][3]

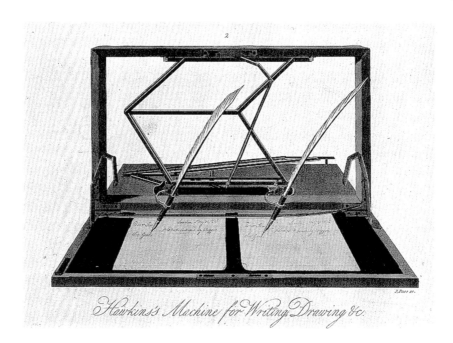

The Hawkins
Polygraph

Anna Isabella was christened by her father in Bow Church on 5 April, an event marked by an evening party at the school attended by about 100 guests. Anna Isabella outlived three husbands but had no children; she died in 1926.

Meanwhile the school's 'Lady-day Quarter' started on Monday 15 January, with 472 boys on the roll. The newly-elected William Cook, Master of the Fourth Class, soon made an important move to broaden the curriculum. On 7 February Giles requested the Committee

> to give directions for providing the following Articles to be used in explaining the principles of Natural Philosophy in the Lectures to be given in the Theatre of the School, viz.
>
> An Air Pump
> Glass Tubes etc.
> Condensing Syringe
> A small quantity of Mercury
> A Lathe etc. for constructing any necessary Appendages.[4]

The Committee agreed, leaving it to the Sub Committee to deal with the details. They consulted Cook and Edkins on 23 February, when the purchases were confirmed and Cook was allocated a room (perhaps one of the cellars?) in which to store the equipment. William Cook's science lectures seem to have been the earliest in any English school that were accompanied by practical demonstrations. In November 1838 Cook resigned to take up an appointment as a master at University College School, but offered to continue to deliver occasional lectures "as he felt convinced that the Lectures were highly useful to the Pupils and creditable to the School generally (to which he felt a strong attachment)." His offer was accepted.[5]

At the meeting on 7 February Giles also informed the Committee that he had invited the Lord Mayor to visit the school, and that his Lordship had agreed. Giles argued that since the previous Lord Mayor had visited the school it was reasonable to ask his successor to do the same, "considering that it might probably lead to the observance of the same practice on the part of future Chief Magistrates." The Committee made it clear to him that he had overstepped his authority: such invitations should come from them, not the Head Master. But as the invitation had been given it was honoured, so the Lord Mayor, Sir John Cowan, came on Monday 9 April and inspected the various classes. He said that he thought the pupils would expect an extra holiday from him, but he would leave that in the hands of the Committee. The boys were to be disappointed, as on 11 April the Sub Committee resolved that they "see no reason to sanction any additional holiday being given on the present occasion." After further discussion it was agreed that the Lord Mayor should be invited to attend the Annual Examination each year, and to dine with the Committee and other guests afterwards.[6]

On 2 March Giles wrote to invite his father for his first visit (he eventually came on 28 April), and to tell him about the Windlesham property which, surprisingly, he had not previously mentioned:

I write to say that on Monday week Miss Roberts will leave us. We shall then hope to see you as soon as you can make it convenient to come. Our house has for the last six weeks been a perfect Inn, but I hope for some months it will be as quiet as it has hitherto been noisy. [...] Some little time ago I bought 60 acres of land, freehold and tithe-free between Virginia Water and Bagshot, and have been lately engaged in building a Gothic house upon it. I had hoped to finish it in time for you to have stopped there on your way either up or down, but it requires longer time than I had calculated. [...] The land cost me £540: it is of course very inferior at such a price, but it will answer my purpose, which is to have an excuse for going out of town frequently on a Saturday afternoon: we find the closeness of the City renders such a change desirable. [...][7]

The "closeness of the City", the large number of pupils and the complete lack of outdoor space were also causing problems at the school. In April the Committee agreed that the Boarders' Sitting Room should be used for the Drawing and Mapping Classes. They also viewed the "Laboratory" room in the basement, now used by those who did not go home for lunch, and ordered that iron guards be put up to protect the windows from being broken by the boys. It was also agreed that "the space under the Theatre be appropriated for their use as a Play Room" and should be paved.[8]

At the same April meeting Hale reported complaints made to him by Mr Robert Obbard, a member of the Court of Common Council with two sons at the school. The Sub Committee considered this and instructed Brewer to write to Mr Obbard.[9]

City of London School 19 April 1838

Sir

The Committee of this School having been informed that, in a Meeting of one of the Committees of the Corporation, a statement was recently made by you to the effect that the School is in a very poor state of discipline, and that language of a most improper and reprehensible description is in use amongst the Pupils – and not being aware that there are any grounds for charges of so serious a nature to be made against the School – have directed me to request that you will favour them with any information on the subject which you may be in possession of and which may appear to you to warrant the above statement, in order that a proper investigation may be entered into by the Committee and such remedies applied as may appear to be necessary.

I am &c.

Thomas Brewer,   Secy.

Obbard's reply is lost, but prompted this response:[10]

City of London School 26 April 1838

Sir

I am directed by the Sub Committee of this School to acknowledge the receipt of your Letter of yesterday's date, and respectfully to acquaint you that as it does not appear to them to contain sufficient information to enable them to enter into an investigation of the subject referred to in my Letter of the 19th Instant they will feel obliged by your attendance at the next meeting of the Committee, which will be held here of Wednesday next the 2nd of May at One o'clock in the afternoon precisely.

I am &c.

Thomas Brewer,   Secy.

Mr Obbard did not reply or attend as requested. No further action was taken, and the Obbard boys, Arthur and Harry, remained at school until Michaelmas 1839 and Easter 1840 respectively.

Having made some progress in providing instruction in "natural philosophy", the Committee turned its attention to another item in the published Course of Study which had so far been neglected. They asked the Sub Committee "to consider and report what arrangements are necessary to be made for the 'Elements of Choral Singing' to be taught in the School, [...] and that they be instructed to confer with Edward Taylor Esq., the Gresham Professor of Music, on the subject."[11] There is no evidence that Taylor was asked about this, as when the Sub Committee eventually got round to the subject they resolved that "it is not expedient at present to take any steps for the introduction of Choral Singing as the subjects taught in the School appear to require the whole of the time during which the Pupils are in attendance."[12] Nothing more is heard of singing in the curriculum until 1841; optional lessons taught by Nathaniel Woodroffe started in September 1842.[13]

In May planning began for the first external examination of the school; this was fixed for the week beginning 18 June, with the presentation of prizes to be on Friday 22 June. Joseph Pullen, the highly regarded Gresham Professor of Astronomy, agreed to act as examiner, as did John Bradley Dyne, Fellow of Wadham College Oxford. Dyne and Giles had first met when they were competing for the Oxford scholarship that Giles won; later in 1838 Dyne was to become Head Master of Highgate School[14], a post he occupied with distinction until 1874. Giles recalled 42 years later that he had cut his hand badly "at breakfast when Dr Dyne came to examine the boys of the City of London School, and worried me by talking when I wanted to be eating."[15] The examiners for French and German were Isidore Brasseur and Dr Adolphus Bernays, respectively professors of those languages at King's College.

Perhaps it was the wish to make a good impression at the School's first public showing that led some of the Committee to ask Giles to take a Doctor's degree as soon as he could, since "the Head Master of every great public school should have a superior degree". Giles wrote to Dr Bliss, Registrar of Oxford University, about this. What followed is best told in Giles's words.[16]

Dr Bliss, being a bit of a wag, sent me this reply.

Oxford, June 1 1838

My dear Sir,

We cannot quite make Doctors of Law by steam,[17] but we will do all we can for you. The President of Corpus will propose your commutation on Monday next, and on Wednesday you may consider yourself B.C.L. You shall have a dispensation to do your exercises *in one day*, which may be on Thursday at any hour convenient to yourself so that you may come down that morning as early as you can leave London say 7 o'clock, and if the Vice Chancellor will, as I doubt not he will, give you a private day on Friday you might return to town by 11 or at latest 12 o'clock on that day.

It will be impossible to do what you wish earlier, for your exercises must be done *in Term*, & the Term, as you know, commences only on Wednesday.

Pray write to me by return of Post, because if this arrangement does not suit you we shall not get the Chancellor's Letter to commute your M.A. for B.C.L., for that Letter once read, you will be a bachelor of Law which, unless you proceed to your superior degree, may not be convenient.

Your's, Dear Sir, very faithfully

Philip Bliss

June 5, Tuesday. I went to Oxford this day wishing to have a little spare time before the Degree was given me. The Birmingham train starting at 12 o'clock brought me by one o'clock to Tring,[18] and from thence I went by coach to Oxford & slept at the Mitre Inn.

June 6, Wednesday. I called on Dr Bliss, and spent half an hour reading the thirty-nine Articles, this being a necessary procedure before one can take a degree. And the mention of this reminds me of the mode in which I went through the same ceremony with Thorpe the tutor of Corpus before taking the degree of bachelor of Arts. I went to Thorpe's rooms between 9 and 10 o'clock on the morning appointed, and found him dressing, - tying on his cravatte. He rejected two before he got to one of his taste. Then he came out in shirt-sleeves and said, "Well Giles, we must look sharp; for it is late. The law requires that you must read the Articles to me, or I to you: so you begin at the top of this page and I of the opposite page, each of us reading half of the whole." We did so, but he came to the bottom of his page before I had read six lines, and then turned over two leaves at once. In three minutes we had done, and nobody the wiser. The whole affair is an absurdity. Dr Bliss however heard me read all, barring a few skips. I then paid him the fees – a pretty sum in all £63–13–6. In the course of the day I met many old friends, and at ½ past 5 dined in the Hall at Wadham College. There was some speechifying in the Common Room after dinner and much eloquence was exhibited.

June 7, Thursday. The annexed letter to Anna will explain the events of today.

Oxon Scholae Philosophiae Naturalis, Thursday M.g. [morning?]

My dear Anna

I should certainly not have deemed it necessary to favour you with a letter during so short an absence from home, but severe destiny compels me to do so in order to slay that old enemy of the human race, time. I yesterday heard Dr Bliss ask the Convocation to suffer my degree of M.A. to be commuted for that of B.C.L. upon which the Proctors, rising from their seats, whisked down the Convocation-House between the lines of Masters, and back again to their seats: no one *plucked* their gowns i.e. made opposition, and I was consequently by way of this proceeding changed into a B.C.L.. I did not however feel any internal change take place, and I went out of the Convocation as I went in. After this I sat with Dr Bliss half an hour reading the thirty-nine Articles, and was then informed by him that all Candidates for Doctoral dignities must sit in the Schools three days, an hour each day, exposed to the questions of any one who might choose to come and dispute with them and see whether they are fit or not for their degree. A grace is sometimes passed allowing the three hours to be undergone on one & the same day. This bountiful consideration on the part of the University has been extended to me, and I am now accordingly awaiting my fate this morning from ½ past nine till ½ past 12; unless, when Purdue the clerk of the Schools comes at ½ past 11, I shall choose to go out for half an hour, in which case my punishment will extend to 1 o'clock. Under this heavy infliction it is some consolation to find that, although anyone may come & question me, there is an insuperable difficulty to be got over, which in fact saves me altogether from being questioned. The door is locked! Whether this is a merciful provision in my favour to keep out the inquisitive, or whether it is not more thoughtfully adopted in order to keep me from escaping, is a question that I will not take upon me to answer. Thus you see I am in durance vile, and among other expedients have thought of writing to you as a mode of occupying my time – As soon as this letter is finished, I see another mode presented by Providence of employing my prison-hours. A scarlet DCL gown has been most mercifully left in the Schools where I am, and at least ¼ of an hour may be profitably occupied in fitting it on, and admiring myself in it – Giles the tailor tells me that it will be impossible to make my academicals in time to bring home with me. The articles necessary to complete a doctorial wardrobe are as follows – 1 Black civilian's gown, worn in the Street and on ordinary occasions – 2 Black lace dress gown, worn at dinner & on extraordinary occasions – 3 Pink full dress gown worn at Court and in Convocation – 4 Pink hood worn on the surplice – 5 Cap worn on all occasions – The only one of these which I can get is the first, which I shall bring home with me; unless I choose to sport a pink, which I can get ready made - Now then to business. If you wish to show yourself a thoughtful spouse, you will instantly perceive that it is necessary to restore my cassock to some little degree of splendour for use until my new one is sent me. You will therefore, without fail, immediately on receipt of this, mend the sleeves thereof & put new cuffs, preparatory to Saturday M.g. You may make use of my gown for materials, as I shall bring a new one with me. And now, having come to the end of my paper, I am going to try on the gown.

Give young Patch [Isabella] a kiss and believe me

Your affectionate Husband

J.A.G.

June 8, Friday. I went to the Convocation House, and had all the honours of a DCL conferred on me. As it was a case of Doctorship, I claimed to have an extraordinary convocation expressly for myself; but was obliged to get together nine members to make a House.

At one o'clock I started for London, and as part of the road was by train, we passed over 32 miles in an hour and a quarter, but nevertheless did not get to London till 6 o'clock.

It is to be hoped that the 'pink full dress gown' had arrived in time to be worn at the first public prize giving on 22 June, to add some extra colour to the black gowns of the masters and the violet gowns worn by members of the Court of Common Council. The reports of examiners on the achievements of 484 boys divided into seven classes were read. These were printed at length in *The Times* some time later.[19]

For example:

> The sixth class were examined on portions of Xenophon's Anabasis, the Odes of Horace, the Jugurthine War of Sallust, arithmetic, algebra, 1st, 2nd, 3rd, 4th, 6th, and 11th books of Euclid, and the elements of trigonometry. Their construing of both of Latin and Greek was very good, and displayed, with a few exceptions, care and attention to this department of their studies. Their knowledge of the principles of algebra, as well as their power of applying them, was creditable. Their proficiency in geometry deserves especial mention both in respect of its extent and accuracy.

The examiners concluded:

> The recent origin of the establishment, would lead them to expect neither a great extent of acquirement on the part of boys nor that marked distinction between the several classes generally found in schools which have been established long enough to admit of a progressive course of study. On this account, therefore, the condition of the junior classes may perhaps be considered the best criterion, as

well of the efficiency of the system adopted for the management of the school as of its future prospects. From these circumstances, added to the zealous interest and attention of the several masters as proved by the result of the examination, the examiners have every reason to hope that the City of London School will gradually exhibit fresh evidence of its utility, and become the efficient means of promoting the true interests of the metropolis, by extending sound religion and morality combined with useful learning.

Book prizes to a total value of £50 6s 8d (supplied by Mr J. Souter of 73 St Paul's Churchyard) were presented by Dr Birkbeck. The winner of Dr Conquest's Gold Medal was Henry Judge Hose, and it was reported that Sir James Shaw, Chamberlain, had given £100 for prizes, and Under Sheriff Wire a further 10 guineas, and that the £400 fine paid by Mr Thomas Tegg to be excused service as Sheriff was to be used to endow an exhibition at one of the Universities, to be enjoyed by students who had been pupils in the school.

After the ceremony the Committee, Examiners, Secretary and Masters dined at the Albion Tavern, Aldersgate Street, with guests including Lord Brougham, Dr Birkbeck, Dr Conquest, and the Lord Mayor, Sheriffs and Chamberlain. Giles had with him as personal guest an old family friend, Dr S.J.Bloomfield,[20] who "was much pleased with the whole affair - but he made a fearfully prosy speech."[21]

It was presumably around this time (he was then 30) that the portrait of Dr Giles in his "pink" (actually scarlet) gown was painted; in 1937 this was given to the school by an unknown Giles descendant; it now hangs in the Great Hall. The artist was Charles Grant.[22] In his diary for 16 February 1835 Giles records that "Mr Charles Grant, who had taken the pencil drawing (coloured) of me several years before at Oxford, took a sitting of Anna and me for the oil painting which we still have." It is not known where this double portrait is now, and there is no mention in the diary of when the "pink gown" portrait was created.

The prize-giving concluded the term, with five weeks' holiday to follow. While their house was being finished Giles and Anna took lodgings nearby in Windlesham. Anna had gone there with Isabella on 16 June, and Giles with his brother Charles and nephew John Dalley joined them a week later. During 1838 Giles produced editions of six Latin authors (all published by James Bohn), and was preparing a Greek lexicon and grammar and an enlarged edition of *Murray's abridged English grammar* for publication in 1839. So there was plenty to occupy him during the holiday.

The school's third quarter started on Monday 30 July and lasted the eight weeks until Michaelmas (29 September) followed, apparently without a break, by the fourth quarter of 12 weeks up to Christmas. The number of pupils dropped by over 50 to 432 in the third quarter and rose slightly to 440 in the fourth. The reduced roll caused concern to the Committee, as did a number of specific issues. In August the Committee received a letter from Mr A. K Gifford "announcing his intention of removing his son from the school and stating several particulars on which, in his opinion, complaint can be made as to the conduct and management of the School."[23] The Sub Committee's investigation of this dragged on until November when Brewer wrote to Gifford asking him to attend a meeting to explain the circumstances alluded to in his letter, but nothing came of this, and we do not know what the "several particulars" were. Meanwhile on 5 September the architect Bunning, having examined the roof, reported that "slops are thrown down the North West gutter, and that such practice if continued will cause damage to the Lead."[24] Giles was firmly reminded that similar problems had occurred less than a year before, and requested to put a stop to the practice: "otherwise the Committee will be under the necessity of ordering the Door [to the roof] to be fastened up." His reply of 28 September raised yet another problem:

> I am extremely sorry that the improper conduct of my servants should have needed your interference. I have reproved them for it & flatter myself that, after what has taken place, they will not do any further injury to the roof of the building, in the same or any other manner.
>
> I beg leave to call your attention to an important subject. Many of the boys have lost umbrellas or have taken away old ones instead of good ones which they had brought with them. Repeated complaints have been made, some of them in an angry tone. The evil is without remedy so long as all the classes are allowed to put their umbrellas together in the same place, which causes great confusion. The porter has in his possession 48 old umbrellas! I beg to suggest the propriety of dividing the umbrella stand into 3 or 4 parts & placing them so that each may stand near the door of one or more of the class rooms.

An example of such a complaint (though hardly "in an angry tone") has survived in the school archive:

> 31 Upper North Place
> Grays Inn Road
> 2 October 1838
>
> Sir
>
> I am desirous to call your attention to a practise [sic] that I fear is too common in your School namely that of some of your pupils taking away good Umbrellas and not returning them.
>
>   My Son took a new Umbrella last Autumn it disappeared the first day, he took a new one last week it disappeared the first day, but he did not lose the old one he made use of last winter.
>
>   I presume not to dictate the best method to check a system that if left to grow will bring the School into disgrace but as the Munificence of the City of London has built a spacious Hall and Lobbies, and appointed two Porters to attend at the

assembling and dismissal of the Classes it seems to me that the Committee would cheerfully allot a separate place of depot for each class and so far reduce the number of chances and simplify the examination when an error occurs.

I pray you to excuse this intrusion and am

Sir

Your ob[t] Servant

Joseph Mitchell

The "important matter" of umbrella stands was of course referred to the Sub Committee, who on 29 October decided to leave the matter for the Chairman to resolve; the outcome is unknown. The fact that, 18 months after the school had opened, Giles had not felt empowered to resolve such a minor issue is an example of how tightly the Committee kept control over the everyday running of the school, and there are hints of Giles's frustration in the terms of his letter.

Meanwhile Giles had been preparing a proposal of real significance. When the London University was established in 1826 it did not have the power to confer degrees. Its petition for this to be granted was controversial, with opposition expressed by the universities of Oxford and Cambridge, the London medical schools, and the Anglican church. In 1836 two royal charters were granted simultaneously, one incorporating the University of London, with its name changed to University College, and the other "establishing a Metropolitan University, with power to grant academical degrees to those who should study at the London University College, or at any similar institution which his Majesty might please hereafter to name."[25] Giles spotted an opportunity, which he presented at the Committee's September meeting.

To the Committee of the City of London School
City of London School
Sept 11th 1838

Gentlemen

Permit me to invite your attention to the following statement. The benefit of the Institution, at the head of which I have the honour of being placed, induces me to address you, and I am well persuaded that, whatever can promote the interests of this Establishment, will meet with your prompt support.

It will be remembered that, some time ago, the Common Council petitioned the King to grant a Charter to the London University (as University College was then called) similar to the Charters of Oxford and Cambridge. The Queen's Government have lately granted this request, but in a different form from that in which it was first made. They have granted a charter, not confined to University College (in Gower Street) alone, but comprising also King's College in the Strand, and intended to comprise any other College in the United Kingdom which, on application to the Secretary of State, shall be admitted to that privilege.

The question then which is proposed to your serious considerations is: Whether the privilege of becoming a College, attached to the University of London, and of receiving degrees from the Senate, may not reasonably & with propriety be obtained for the City of London School?

I will now state my reasons for suggesting the propriety of endeavouring to obtain the privilege of graduating in Arts, Laws, and Medicine for such Students of the City of London School as may become Members for that purpose.

I. The business of the School, being now well settled and in efficient operation, will not be interfered with, and none of its arrangements or regulations will be disturbed by the plan now under consideration.

II. The building offers ample accommodation for the delivery of Lectures to the limited number of students who would be likely to enter as Members of the Senior Department; and the circumstance of their [sic] being two places of entrance renders it possible to keep the Collegiate & Scholastic portions of the Institution in every way apart.

III. Scholarships, Exhibitions and other encouragements to Learning and Science, are offered by the University, & would without a doubt excite great emulation among our Scholars.

IV. There are at least 100 more pupils in the City of London School, than in the Schools either of University or King's College; our School therefore would fairly appear to be qualified to receive the same privilege.

V. The arrangement will be beneficial to several classes of persons:

1. To young legal students, who at present have no opportunity of displaying their attainments.

2. To medical students, of whom great numbers reside in the city: and it may be asserted that these would have greater advantages with us than elsewhere, from the numerous & large Hospitals in the immediate neighbourhood.

3. To numerous young men engaged in tuition, who may thus, by graduating with us, have an opportunity of rising in the world which want of means, neglected opportunity, and other circumstances debar them from doing at Oxford and Cambridge.

4. To many other individuals, who from conscientious motives cannot graduate at our older Universities.

5. To all those who pursue Literature and Science at their leisure-moments, and whose bias of mind at present shows itself by joining one or other of the Literary & Scientific Institutions with which the City abounds.

VI. The City and Eastern parts of the Metropolis are, if possible, more populous than the Western; and, as both the existing Colleges are to the West of Temple Bar, it may reasonably be supposed that there is ample room for a third in the City.

VII. If it be supposed that the two Colleges, already existing, are sufficient, let it be remembered that Oxford and Cambridge contain each 20 colleges, most of which contain more students than the Senior Departments of King's College and University College put together.

VIII. The present moment is favourable to a consideration of this question

1. Because the University-Senate will begin their Examinations for the Matriculation of Members on the 5th of November.

2. Because the Common Council have recently attached a Scholarship to our School, to be given to a student who is going to College. This would at once enable <u>one</u> to pursue his studies for his degree in our own senior department.

His timing was perhaps unfortunate. In the light of falling rolls, umbrella stands, slops on the roof and other complaints one can imagine eyebrows being raised at the "well settled and in efficient operation" claim. The outcome was sadly predictable: reference to the Sub Committee and then on 3 October the Resolution "that this Committee, having fully considered the Letter of Dr Giles, are of opinion that the proposition therein contained does not come within the limits and objects of this School, and that therefore it is inexpedient for this Committee to take any steps therein." So the opportunity to create a City University passed, and was not to be realised for another 128 years.[26]

At the end of October 1838 the Committee further tightened its control of the School (and further reduced the Head Master's autonomy) by accepting the Sub Committee's proposal that a Committee of Visitors should be appointed, consisting of the Chairman and three members, one of whom would retire each month in rotation. Their duty would be "to visit and inspect the School at such times as they may think proper, and to report any suggestions or observations which they may have to make" to the Committee. The Visitors soon stirred things up by prohibiting a testimonial collection which was being organised by the boys as a leaving gift for the popular William Cook. A letter from the Visitors banning this came to the attention of the Committee, who invidiously summoned Cook to give his views. A motion that "the Committee [...] consider it unadvisable to give their sanction to the said Letter," was proposed but defeated.[27]

The annual re-election of the Masters to their posts occurred each November; this was normally a matter of routine, but it did occasionally provide the Committee with a useful weapon. At their meeting of 29 November –

The Committee having understood that Mr Thomas Ward, the Assistant Master of the Junior Class, had been repeatedly absent from duty without assigning any cause, and appeared to fail in giving satisfaction in other respects, The Revd Dr

> Giles the Head Master was requested to attend the Committee on the subject, when he stated that he was not aware that any complaint existed against Mr Ward with respect to his attendance, but that as the Committee desired his opinion as to his efficiency he felt bound to state that he did not consider Mr Ward calculated to teach a Class, particularly of Boys so young as those which were under his care, and that the School suffered in consequence of the inefficient manner in which he discharged his duties. Resolved that the Election of [the] Assistant Master of the Junior Class be postponed.

Postponing his re-election gave a sufficient message: Thomas Ward resigned, and Thomas Hall was promoted to fill his place. But the way this matter had come to the Committee in the first place raises questions. If Ward really had been repeatedly absent why was Giles not aware of this? Who raised the issue with the Committee, and why was that not recorded? If the allegation came from a Master (perhaps the Second or Third Master, or Thomas MacDougal, First Master of the Junior Class) why did that person not act via the Head Master? Or could it have been the Secretary, Thomas Brewer, whose duties included writing the Committee minutes? There are certainly signs of disunity in this episode.

Again Giles saw an opportunity for improvement, writing to the Committee on 29 November:

> Gentlemen
>
> As you will shortly be called upon to appoint an Assistant Writing Master, I cannot neglect the opportunity of recommending that he should be appointed subject to the performance of a slight additional duty, which would be of the greatest possible benefit to the School.
>
> I have myself laid down a rule that no boys shall be detained after school-hours without the presence of one of the Masters. Now this is certainly an encroachment on the leisure of the Masters which it would be desirable to avoid. If you would make it conditional for the new Writing Assistant to take this daily duty & to keep order amongst the boys who stop here from 12 to 2, it would be of the most essential advantage to the whole School.
> I am
> your obd[t] serv[t]
>
> J A Giles
> P.S. The addition of a small sum to his Salary would be an ample compensation for the increase of duty.

But again he got nowhere, the Committee resolving a week later that "it is not advisable to adopt the suggestion." Thomas Hall was promoted to take the place of Thomas Ward, and in January Peter Flowers was appointed Assistant Writing Master.

Secretary Thomas Brewer's personality rarely shows in his voluminous official correspondence and minutes, but there is a hint of annoyance in the letter he felt obliged to write to Giles (whom presumably he could talk to every day if he wished) on Friday 14 December:

Dear Sir

I find that a Letter to me of an official nature, and which required immediate attention, was presented at the House door last night after the Porters had left, and was refused to be taken in.

It is very far from my wishes to be the occasion of any trouble for your family or servants, and, <u>on my own account</u> (whatever I might feel) I should not complain of such a circumstance, but as the Letters which are addressed to me here are generally of an official nature, and concern the Committee and others connected with the Establishment more than myself privately, and as considerable inconvenience may result from their being refused, I trust that you will give directions that whatever communications may in future be brought for me after the Porters have left may be at once received, and delivered at the first opportunity.

The third and fourth quarters of the school year were in effect a single term of twenty 5½-day weeks, with only Lord Mayor's Day (Friday 9 November) as a holiday. So the three week Christmas holiday must have come as a great relief to all, and Giles quickly escaped to Windlesham. It seems that work on the house was now complete, for on 13 December Giles "borrowed £600 of Mr Dugmore [a family friend] on depositing the Windlesham Deeds."[28]

On the right of the western road, about a mile from Bagshot, is Windlesham Hall, the seat of the Rev. Dr. Giles, the donor of the eastern window in Windlesham church. This is a new and handsome building in the Tudor style of architecture: it is constructed of red brick, with stone dressing, and is intended to be enlarged by wings. The gable is remarkably lofty; and in the great-hall window, which rises to the roof, is a stained-glass compartment, by Willement; including figures, arms, and badges.[29]

Giles was acquainted with Thomas Willement (1786 – 1871) "the Father of Victorian Stained Glass",[30] and was firm in negotiating with him: "I cannot afford to lay out one farthing more than £30 on each of the two windows." His donation of the church window seems to have been calculated to make sure his arrival in the district was duly noticed. The design for this included "my own two badges, the pelican & pansy-flower [...], instead of the Bishops' arms",[31] and the saint depicted was St Giles, though resemblances between this ascetic, solitary, vegetarian hermit and his namesake are not obvious.

For no stated reason the family were not together on Christmas Day: Anna and Isabella remained in London while Giles "took the opportunity of accepting Mr Onslow's[32] invitation to Dunsborough House in the parish of Ripley [in Surrey]. We had a most jolly day, dancing and other amusements. But as the house was quite full of the Onslow family, they got me a bed at the village inn." It is good that Giles enjoyed himself that year, for his next Christmas was to be far from jolly.

7

Dr Bialloblotzky

The Reverend Doctor Christoph Heinrich Friedrich Bialloblotzky was born in 1799 in Pattensen, near Hanover.[1] The Bialloblotzky family were originally from Poland, a strongly Catholic country which they left because of their fervent Protestant beliefs. Friedrich's father was superintendent (the Lutheran equivalent of bishop) for the diocese of Wunstorf. In 1818 Friedrich matriculated at the University of Göttingen, about 60 miles south of Hanover, and studied theology. He was a prize-winning student who within six years was a Doctor of Philosophy giving lectures in Christian Apologetics at the University. In 1824 he was ordained in Hanover as a clergyman of the Established Lutheran Church, and was appointed chaplain to students at the University of Göttingen. With his scholastic gifts and influential relatives he seemed set for a distinguished career in the Hanoverian Church, but this was not to be.

From 1822 Bialloblotzky was in contact with and much influenced by the leaders of the Lutheran *Erweckung* (awakening or revival) movement. This aimed to replace the formalised routine and rationalist theology of the established church with more heart-felt devotion and emphasis on personal religious commitment. In summer 1825 Bialloblotzky gained leave of absence to spend a year in England and Scotland, travelling with Friedrich Tholuck, a fellow pietistic theologian from Berlin, to meet followers of the similar British Methodist and Evangelical movements. One consequence was that Bialloblotzky was employed by the Continental Society[2] to work in north German universities to "check the progress of Neological [= rationalistic] infidelity, that so awfully prevails in those seats of literature." The arrangement did not run smoothly: the Continental Society complained that he did not keep in touch with them; he suspected that his letters were being intercepted by the Hanoverian authorities (which was later shown to be true). The Society was short of funds and failed to pay him the £75 per annum which had been agreed. At the end of 1827 he made contact with the Wesleyan Methodist Missionary Society (WMMS) in London, and was soon doing similar work for them instead of the Continental Society.

His revival mission was conducted mainly through home meetings "twice per week [...] in order to pray, to read the scriptures, missionary notices and other spiritual books" and through his publications. These activities were seen by his superiors in the church and the university as undermining the authority of the Lutheran church (of which he was still an ordained minister). In September 1827, after prolonged controversy, Bialloblotzky was dismissed from his post and obliged to leave Göttingen. He moved to London and was accepted as a missionary candidate by the WMMS. He first returned to Germany via Holland to distribute one hundred Bibles and two hundred New Testaments for the British and Foreign Bible Society; for this activity legal proceedings were started against him in Hanover. These he avoided by continuing his journey through Italy to Zante, as the Italians called the Greek island of Zakynthos in the Ionian Sea. He arrived in December 1828, having been commissioned by the WMMS to assist Walter Croggan[3] who had been working there for two years. Zante was then a war zone as the Greeks fought to gain their independence from the Ottoman Empire.[4]

Despite periods of illness and depression Bialloblotzky soon began to learn modern Greek and was busy teaching and preaching. With a fellow missionary from America he explored other Greek islands and much of the Peloponnese. Letters from England had hinted that he might be sent on to Alexandria, so in September 1829, despite Croggan's attempts to persuade him to wait for formal instructions from the WMMS, he decided to move there. Croggan did not regret his departure, reporting to the WMMS: "He is a clever man and will do well as a Travelling Missionary but I believe he will never be under the direction of anyone. He is more eccentric than you thought."

Bialloblotzky found the Methodist mission station in Alexandria, established in 1825, in a state of disrepair and disorganisation. With help from members of the small English-speaking community he got things back in order, began ministering to English patients in the hospital and the crews of ships, and added Arabic to his collection of languages. In June 1830 he was joined by James Bartholomew, who had been sent by the WMMS Committee to assist (and perhaps keep an eye on) him. With Bartholomew now able to look after things in Alexandria, Bialloblotzky felt able to follow his inclination for "evangelistic travel". His journeys between Alexandria and Cairo during the next three months confirmed his feeling that his calling was to be a travelling missionary, doing without all comforts and throwing himself upon the grace and mercy of God for food and shelter. This was very different from the procedures and intentions of the WMMS, and tensions arose between him and Bartholomew. In February 1831 Bialloblotzky returned to London and met with the WMMS Committee for a thorough discussion of various theological and organisational issues. The result was the termination of his employment by the WMMS, though he was given a letter of reference which, while mentioning "certain differences of religious sentiments and views", emphasised the he "is and has invariably been regarded as an amiable, learned and pious character". He also severed his connection with the British and Foreign Bible Society, who were embroiled in controversy over whether or not the Apocrypha should be included in the Bibles they distributed, and had, he thought, lost touch with the realities of life on the continent.

He decided to live in London "not as an exile, but from my own choice", and his primary interest switched from theological issues to the need to settle down and find work. His evangelical connections were of practical help to him. He found accommodation at Albury House in Cheshunt, Hertfordshire. Here he was in close contact with the staff of Cheshunt College[5], a theological college for training non-conformist ministers, and from December 1837 to 1840 he was employed there part-time to teach Hebrew and Classics.

At first Bialloblotzky's main source of income was teaching German privately; for seven lessons he charged 2 guineas if they were given at Albury House, or 3 guineas at the student's home. During school and university vacations he also took boarders at Albury House, at 2 guineas per week for residence, board and instruction. To aid his teaching he revised and edited Noehden's *A Grammar of the German language*, and produced two volumes of his own *German Reading Lessons*. In 1833 he also published a book on Hebrew grammar, and a translation into Hebrew of the morning and evening prayers as used in the Church of England.

In April 1834 he married Sarah Maria Batley (1802-66). Their first child Frederick was born in February 1835, followed by three daughters, Elizabeth, Rosina and Minna. By the autumn of 1836 he was living in Crouch End and teaching four hours per week (for £50 per annum) at the Forest Proprietary Grammar School[6] near Snaresbrook, where he was on friendly terms with the Headmaster, the Revd Dr Thomas Dry. He also taught for a while at Hanwell Collegiate School, started by the Revd J.A.Emerton in about 1832, which specialised in preparing boys who were to enter the army.

Bialloblotzky's application for the post of German and Hebrew teacher at the City of London School in December 1836 was fulsomely supported by Dr Dry who concluded "I believe the Directors of our Establishment agree with me in opinion that Dr Bialloblotzky's department is most ably and satisfactorily sustained". Like Giles, Bialloblotzky had been assiduous in preparing the ground for his job application. There were five further testimonials, including one from the chaplain to the Royal Lutheran Chapel[7] at St James's, and one signed by twelve members of the staff of the British Museum, headed by Antonio Panizzi. On 11 January 1837 the School Committee interviewed four candidates for the post, and Bialloblotzky was duly appointed to teach on Mondays and Thursdays for £100 per annum.

It is hardly surprising that Giles and Bialloblotzky did not get on well. Both were in holy orders, and both were scholars of some renown, but Bialloblotzky's fervent evangelicism was in marked contrast to the relaxed scepticism of the reluctantly-ordained Giles. This might not have mattered too much (things seemed to go smoothly enough at Forest School) had there not been friction generated by Giles's lack of esteem for the teaching of German and failure to resolve obvious clashes caused by timetabling German (an optional subject) at the same time as classics or mathematics.

The first evidence of these problems was a letter to the Committee of 25 August 1837[8] in which Giles states that "the German and Hebrew Classes in the School under the care of Dr Bialloblotzky are in a very unsatisfactory state, there is a great want of discipline and good order in them, the Master is not so punctual as he should be in his attendance, and the Boys appear to be making little or no progress in those departments." The Sub Committee investigated, and on 20 September received a long letter from Bialloblotzky, whose first paragraph shows his grasp of English rhetoric:

Gentlemen

Aware of the difficulties attending the first organisation of so large a body as the City of London Corporation School, presenting as it does points so numerous and so nice which required consideration and control, I have patiently endured and sedulously endeavoured to supply by increased exertion the deficiencies which interfered with the easy and successful discharge of my duties. I endured these disadvantages because I confidently believed that the Head Master, to whom I imparted my complaints, was endeavouring from desire for the welfare of the Institution and regard to my first complaints to remove every impediment – but since these impediments so far from being removed are increased I deem it due both to the Institution and to myself to bring the whole matter before the Committee.

Both the German and the Hebrew languages, on account of their pronunciation differing so widely from the English, require every advantage that may be given to the Master's voice and the pupils' attention but during the former half year it very frequently happened that another master taught another class in the same room at the same time that I was employed teaching mine. I expected that this evil would be entirely obviated by the completion of the German Class Room which I have lately occupied – but on Monday last when I arrived at the school I found this room pre-occupied by the Writing Master who informed me that he was expressly directed by the Head Master to station himself in this room. I subsequently learned from the Revd Mr Webster that he had expected the Writing Master in his room, it being his turn to receive him.

The boys are repeatedly prevented attending the German and Hebrew classes – on Thursday 7th September only one boy attended the Hebrew class, on the following Monday some boys attended but were almost immediately called out again by the Head Master – on the following Thursday a few were present, but last Monday the boys were called out almost as soon as they had opened their books. One boy stated in my presence to Mr Brewer that he had been prevented from attending four successive times.

The boys have not been provided with books. When I submitted to the Head Master the propriety of supplying the boys with books I was requested to desist from urging the purchase of books at that time as the expenses incurred for books of other kinds had amounted to too large a sum. I afterwards induced the booksellers to provide the boys gratuitously with the first sheets of some works which I have compiled for the express use of this school. At the express wish of the Head Master I compiled these books, the plan of which was originally approved by the Head Master and the proof sheets of which have been submitted to his inspection from time to time – these works have received Dr Giles' express approbation but although most of the boys have themselves purchased these books the deficiency is still but partially removed.

I have never been allowed to class boys according to their proficiency, but have to take them as they can be absent from other classes.

Other complaints I might make, but I will come to the practical point of making the following suggestions to the Committee –

1st That the necessary books be sanctioned by the Committee

2nd That no other Instruction be allowed to interfere with the times allotted to German and Hebrew Instruction.

3rd That I may be allowed to class the students according to their proficiency.

4th That the students may be examined in German and Hebrew in the same manner as in the other subjects taught in the school and that prizes may be awarded to those who make the greatest improvement.

5th That all communications may be avoided which have hitherto tended to impress the pupils with the idea that their progress in German and Hebrew was of minor importance.

6th That the Head Master be requested to accede to the wish which the German Master has repeatedly expressed to him that he should occasionally visit the German and Hebrew Classes and suggest to the Master of those classes any improvements of method which might occur to him [and] converse freely with him of the various circumstances affecting the progress of the Pupils.

Should these requests as far as circumstances may admit be carried into effect I can reasonably hope to have in the City of London School the same success that I have had in other schools.

If some points of this communication should appear indistinct I shall feel very happy to be afforded an opportunity of explaining myself verbally, and in the presence of Mr Giles before the Committee.

If, as Bialloblotzky alleged, Giles did not visit the classes, how could he be so sure that the discipline was so poor and progress so limited? Perhaps he relied on reports from the Writing Master and others.

Bialloblotzky's pleas were taken seriously: the Sub Committee proposed that books should be supplied and suggested a number of changes.[9] But before these could be discussed by the Grand Committee another highly critical letter arrived from Giles, dated 21 September.

I beg to call your attention the subject of the German and Hebrew classes in the City of London School. It is my duty to inform you that the Master of those classes has placed a Deputy to act in his place, and the result is that his own attendance is very much shortened and occasionally dispensed with altogether. In addition to this, the Pupils who profess to be studying Hebrew and German do not appear to me to have made any progress whatever. I cannot refrain from expressing my conviction that the present Master is far less qualified for teaching large classes in a School than (from his literary attainments) we might fancy him to be for teaching a few private pupils. You will have the kindness to take the matter into your early consideration, for the evil is not confined to itself, but influences the rest of the School also. It may not be amiss to add that the number of those who learn German and Hebrew does not warrant the attendance of a German and Hebrew Master during two whole days, as at present arranged.

At its meeting on 4 October the Grand Committee told the Sub Committee to confer with Giles and Bialloblotzky with a view to resolving their conflict. This discussion took place five days later: Giles and Bialloblotzky stated their views, and eventually agreed that the regulations proposed by the Sub Committee could work. These were that German and Hebrew lessons (two per week) were to be optional, and at the wish of the parents. Hebrew lessons (open to all) were to be held from 12 to 1 in the lunch break, thus avoiding clashes with other lessons. German lessons were restricted to boys in the 4th, 5th and 6th Classes, and were to take priority over all other subjects. The German and Hebrew Master should be allowed to class his pupils according to their proficiency. Pupils should be examined in German and Hebrew in the same way as for other subjects, and prizes awarded. There is no further mention of using a Deputy, an issue which, if it were established, would surely have attracted official censure. On 11 October the Grand Committee approved the new regulations, and made sure that Giles and Bialloblotzky had written copies "for their information and guidance". This uneasy truce (which had not solved the fundamental problem that German clashed with classics and mathematics) lasted until the Annual Examination in June 1838.

This first external examination of the German class was conducted by Dr Adolphus Bernays, who since 1831 had been the first Professor of German at King's College, London, where his duties included teaching at King's College School. There is no mention that he also examined Hebrew, which was taken by only five or six boys, though he was qualified to do so, his brother being the Chief Rabbi of Hamburg. His report on examining 31 boys in three divisions was largely positive:

[The First Division of the class] all read fluently and correctly so that they could be well understood by any German. Most of them construed the German extracts they read with facility and gave a satisfactory account of nearly all the words on which I questioned them. They all understood their Master when he questioned them in German[10] upon the subject of their reading and generally answered him well in the same language. [...] Their grammatical knowledge, however, is less than is found among such Boys, owing to your Master's plan of teaching more practically than theoretically. Upon the whole I would venture to affirm that if any of those Boys were, with his present knowledge, to spend three months at a good German School, he would speak and write the language as correctly as the mass of German Schoolboys at his age generally do – a result, I should say, which speaks satisfactorily for the plan pursued by your School and the zeal of your German Master.

Such commendation from an expert dampened criticism, but the fundamental problem of Giles's lack of support for German remained. This appeared again in the Plan of Studies he produced in October 1838. Part of this was a homework timetable in which, despite the agreement of the year before, German did not appear at all – the evenings before German lessons were to be devoted to preparing Mathematics and Greek. The scheduling continued to cause friction with other Masters: in March 1839 the Second Master, Edkins, pointed out to the Sub Committee: "the inconvenience which is sustained in my [Fifth] Class by the interference of the German Studies with the ordinary business of the Class; the study of German being optional and not extending to the whole Class, a large portion of my boys are frequently withdrawn in order to attend the German Master, by which means the Class is so broken up that it is impossible to proceed with the regular studies in a satisfactory manner with the few boys who remain." Edkins suggested that either the whole class should be required to learn German (as was the case with French), or the German classes should be moved to other days where they would not clash with major subjects (by which he meant mathematics and classics). Bialloblotzky was willing to change to attending on other days, and William Webster, Third Master, said he had "always found him extremely willing and obliging in making rearrangements to meet the wishes of the other Masters." But still no substantial changes were made.

In June 1839 Dr Bernays examined the German class again, recording that there were 13 boys in the 1st Division and 17 in the 2nd Division. He noted that the boys' behaviour throughout the morning's examination "was highly creditable to themselves and spoke very much in favor [*sic*] of the discipline of the Establishment." As before he praised their oral work and comprehension, but continued:

> But here I regret my commendations must end. I found both the Divisions utterly unacquainted with the simplest elements of the language such as the auxiliary verbs, the declension of pronouns and adjectives, both in theory and practice, for they neither could say them by rote, nor employ them correctly in the formation of easy sentences with which I tried the first Division both orally and in writing. It would be more painful for me to have to state such a deficiency to you if I were not convinced of the ability of Dr Bialloblotzky to remove it, if he has sufficient time given to him, and the Boys <u>be encouraged to consider this branch of instruction as important as others.</u>

Bialloblotzky reacted with a long letter attacking this assessment, which he claimed "contradicts itself and contradicts the Report of 1838". He pointed out that in 1838 the boys had been examined on just one prepared chapter of their prose Reading

Book, but in 1839 the same boys had offered to explain any part of the Reading Book, plus some pieces of poetry from Goethe and Schiller – surely a sign of progress. He mentions that the boys Dr Bernays placed at the head of the First and Second Divisions (Henry Nathan and George Lamerte respectively) had both begun learning German "from A B C" within the past nine months (he enclosed statements from Nathan and Lamerte confirming this), and had been judged more accomplished than other boys who had been educated in Germany. "As long as I can effect that Boys who have learned German from me a few months only advance before others who have had apparently greater advantages, I hope that the justice of the Committee will protect me against an Examiner from whom I differ in the System of Grammar as well as in terminology."

By August 1839 the Committee was concerned about other things too (see Chapter 8), and asked Giles to report on the state and condition of the School. His response of 4 September included his familiar view of the German class: "I am convinced that nothing is learnt and what is worse the state of things therein causes great disorder throughout the School." "Events" (to be described later) caused further consideration of the German class to be delayed until a Special Committee of Inquiry into the management of the School had been set up, with investigation of the German class as part of its remit.

Meanwhile Bialloblotzky's real opinions on Giles and Bernays are clear from a letter he wrote to Thomas Brewer on Thursday 19 September 1839:

> I regret a slight degree of fever arising from cold has prevented me this morning from setting out for London. I feel however already so much better that I may confidently hope to be at my post on Monday next. I regret my absence this day the more, because I know that a certain individual watches me with an evil eye. I trust, however, that a fair examination will prove that in spite of his secret opposition, in spite of his clandestine attempts to render my efforts fruitless, and in spite of his discouraging tampering with my rivals, the boys are, on the whole, quite as far advanced in German as they will be found to be in any branch of knowledge in which he himself instructs. I know this because in my illustrations of German grammar I habitually take cognizance of similar features in Latin and Greek. Now if there comes an examiner who is himself unacquainted with classical literature, who never had a university education, and who only obtained his degree, of late, from one of the smallest German Universities[11] which may rank with Aberdeen or St Andrews, and whose feelings have been excited into rivalry, he may begin to seek in the German students for ignorance instead of knowledge. Consequently he will find what he seeks, for in this sense also it is true what the truth itself has spoken "seek and ye shall find". But I appeal to the Committee at large. I am convinced that if they will trust to their common sense, I shall have an opportunity of proving that I am their efficient master as well as

> obedient humble servant
> F.Bialloblotzky

Writing in such terms shows that Bialloblotzky considered Brewer an ally in his battle with Giles, and an eight-page letter from Brewer to Hale ten days later reveals

117

that Brewer was much more closely involved with the school's internal disputes than the detachment of his minute writing and official communications might suggest:

Although I may perhaps be considered as overstepping the line of official duty in addressing the present communication to you I trust no apology is necessary from me for so doing, as my object is merely to arrive at a right conclusion, by right means, on a subject which will necessarily occupy your and their [the Special Committee's] attention.

The subject to which I allude relates to the German class in the School, the report of Dr Bernays and the letter from the Head Master [of 4 September] [...] The tendency of both these communications appears to be the same, viz. to lead to the belief that the German master is unfit for his position. [...] It may perhaps appear like presumption on my part to raise the smallest doubt on the subject when such decisive testimony is offered by those who may be supposed to be best qualified to judge of the matter; but if the value of a person's testimony depends on the consistency of his statements, or the steps which he has taken to arrive at a correct opinion, it is not presumptuous in any one who has the means of doing so to apply these principles as tests to any statement that may be offered for his reception. It is because I think there _are_ the means in the present case that I feel anxious that the Committee, as well for their own sake as for the interests which may be affected by their proceedings, should _judge for themselves_ rather than run the risk of being misled by the statements of others. [Brewer restates the inconsistencies of Dr Bernays reports, both within the 1839 report and between this and the 1838 report.] Dr Bialloblotzky has himself forcibly pointed out these inconsistencies in the letter which he addressed to the Committee when the report was presented, but which letter I beg to remind you has never yet been read in Committee, as, I venture to suggest, it should be when the matter is under consideration.

The other test which I suggested seems applicable only to the statements made by Dr Giles, and its application seems desirable by the very manner in which he has couched that statement. He says "I am _convinced_ that nothing is learnt". Now it is well known that while some persons are rather _hard_ to be convinced, others are very _easy_, and the same individual may be proof _against_ conviction on some points who finds little difficulty in _yielding_ to it on others. _When a person says he is convinced,_ altho' we may be disposed to give him credit for sincerity, it is not necessary we should own _ourselves_ convinced too, without knowing the grounds on which his conviction rests. In the present instance we are not favoured with the means by which Dr Giles has arrived at his conclusion – for aught that appears he _may_ have only adopted the views and opinions of others; - or, he _may_ have taken the surer course of investigating and judging for himself. Frequent personal inspection of the class, and an examination into the mode of teaching adopted by the Master appear to be among the means best calculated to assist in forming a correct judgment, and it would add much to the weight of Dr Giles's opinion if it were known that he had arrived at it by the use of these means, but from what I know I cannot state it as _my_ belief that such is the case. [...]

Since so much has been said on this subject I have for my own satisfaction made a point of attending several times in the German class, and from what I have there witnessed I have not the slightest hesitation in saying that the statements which have been made as to the entire want of knowledge on the part of the boys are not borne out by the facts [...] for instance I have seen the boys commence with reading something in German and correct each other[']s mistakes as they go on, they have then translated what they have read into English – afterwards they have been questioned on the different words which occurred in the sentence read, and have been required to name what parts of speech they were [...] and in some instances the progress made has appeared to me much greater than could have been expected from the time occupied in the study. [...]

I know that some inconvenience is felt by the Masters of some of the classes from the system on which the German class is formed, but this inconvenience seems inevitable so long as the system (which however is not the work of the German master) is acted upon. [...] I am quite free from any bias on the subject having no object to serve but the advantage of the School and the reputation of those who have the administration of its affairs.

Allow me to add that the present communication is solely designed for your own information and that both the German Master and the Head Master are alike ignorant of its existence.

When the eight members of this Special Committee met on 10 October they had before them written submissions from Giles, Edkins and Bialloblotzky. These covered by now familiar territory, but with sharper emphasis.

Giles:
[...] Since my last communication I endeavoured to persuade Dr Bialloblotzky to adopt a mode by which the evil of disarranging the regular Classes would be avoided, and the same or nearly the same facilities left him for prosecuting the German Lessons. This proposition was cheerfully acceded to at the moment, but has this afternoon [7 October] been suddenly reversed by Dr Bialloblotzky without notice and accompanied by remarks in the hearing of the Boys calculated to lower his moral influence over them and to make it very difficult for myself to act in any way so as to accommodate the difference of opinion that exists. [...] I have hitherto shewn every consideration to Dr B but I cannot refrain from saying that the German department is very inefficiently filled and I see no hope of amendment. [...]

Edkins:
"[...] I have in the first instance adopted what appeared to be the regular mode of obtaining redress, an appeal to the Head Master, but he informed me that Dr Bialloblotzky has an absolute power of arranging or altering the 6th Class during Monday and Thursday, without consulting or previously informing their regular instructors. [...] It would not be easy to state briefly the details of the disarrangement for teaching German, but I am sure if the Committee will

take the trouble to inquire they will soon be convinced there is something wrong. [...]"

Bialloblotzky:

[...] The Head Master does not co-operate with me in classing the Scholars according to their proficiency in German. Studies of <u>primary</u>, instead of those of secondary importance, are appointed for the same hours in which the German Classes must be given. There seems to be no necessity for such misarrangements. [...] An absurdity like this cannot be demanded by a man who is fit to be Head Master.

[...] I have been informed that with the concurrence of the Master of another school my salary has been increased for the <u>last</u> quarter and for the <u>future</u> by the Committee of that school; and the Master of a third school wishes to effect the same. I mention this in order to show that it is not my misfortune to disagree with Head Masters generally. I entertain the hope that the insinuations of Dr Giles will lead to a full investigation not conducted by a few prejudicial individuals, but by a full Committee. If this Committee should perceive that in spite of the Head Master's counteraction I have taught as effectually as under existing circumstances could be done, I beg that they will not withhold from me their approbation, so that I may devote myself cheerfully and without care to my Office, while I maintain that decorum which the Committee would be glad to observe in their Servants.

A cheerful and carefree Dr Bialloblotzky takes some imagining.

The Special Committee also heard oral testimony from these three plus Third Master Webster. Edkins was even more emphatic than before: "we have the worst plan that could be advised. [...] German interferes so seriously with the discipline and progress of the School that rather than continue as it does it would be better for German to be excluded altogether." Webster confirmed the severe disruption that the German arrangements were causing. Bialloblotzky claimed Giles had previously deviated from the regulations agreed a year ago, but "During the last few weeks the Boys have attended as I would wish and I have at present no complaint to make on that subject. Though the Head Master has not been accustomed to visit the Class [...] he lately spent two hours in the Class, and when he left [...] he said that he did not know that he could suggest any alteration for the better in my plans."

Giles stated "I do not think (and I believe it is the general impression) that since the School was opened, the German class has been taught well. I attribute it to the Master being better capable of teaching Adults than Boys – he uses language above their comprehension – and that which he says makes the Boys laugh at him. I have not examined the German Class but I derive my knowledge chiefly from incidental inquiries. About a month ago I spent the whole morning in the Class but I did not deem the result satisfactory. I cannot venture to say that I made any suggestions to the Master – he asked me if I could suggest any thing and my reply was that I had nothing to say. I did not express dissatisfaction. During my visit there was on the whole very good behaviour in the class. [...] I have no doubt that a Plan could be devised which could secure the efficiency of the German Class without interfering so much as at present with the other Studies." This mixture of unsupported assertion and feebleness cannot have raised Giles in the esteem of Hale and Brewer.

The Special Committee felt unable to judge for themselves whether, as Giles claimed, Bialloblotzky was unfit for his post, and decided that a "fair and impartial Examination of the Class should be made by some competent person", asking the Secretary to arrange this. Invitations were sent to William (Wilhelm) Wittich of University College[12], G.M.Heilner[13], H.C.Robinson and James Yates; Heilner and Robinson were recommended by Richard Taylor, and Yates by Robinson. Dr Bialloblotzky was unhappy with some of these suggestions, remarking that the pool of competent Germanists in London was small, and there were rivalries between them; at his suggestion W.T.Brande (Humphry Davy's successor as Professor of Chemistry at the Royal Institution) was added, and Heilner did not take part.

The examination took place on Thursday 12th December. Chairman Hale and three other members of the Special Committee (Croucher, Hardwick and Pewtress) met the four examiners at about 1.30, with Secretary Brewer in attendance and taking notes. Hale explained the object of the exercise, and Brewer supplied a list of the 54 boys in the German class, giving how long each of them had been studying the language – 40 of them had started since Dr Bernays' midsummer examination. Each boy received (in theory) two two-hour lessons per week. Suitably briefed, the whole party went to the German class soon after 2 o'clock, and stayed until past 4. The other members of the Special Committee (Stevens, Stacy and Lawrence) came for part of the afternoon, and some left early, but Hale, Croucher and Brewer were present all the time. It was remarked that "throughout the examination the Boys were very attentive and their conduct very satisfactory", which is hardly surprising given the presence of up to a dozen strange and no doubt impressive gentlemen – this unique circumstance could give no indication of how they might have behaved normally.

Then the examiners retired to the Secretary's office with Hale and Brewer. They agreed not to write a formal report, and Brewer undertook to represent their views and opinions to the Committee. They declined to pass judgement on Giles's claims that nothing was learnt and Bialloblotzky was unfit to teach, preferring to confine themselves to the results of his teaching as they had appeared in the examination. Their impressions "were by no means unfavourable as regards either the qualifications or the system of Dr Bialloblotzky". Mr Yates went further: "he considered him an able and zealous Teacher, and was convinced that he had succeeded in inspiring the Boys with a great fondness for the study of the language, and was in other respects a favorite [sic] Master with them." He also commended the teaching system adopted as "the most correct" and found the comparisons made with other languages "highly important and interesting." The examiners agreed that "taking into account the time that the Boys have been in the Class, the opportunities which are afforded for the study, and that it is an extra subject [...] a great deal has been learnt that is very important in the acquisition of the language." They did however suggest that "more attention should be paid to the elementary portions of the language, especially to the construction, and that pupils should be accustomed to the practice of translating from the English language into the German." They also suggested that the Class should be taught in three divisions of not more than 25 pupils, but had no further comment, and were willing to return to check on progress "if their services should be considered desirable by Committee."

Though the examiners (each of whom was later sent two guineas for his service) declined to adopt a judicial role, the members of the Special Committee felt no such inhibition, and firmly sided with Bialloblotzky against Giles. In their view the fundamental problem was that "the study of the German language has, from some cause or other, not received that degree of sanction and attention from the Head Master, as the Principal governing authority of the School under the Committee, to which in common with other Studies it was fairly entitled; on the contrary it appears by the statement of the German Master that nearly all the difficulties which he has experienced have proceeded from that quarter."[14] They cited Giles's initial failure to resolve the clash between optional German and compulsory classics and mathematics, which required the Committee to introduce Regulations agreed in October 1837, then his Plan of Study a year later which broke that agreement, and then his refusal to change the "disarrangements" despite claiming that a better plan could be devised. They conclude:

> We have thought it necessary to offer these remarks for two reasons, - first, because whatever may be the result of this inquiry as regards the present German Master, we are of opinion that while the present system, or want of system, prevails the evils which have been so loudly complained of must continue to exist. And, secondly, because we wish to convey our opinion that the want of co-operation between the Head and any other Master in the School is both unseemly and injurious, and that it is the duty of the Head Master, with regard to every appointed study, whatever may be his own views as to its importance, rather to extend to it his protection and countenance than either to depreciate it, or suffer, much less occasion, obstacles to its successful prosecution.[15]

So Bialloblotzky's position was secure, at least for a while. There are two descriptions of his teaching style. The Head Master of Forest School, Thomas Dry, wrote to support Bialloblotzky's application in December 1836:

> As having had myself considerable experience in tuition, I may perhaps be permitted to say that his accurate and grammatical knowledge of our language, the perspicuity of his elucidations, the facility with which he brings to bear upon the illustration of his subjects an extensive acquaintance with the range of classical literature, eminently qualify him for the efficient duties of tuition, where sound judgement, refined taste, and considerable critical acumen are to be considered indispensable requisites.[16]

Henry Fagan[17] joined the School in Midsummer 1840. He became School Captain (now called Head of School) and was the first boy to gain an Oxford scholarship. He went on to be Head Master of three grammar schools and Rector of three parishes. In 1883 he wrote reminiscences of his school days,[18] including this about Bialloblotzky:

> He, poor fellow, was at loggerheads with the committee, and every now and then he would take a wild dislike to some boy whom he would accuse of being "von shpy," employed to report on his teaching. He did not do us as much good as his colleague [the French Master Delille] did: for, as we could not rub along in German as we did in French, he talked to us in English, and was just as easily thrown off the groove of lesson exercises by a question about the Talmud, or about early Teutonic myths, as the other was by a discussion of French politics. His English was very broken. I remember the length of the "divine primitive cow who out of the salt rock forth licked became was," and who was the ancestress of all the Germans.

Fagan's claim "his English was very broken" must be referring to his manner of speaking: all Bialloblotzky's surviving letters in English are fluent and correct, as Dry asserts. These seemingly contradictory accounts perhaps merely reflect how differently this learned but somewhat obsessive man appeared to a fellow pedagogue and a 13 year old schoolboy.

Bialloblotzky lasted another year at the school. In May 1840 the teaching of Hebrew ceased and the German classes were moved to Wednesday and Saturday afternoons, thus at last removing the timetable clash which had caused so much trouble (though Fagan thought that putting lessons into the Saturday half holiday was "despicable"). The external examiner's report on the German class was satisfactory, but the new Head Master, Dr Mortimer, thought it was "more favourable than I think I should have felt warranted in making had I been in his place" and in September 1840 he wrote to the Committee in by now familiar terms: the German class was in a very unsatisfactory state, scarcely any of the boys knew anything of the language, and the lessons were generally confined to a few bright pupils in the class, the poorer ones hardly having a question put to them. Further rounds of written representations and discussion ended on 20 October when Bialloblotzky, who had declined to resign, was told that it was "not probable" that he would be re-elected to his post in November. He asked the Committee to continue to pay his salary until Christmas without requiring him to attend the school any further. This was granted, perhaps with a collective sigh of relief. His successor, Charles Augustus Feiling, was appointed on 8 December, though only for three hours per week at an annual salary of £75.

After he left the City of London School Friedrich Bialloblotzky continued with a wide variety of teaching, examining, writing and publishing, mainly in Hebrew studies. One major publication, which attracted many distinguished subscribers, was the first book of Psalms in the *Hexapla* form (six parallel versions, two in Hebrew and four in Greek). This was dedicated (with permission) to Prince Albert and printed in 1847 on Bialloblotzky's private press in Winchmore Hill, where he was then living. He was also deeply involved with the founding in 1846 of the Evangelical Alliance.

Any hopes he may have had of securing a permanent senior post in education ended when in December 1847 his wife Sarah, in an action very unusual at that time, brought a case against him in the Consistory Court[19] in London, petitioning for a divorce on the grounds of cruelty. The outcome was reported in *The Times* of 15 June 1848:

> The learned Judge [Dr Lushington] had no doubt whatsoever that the charge preferred against the husband of having committed divers acts of cruelty against his wife was sufficiently established by the evidence, and that the character of those acts constituted legal cruelty. Without any provocation at all the husband had on two occasions inflicted gross personal violence on his wife, at one time with a whip and at another with a cane. The judge was satisfied that the evidence proceeded from witnesses who had not the slightest disposition to deceive the Court or exaggerate the facts. He had never seen evidence more fairly or candidly given, and indeed, it was evidence confirmed by the answers of the husband. Mrs Bialloblotzky was entitled to her remedy, and he therefore pronounced for her prayer.

Charles T. Beke with his wife Emily who was connected by marriage to the Giles family.

Bialloblotzky left London in disgrace, and returned home to Pattensen, near Hanover. From there he immediately wrote to a London acquaintance, Dr Charles Tilstone Beke (1800 – 74), a lawyer and businessman with wide interests in Biblical studies, linguistics, geography and geology. From 1840 to 1843 Beke had been in Abyssinia (Ethiopia), where he was the first to determine with anything approaching accuracy the course of the Blue Nile.[20] Bialloblotzky, his academic career ruined, now made an extraordinary proposal: he would travel to the East Coast of Africa and then explore inland to discover the legendary great lake and establish this as the source of the White Nile.

Beke set about raising subscriptions to fund this ambitious scheme. There are 89 names on the subscription list,[21] headed by Prince Albert (£10), and including Alderman David Salomons and Richard Taylor. Beke himself made the largest contribution (£30) to the totals of £182 in 1848 and £67 in 1849. The Directors of the East India Company granted Bialloblotzky free passage from Suez to Aden.

Leaving Aden in December 1848, Bialloblotzky arrived in Zanzibar in February 1849. There the Imam of Muscat (who ruled over the whole East African coastal region) and Captain Atkins Hamerton of the Indian Navy, Her Majesty's Consul in Zanzibar and the East India Company's representative to the Imam, gave him a hospitable welcome. But they objected strongly to his plans to travel into the African interior. They thought he was too old, inexperienced, ill-equipped and under-funded to embark on such a journey, and probably feared that they would have to mount an operation to rescue him. In the face of such opposition Bialloblotzky had no alternative but to abandon his plans and return to Aden.[22]

For the next four years he continued to travel in the Middle East, and possibly as far as Ceylon (Sri Lanka). By the beginning of 1854 he was in Göttingen lecturing at the university, officially in philosophy but later also in French, Italian, Spanish and Hebrew, and in archaeology and the Bible. He applied for a permanent post in the University Library. The head librarian reported that he "had very wide-ranging knowledge as well as a sound education [...] but he lacks the ability to concentrate all his powers and persevere in an academic piece of work." Moreover "his handwriting is so bad that the catalogues of books would almost certainly be disfigured if he were employed."[23] Not surprisingly he was not appointed.

His principal interest now shifted from religion to science, and he put much effort into promoting the idea of an international meeting of scientists, modelled on national conferences which had been established in Germany and Great Britain.[24] He attended such conferences in Germany, France and England. In particular he was in Oxford in 1860 for the British Association meeting which included the notorious clash on Darwinian theory between Professor Thomas Huxley and the Bishop of Oxford, Samuel Wilberforce. Bialloblotzky's vigorous lobbying for a "Universal Scientific Congress" gained support from a wide range of correspondents, but by the time of his last publication in 1866 nothing practical had been achieved – the idea was ahead of its time, though in the 20th century international conferences of all types proliferated.

In March 1869 Bialloblotzky went to stay with his sister Marie at Ahlden in Lower Saxony, where her husband was pastor. There he died on 28 March, aged 69, and was buried in Ahlden cemetery. A short obituary in the local paper describes him as "a sprightly old man" who had become "rather generally well known". His life might be seen as a series of failures, as evangelist, missionary, teacher, husband, explorer and promoter of international co-operation, but he was a memorable character of whom it was written "he works like a thunder-cloud, which, even as it refreshes and reinvigorates, showers electric sparks over all the prominent subjects which cross its path."[25]

8

1839

In 1838 and 1839 Giles was busy with several scholarly publications, most of them printed by James Bohn[1]: these included the works of five minor Latin poets, and editions of Antimachus and of Terence ("Elegantly printed in 8vo, pp. 856, price 16s."). Around the same time William Pickering,[2] whom Giles had known socially since 1835, produced two volumes of the writings of George Herbert and four volumes by Matthew Hole on Anglican liturgy, all edited by Giles.

In the twenty months since he had first mentioned them Giles's frustrations at his lack of power as Head Master had grown, and now he was thinking of his next move. "I had already in the beginning of the year 1839 made up my mind to resign when a good opportunity offered, and I at the same time felt sure that a good opportunity would offer soon."[3]

A dinner guest, Dr John Whitaker, who had been vicar of Blackburn since 1822, mentioned that the small living of Lower Darwen in Lancashire was available.[4] This was in the diocese of Chester, whose bishop, John Bird Sumner (later Archbishop of Canterbury), happened to be a brother of Charles Sumner, the bishop of Winchester and Patron of the Camberwell Collegiate School who had ordained Giles priest. Through this connection Giles contacted the Bishop of Chester, and on 22 March went to see him with a proposition:

> I told him that I could not immediately resign the Mastership of the City of London School, but if the bishop would allow me non-residence for a couple of years, I would place a curate there, who should receive the whole value of the living, and I expected to resign the mastership at the end of that time. [...] The office is burdensome, and cannot be held many years, but a living is not to be had at a moment's notice, and it is fair to allow a little latitude in such cases. The bishop of Chester said he would think the case over and write to me.[5]

The answer came three days later and was a definite "no": the proposed arrangement "would be so absolute a violation of the Law, that I could not recommend the case to the Archbishop for a licence: & personally I have not authority to grant it." Giles says he was relieved to find that the procedural formalities such an appointment would require "were now all swept away by the conscientious scruples of the bishop of Chester." But he does claim that such appointments were common among the heads of large schools.[6]

Meanwhile the first quarter of 1839 started with 423 boys on the roll, a drop of 17 from the previous quarter and well below the averages of 467 for 1837 and 457 for 1838. This was a cause for concern, particularly to the statistically-minded Thomas Brewer. In January Henry Riley was appointed to replace Thomas Cook, and in February the committee followed up Cook's offer to give occasional science lectures, agreeing that there should be between 10 and 12 of these each year, to be delivered in the afternoon immediately after the end of normal lessons, and attended by two Masters in rotation.

Despite the falling numbers, the French classes were thought to be too large. This issue had been raised the previous October, when the versatile C. N. Woodroffe had stepped in occasionally to ease the pressure. The committee commended this, and Woodroffe was one of six masters to be awarded a £50 pay rise then, but this was not a long-term solution. Unlike Dr Bialloblotzky, the French master Charles Delille (who stayed until his retirement in 1858) was an enlightened teacher, popular particularly with the senior classes. H.S.Fagan describes "delightful evenings at [Delille's] home to which we elder boys were at rare intervals invited" and adds "he taught me the use of my voice – he was recitation-master and prompter at our theatrical scenes: and what a delight it was to be allowed to go now and then and see him act in something out of the *Bourgeois Gentilhomme*, or the *Plaideurs*, at one of his young men's [evening] classes."[7] In February the committee agreed that Delille needed more help, and in April William Chapman (the only non-French candidate) was elected Assistant French Master at an annual salary of £80.

The committee would no doubt have been surprised to know that, just before the first quarter ended on Lady Day (25 March), Giles also had a brief excursion into body-snatching. He had first met Edmund Barker[8] on 2 January 1837 at Jackson's Coffee House in Bow Street.[9] They became friends, and Barker accompanied Giles at the end of the month when he first went to view the land in Windlesham which he later bought.[10] Barker was not a good business man; in particular he got into financial difficulty by ordering a Great Yarmouth printer, Mr Skill, to print a large quantity of his books which he had no realistic hope of selling. On 13 May 1837 Barker was arrested after Skill brought a suit against him for debts of £40; Barker was put into the Fleet Prison as a debtor, where Giles visited him that evening, despite having buried his infant son Henry on the same day. Giles himself used Skill to print some of his own books, though the relationship was not a happy one. In one letter Giles is pretty blunt:[11]

> How can you for a moment suppose that I will consent to pay Mr Barker's costs? You might as well ask the Queen to do so. Your wisest step will be to stop all legal proceedings even now at this eleventh house. Mr B. cannot pay one farthing, and it must all recoil on yourself.

Nevertheless, by July 1838 Giles had advanced sufficient funds to settle the debt; Barker was released, though he never recovered his position in the world:

March 21 [1839], Thursday. Mrs Reynolds, wife of G.W.M.Reynolds,[12] called about 11 o'clock this day, and told me that Edmund Henry Barker was lying dead at a lodging house in Covent Garden Market; that since his release from the Fleet Prison, he had left the Globe Coffee-house where he had lodged for some time, and had lived for the last two or three weeks with a woman named Bayes; that in order to obtain credit, for he had been for some time without money, he had taken her name and they passed for man and wife. Immediately on receipt of this news I hurried off to the house named by Mrs Reynolds, and found the poor man lying dead, and Mrs Bayes weeping with sorrow for his loss. I could not help feeling for the woman: her sorrow was deep and unfeigned. She exclaimed bitterly against his wife, who had allowed him to live so lonely in London at lodging-houses, and said how proud she should have been to call so learned a man her husband. I went from the house to [my solicitor] Mr Maxon in Little Friday Street, and again went back to Covent Garden. Mr Maxon told me he was entitled to £1000 insurance on Mr Barker's death, and he would therefore pay all expenses of the funeral.

March 23, Saturday. We this day procured a coffin for Mr Barker, & went to the house where he had died, to see the landlady who was an Irish woman. She was not at home, but the servant said she was sure the landlady would not let the body be taken away, until her bill was paid, amounting to several pounds. As Mr Maxon meant to pay this, but had not got the money in his pocket, we sent for the coffin which was not far off; four men brought it, and when the door was again opened, we prevented the servant from shutting it; the four men made all speed up the stair case, put the body in the coffin, and carried it off to the back street where the carpenter who undertook the funeral had his workshop. As we issued from the door into the street, we met the landlady returning home. "Oh, and is it your riverence that can play such tricks upon a poor widow, and carry off a dead body without paying the rint?"[13]

The second quarter started on Tuesday 2 April, and passed smoothly, though of course the problems with the German class rumbled on in the background. In May it was agreed that the Foundation Scholars could, if their parents wished, live at home instead of in the school, and be paid an allowance of £25 for their board and clothing. The Committee of Visitors was increased to five plus the Chairman, and was asked to look at the arrangements for the Scholars who boarded at the school. Their recommendations suggest that Giles may have been somewhat negligent in this regard. They wanted the Scholars to have "a Sleeping Room appropriated and preserved for their sole and exclusive use", to take breakfast and dinner ("at least") in the apartments of the Head Master, and to remain at school on Sundays unless their parents requested in writing for them to be at home, and they asked the Head Master to see that the Scholars were "punctual and regular in their attendance to their School duties."[14]

On the morning of 21 June the committee met to receive the reports of the examiners (the same as in 1838: Dyne, Pullen, Brasseur and Bernays) before the distribution of prizes that afternoon by Lord Brougham. But there were complications. First Giles informed the committee that the boys placed first in Classics and General Proficiency were the same as in 1838 (Henry Watson and George Heppel), and so were precluded by the committee's regulations from receiving prize medals for a second time. These medals would therefore go to those placed second, Henry Hose and Alfred Bousfield. But Hose had come first in Mathematics too, and so would receive two medals, which was against customary practice. Giles proposed that Hose should receive the Mathematics medal and the Classics books ("Bacon's Works, value 10 guineas"), with the Classics medal (but no books) going to Henry Baxter, and the mathematics books to William Emery instead. Second Master Edkins, always keen to defend the standing of mathematics in the school, spoke against this arrangement, which deprived Hose of his mathematics books, but the Committee agreed to do as Giles suggested "without prejudice to the future".[15] A letter from Dr Bialloblotzky objecting to the German report (as described in the previous chapter), was read but discussion of this was postponed. Then a message arrived from Lord Brougham:

4 Grafton St, 12 o'clock

Lord Brougham presents his compliments to Mr Brewer, and is extremely sorry that he is obliged to attend a Committee of the House of Lords, and cannot postpone his attendance as one of the Irish Judges who is summoned at that hour is obliged to return immediately to Ireland.

Lord B. exceedingly regrets that this circumstance deprives him of the opportunity of meeting the London School Committee, but it is wholly out of his power.

The arrangements for the afternoon ceremony were hastily rejigged, with Hale presiding and presenting the John Carpenter Scholarship, Giles presenting Dr Conquest's Gold Medal for General Proficiency, Dyne and Pullen giving the medals and books for Classics and Mathematics respectively, and the remaining class prizes given by the Masters of the respective classes.[16]

Giles also had a domestic distraction that day. Writing in 1877 he recalled:

During the months of June and July [1839] we spent time quietly and without much incident. I have kept no diary of those months, and the only important incident was the birth of our present eldest son Arthur Henry, which took place on Friday June 21. The examination of the boys at the City of London School took place in the morning, and I dined with the Common Council in the evening. Having as usual on such occasions to make a speech, I alluded to the birth of the child; upon which there was a great shout, "A new pupil for the School!" I knew however even then that I should not remain in the position of Head Master until the little baby could enter the school. In the year 1839 the Common Council had not regained the respect of the whole people. The reforms that had been made to its constitution[17] had let in a lot of noisy persons, who belonged to a lower class, had received little or no education, and had clamoured themselves into civic offices, to which formerly they would have aspired in vain. I will give an instance of what constantly took place. One day one of them named Hoard[18], a baker who lived in Houndsditch, came into my room where I was engaged with one of the classes, and said "Dr Giles, how is it that I find boys of great talent in the same class with others who are very dull?" I replied "You must apply to a higher authority than me for an answer to that question. Did you ever know any class of men who all had the same talents?" And this man, who asked such a stupid question, was appointed a member of the Committee to manage the school and to interfere at their monthly meetings with the authority of the Master. Nor did they all observe decorum in their visits. Several of them walked into my room with their hats on, and seemed to look on me as a shopman behind the Counter. Yet they did not scruple to cabal with the under-masters, and to exempt them as much as possible from my jurisdiction, until at last I gave up on many things, on which I ought to have insisted, and I of course found that I was still responsible, although my powers of action were limited.[19]

The prize giving marked the end of the Midsummer quarter, followed by five weeks holiday. Giles was at Windlesham, where on 22 July "I sat up this day to a late hour in the drawing room putting in chronological order the various scraps of paper on which I had recorded the various events, so that at some future time I might put them in a regular journal. Interspersed with these fragments were copies of letters which I had made from time to time. These documents form the basis of my present work [the *Diary and Memoirs*]."[20]

School resumed on Monday 29 July 1839, and a week later Brewer presented to the Committee a report[21] on the number of pupils attending, which by Midsummer 1839 was down to 416, adding that "from the present state of the school there is reason to fear that the number this quarter will be even considerably lower". Giles was asked to submit a report on the state and condition of the school, and further consideration was adjourned to the next meeting (4 September). By then it was known that Brewer's fears had been realised: 97 boys left at Midsummer, and at the start of the Michaelmas quarter 33 new boys and 3 returning after absence brought the total roll to 355. Giles's report was flimsy, making only one substantial point: that the rigorous requirement restricting admission to sons of residents of the City or Freemen might be relaxed as this had, in Brewer's estimation, caused 30 to 40 applicants to be rejected. Otherwise he repeated suggestions he had made elsewhere about introducing French in the junior classes, establishing a small commercial class, and (of course) dealing with the "great disorder" of the German class.

Meanwhile Brewer had added much more detail to his statements about the number of admissions. He listed by name all 97 boys who had left at Midsummer, with their reasons for leaving, and summarised his findings in these tables.

Ages of boys who have left		Time they were in the school		Causes of Leaving	
Between					
15 & 16 -	8	¼ years -	1	Dead	5
14 & 15 -	18	½ " -	8	Finished & gone to business	28
13 & 14 -	24	¾ " -	6	Gone abroad	5
12 & 13 -	10	1 " -	4	Change of residence & distance	5
11 & 12 -	12	1¼ " -	4	Family circumstances	2
10 & 11 -	14	1½ " -	9	Gone to a school opened by a friend	2
9 & 10 -	7	1¾ " -	5	Disappointment & dissatisfaction	6
8 & 9 -	3	2 " -	7	Ill health and absence from town	24
7 & 8 -	1	2¼ " -	12	Uncertain (including several believed to	20
		2½ " -	41	have gone to business, or to be ill &c)	
	97		97		97

The 2 last Nos. include 28 Boys who are expected to return.

It is sobering to see that about one third of these boys left for reasons of health, more than the number who had finished their education. The causes of death of the Shankey brothers, Alexander (aged 10¾ years) and John (9¾), and of George Neal (13¼) are not known, but the brothers Henry (8¾) and William (10) Unwin, sons of the printer Jacob Unwin of 31 Bucklersbury, who had joined the school at the start of the year, had burnt to death in a fire at their home on 31 May.[22]

Brewer pointed out that since a large number of the boys who joined the school at the start had been of a similar age it was not surprising that a similar number had left together 2½ years later. He had found that on average boys who had left had been in the school for 1½ years, which he expected might settle at 2 years (as was the case at King's College School). So if the numbers were to remain at 400 then 200 boys must be recruited each year, or 50 each quarter, a target that had been reached only in the first two quarters after the school opened. He doubted whether there were enough "sons of Householders or those free of the City" to keep the roll up to 400, unless these strict entry qualifications were relaxed (the point that Giles had also made). He also gave examples of problems caused by the regulations: sons of those who had been Householders for many years but had recently moved, sons of widows of Householders or Freemen, boys under the guardianship of Householders or Freemen. Brewer's conclusion, expressed in the typically subservient style of his official documents, was "with great submission, to solicit [the Committee's] attention to the general subject, and to the propriety of considering whether a relaxation in the practice which has hitherto prevailed might not be made with great advantage to the School, and without at all impairing the privileges of those classes who have hitherto enjoyed the exclusive right to seek admission into it."[23] The Committee referred the matter to the Sub Committee.

The Sub Committee reported back on 2 October, rejecting the proposals for junior French and Commercial classes. On the admissions policy they pointed out that the regulation was prescribed by the Court of Common Council and that therefore the Committee did not have power to change it. Nor did they think it was advisable "for the present" to apply to the Court for an amendment, but "At the same time we recommend to this Committee to relax the existing regulations as far as they may be able by giving as liberal an interpretation to the Rule as it will admit of without a direct violation of it." The Committee agreed with the report and ordered it to be entered into the Minutes except for this final sentence – all of which is duly recorded in the minutes.[24]

For the remainder of the year much time was occupied by the issues of Gresham College or Dr Bialloblotzky, which have been covered in Chapters 5 and 7, or by the Special Inquiry, which is the subject of the following chapter.

One other serious matter, which must have added to the general concern about the state of the school, came to light on 22 October when Hale summoned the Committee. The minutes recount the sad story:

> The Chairman informed the Committee that they had been convened together this day in consequence of its having been discovered that one of the Boys in the School, named Henry Nathan,[25] had been guilty of purloining Books to a very great extent, which belonged to other Boys, and of selling them for his own advantage to a Bookseller named Joseph Stephens residing at No 7 Hackney Road Crescent, and who also keeps a Shop in Gracechurch Street, two doors north of Fenchurch Street.

> The several circumstances being related to the Committee it appeared (amongst other things) that the Boy had acknowledged his guilt, and had voluntarily made out a List of such articles as he recollected having stolen, comprising 94 to 101 Volumes, besides a pencil case, a pocket book, and mathematical drawing instruments from about 6 cases[26]; and that the number of Books which had been recovered from Stephens was 35.

> The Committee were attended by Mr Walter Joseph of No 15 Broad Street Buildings, Merchant, on behalf of his Uncle, the Boy's Father, who appealed to the merciful feelings of the Committee and entreated them, in consideration of the age and other circumstances of his Uncle, to deal as leniently as possible in the case.

> The Committee having taken the whole of the circumstances into consideration, it was Resolved that Henry Nathan, for his gross dishonesty, be publickly expelled from the School with contempt and ignominy.

> Stephens the Bookseller, and his Wife, were then called in, and after replying to several questions put to them, they were told that in the opinion of the Committee they were exceedingly culpable, that they had by their conduct encouraged the

Boy to the commission of the numerous acts of dishonesty of which he had been guilty, and that there was no doubt they were aware, at the time, that they were doing wrong.

The Boy Nathan was then called in, and also his Cousin Mr Joseph, in whose hearing he again acknowledged his guilt, and he was told of the decision which in consideration of the feelings of his Father, the Committee had come to. At the same time it was stated to him that he was still liable to be proceeded against according to law by the parents of the Boys whom he had robbed.

The whole School, together with the several Masters, being assembled in the Theatre, the Committee proceeded thither, where, after a declaration of his offence, and an impressive address to him and to the Boys generally by the Chairman of the Committee, the Boy Nathan was publickly expelled from the School agreeably to the above Resolution.

There is no record of any further action being taken against Henry Nathan, which was just as well for him as court records for 1840 show boys aged 14 or 15 being sentenced to a minimum of 7 years imprisonment for theft. The bookseller Stephens later wrote to Brewer that "having become convinced that his conduct had been incautious and reprehensible, while he felt perfectly free from the consciousness of having done wrong from a desire for profit or illegal advantage, and being anxious in as far as be in his power to make atonement for his fault, he would not rest until he could trace out and return such of the Books as he had unfortunately sold." He returned a total of five more books.[27]

Meanwhile Giles's prodigious productivity as an author continued. On 13 November he notes "This evening the printers Messrs Spottiswood sent me a complete copy of my Greek Lexicon, a work which has occupied all my leisure for 18 months [...]. I also received the first proof sheet of Bede's *Ecclesiastical History*. Thus my scribblings go on one after the other *velut unda supervenit undam*."[28] Both these books are still available: Giles's translation of Bede runs to 246 pages, while his Lexicon "for the use of colleges and schools" comprises Greek-English and English-Greek ("more copious than any that has yet appeared") sections and a Concise Grammar of the Greek Language, and occupies 939 pages, mostly in three columns. He sent copies to "some of the most eminent schoolmasters", and received appreciative thanks from Dr Hawtrey of Eton College and Dr Kennedy of Shrewsbury School, who added "He is also happy to find many points of coincidence between Dr Giles's judgment & his own in regard to elementary Greek Grammar. Dr Kennedy is engaged in drawing up such a Grammar, & he will not fail to refer to Dr Giles's book in doing so."[29]

Giles clearly preferred scholarly research and writing to the daily challenges of running a large school and fighting its governors. He was preparing to quit his post, but perhaps did not expect the end to come so soon.

9

Special Inquiry

T he end-game started with a letter to Hale from Charles Delille, the French Master:

City of London School
Sept 12th 1839

My dear Sir

I apply to you under circumstances of importance to our school, namely discipline.

One of the oldest of our boys, pupil of Dr Giles, by name Alfred Moul[1], son of Mr Moul of 26 Brudnel Place, New North Road, or 106 Fenchurch Street, has a lesson to write or translate for me, as an imposition for misconduct. This imposition was given to him, by me, yesterday, and ought to have been written on that day between the hours of twelve and one. The boy <u>refused</u> and still refuses to write the imposition, and, consequently, is now detained after school hours. I apprized the Head Master of the boy's conduct yesterday morning, and, in my presence, Dr Giles told the boy that he should be detained until such imposition was written, the boy coolly turned to us both and alluding to the detention said "I am accustomed to dine late". I need not enter into the details of the misconduct, suffice it to say that Alfred Moul and myself are now closeted together and I have the pain of witnessing the most unexampled instance of defiance to a master that can ever had been experienced.

This morning the Head Master invited me to relax in my endeavours, telling me that the boy was leaving in a fortnight and moreover having heard that he threatened to be absent altogether from school, if I detained him as I did yesterday, he, the Head Master, thought it was not worth while for me to insist on this imposition. In my dilemma, being now unprotected by the Head Master, I have recourse to your advice. Far from my wish to disregard the admonition of Dr Giles, but is it not a duty I owe to the trust reposed in me, to enforce the observance of that discipline which ought to exist in our school? I am now in my room with my pupil; could you favour me with a few moments conversation I shall feel grateful to you.

Yours very respectfully

C.J.Delille.

to which was added a postscript:

> My dear Sir
>
> This letter has been kept back until this day. The salutary fear which my application to you created in Alfred Moul brought, on his part, a promise that the imposition should be forthcoming this day (13th September) at twelve o'clock. I have this moment received it, and although this letter, being your property, is forwarded to you, I may express the wish that no further notice be taken of the subject.
>
> Yours faithfully
> C.J.Delille
> 13th Sep., 12 o'C
> City of London School

Delille's final sentence is disingenuous. The letter would not have been Hale's property until he received it, and if Delille really wanted no further notice to be taken he could simply have destroyed it. One suspects that, even though Moul had been brought to submission on this occasion, Delille felt that Giles's lack of support should be brought to Hale's attention, in the expectation that action would be taken.

In this he was right. Hale laid the letter before the Sub Committee on 19 September, who decided that further investigation was needed. They met again on 25 September, when Delille attended and spoke on the general issue of discipline in the school. After a further drafting meeting on 30 September the Sub Committee were ready with a long report which was presented to the Grand Committee two days later. After dealing with the questions of the falling roll, the introduction of junior French and commercial classes, and the regulations for admissions, as described on p.133, they added:

> Before concluding this report we beg to state that while engaged in the consideration of the subjects referred to us by this Committee a variety of circumstances connected with the general management and discipline of the School have been brought under our notice, which appear to us to require the most serious attention; but as we considered that a proper inquiry could not be instituted and completed by us during the short time that we should remain a Sub Committee, and that a subject of so much importance should be confided to a Committee specially appointed for the purpose, and not liable to change by the removal of any of its Members, we have forborne entering into a minute investigation, but we beg to recommend to this Committee to appoint a Special Committee for that purpose, who should be instructed to institute an inquiry into the general management of the School, with the view of ascertaining whether any changes or alterations can be made to promote its future welfare and increase the confidence of the public towards it, and that the result of such inquiries together with any observations that may be deemed advisable thereon should be reported to this Committee for consideration.

The Committee accepted this proposal, and agreed that this Special Committee "do consist of William Stevens Esquire Deputy, Mr William Lawrence, Thomas Corney Esquire Deputy, Mr Benjamin Hardwick, Mr William Croucher, Mr Richard Taylor, Mr George Stacy, Mr Samuel Baylis, Mr Benjamin Bowes and Thomas Pewtress Esquire Deputy, together with Warren Stormes Hale Esquire Chairman." This was an experienced team: seven had been members of the Committee since before the School opened[2], and Hale, Taylor and Pewtress had (with three others) drafted its first curriculum.

The Special Committee met five times, on 10, 14 and 28 October, 18 November and 2 December.[3] What they did is described in their Report[4], presented to the Committee on Wednesday 4 December, which is summarised here.

They had examined individually first the Secretary, then each Assistant Master and then the Head Master. Each was asked the same questions:

1st. Whether the existing regulations applicable to their respective Classes appeared to them suitable and efficient, and whether the power and authority individually possessed by them was such as was sufficient for a satisfactory discharge of their duties.

2nd. Whether the attendance progress and conduct of their respective Classes were such as was satisfactory to themselves and creditable to the School.

3rd. The extent to which the Head Master may be supposed to be acquainted with the state of the several Classes and the means he adopts for obtaining a knowledge thereof, whether he is accustomed, either statedly or occasionally, to visit and inspect the Classes, to examine the Boys and ascertain what progress they are making, and to offer any advice to the Masters.

4th. Whether in cases of doubt or difficulty, especially with regard to the enforcement of discipline, the several Masters are accustomed to appeal to the Head Master for aid, and if such cases have not hitherto occurred what would be the course they would pursue if they did occur.

5th. Whether there is any attempt at uniformity in the proceedings of the several Masters on subjects of discipline etc. either by a system of communication amongst themselves, or between them and the Head Master, or whether each individual Master acts in such cases according as his own judgment dictates.

6th. Whether the several Masters consider the Books which are in general use in the School are well adapted for the purposes to which they are applied, or whether any of them are found to be defective, or considered otherwise objectionable.

7th. And generally whether the Masters can point out any deficiencies in the management of the School, or suggest any alterations or improvements by which it could be benefited.

The general view of the Masters was that the regulations were satisfactory and that they had adequate powers to maintain authority and ensure progress. The two most senior Masters, Webster and Edkins, both complained again about the arrangements for the 5th and 6th classes, the latter being described by Edkins as "bad altogether". Giles agreed that the regulations were adequate, but added that "there were a variety of small things which bring a slur upon the School, such as complaints arising from the loss of Cloaks, Umbrellas, Books and other things, which are not attended to soon enough from a want of power being vested somewhere out of the Committee to remedy them."

Unsurprisingly, every Master thought the conduct and progress of his own class was satisfactory, but Webster took a broader view, stating that he had full power over his own class and that it was progressing well, but that "he feels obliged to accommodate himself to the general tone of discipline prevailing in the School", which he characterized as of "a lax and compromising description", - he also stated that he thought "a stronger tone of discipline" desirable, not only with reference to the time that Boys are actually in attendance at the School, but also as calculated to produce a good effect upon their conduct after leaving it. Edkins took a similar but, predictably, stronger view:

> There are so many irregularities in [the 6th] Class, and the Boys have so much liberty in the choices of their subjects of study, that great disorder is the consequence and the Boys are not nearly so completely under the control of the Masters as the Boys in all the other classes are. The voluntary system of omitting Greek or taking German has been very mischievous – some Boys omit Mathematics and they are always the worst behaved. In the 6th Class [...] there is very little if any discipline, there is no regular system, which is owing partly to the circumstances just mentioned, and partly to the division of the class between two Masters who differ from each other as to discipline – the Boys see that there is a want of encouragement in enforcing my views and they take advantage of it. The evil arises from a want of firmness in execution rather than want of knowledge. The Head Master is not consistent on this point. If a good system were adopted today there is no security that it would be acted upon tomorrow. I do not understand what his system is. Forged notes have frequently been brought by Boys of the 6th Class as excuses for absence &c, and in many cases very little notice has been taken of the circumstances. There is a want of punishment for any great offences that occur, which I think should be left to the treatment of the Parents. The Boys ought in my opinion to be more frequently brought under the cognizance of their Parents, and the Reports of their progress should be sent home twice in the half year instead of once only.

The Inquiry gives several instances of bad behaviour in the 6th Class, in which the annoyance of Brewer, who must have supplied the details, is barely disguised by the formal language:

Again, the extensive loss of books which by the recent inquiry before the Committee has been proved to have taken place in that class must be considered as one of the strongest evidences of a most lamentable deficiency in point of discipline, a fact which is also supported by the following instances (among others which might be mentioned) of injury and destruction to the property of the School, which have no parallel in any other class, viz. the large slate furnished for the use of the Master in setting Lessons to the Boys in Mathematics &c has, through their being left in the room alone[5] or being allowed to have access to it out of school hours, been twice overturned, the first time the frame being fractured and the second time the slate and frame being entirely destroyed, which has recently occasioned an expense of several pounds to replace; in the same room in which this occurrence took place (viz. that occupied by the Division of the Class under Mr Edkins) several keys which have been provided at different times for fastening the door have been made away with, or wilfully secreted, which has also been the case to a very considerable extent with other articles provided at the expense of the School, particularly sponges and cloths, which are required by the Master in effacing Lessons from his large slate which articles there has been good reason to believe have frequently been secreted or utterly destroyed in the most wanton and mischievous manner. In another room occupied by the Division of the 6th Class which is under the care of Dr Giles, considerable injury and expenses have been sustained by the frequent and extensive demolition of the windows; it appears that although every defect which existed when the School broke off at Midsummer was made good before it reassembled after the vacation, in less than 3 months it was found necessary to replace 14 panes of Glass in the two Windows in the room in question which had not been done more than 12 days before the same number were again found to be broken.[6]

Giles took a different view of the general state of discipline: "I am not aware of any deficiency in the discipline of the School, it is well acted up to and I should not wish to augment it. [...] I think it would not be possible to make an alteration for the better." But later he conceded "that there is a slight want of uniformity in the School."

On the third topic of the inquiry, the extent to which the Head Master was aware of the state of the classes, the Masters were unanimous: he never or very rarely visited or examined the classes, and could have little knowledge of the methods of the various Masters. Giles did not contradict this: "I can form an idea of what is the state of the several Classes but there is no regular system of communication between them and myself. I do not visit the Classes periodically but there is hardly a day that I am not in at least two Classes. I have no system of periodical visitation and inspection. I have thought that some unpleasantness might be occasioned if I interfered too much. I satisfy myself that things are going on properly by daily observation."

The next issue was whether the Masters had sought or would seek help from the Head Master in matters of discipline. All except one stated that they had not, and would not, with four adding that they thought they would not receive support anyway, because the Head Master's views on discipline differed from theirs. The exception, Mr Riley, had referred a case, involving a boy inciting another boy to steal from his parents, but had heard nothing until the offender told him that the Head Master had pardoned him. The Report gives Delille's letter to Hale in full, and comments:

> It appears that by Mr Delille's perseverance in this case, although as he says, "left unprotected by the Head Master," not only was this particular boy brought to submit to discipline, but a beneficial affect was produced upon the Class generally. It has already been stated in part of Mr Delille's evidence that that Class (the 6th) he has always found worse than any other, though lately there has been a great improvement in it, "this improvement" (he says) "I attribute to my Appeal to the Committee, rather than to any interference of the Head Master; the Boys know what has occurred and I have no difficulty whatever in managing them to my satisfaction."

Delille's own view was that "A concentrated power is wanted in the School, whose frown would be a punishment and whose smile would be a reward". He added that his experience in several other large Public Schools enabled him to say that such a power was generally resident in, and effectually exercised by, the respective Head Masters of those Establishments, but in this school, in case of a difficulty he should not think of appealing to the Head Master. In response Giles asserted that "The Masters have appealed to me in cases of difficulty, and they have occasionally reported to me the state of their classes and the conduct of Particular Boys, but there is no regular practice of the kind."

On the question of whether there had been any attempt to discuss and form a consistent policy on matters of discipline throughout the school the answer was a clear "No". As with other matters, Giles had let this lapse: "The Masters at first met together, two or three times, but I found no good result from it, on account of diversities of opinion amongst them, and there was an indisposition on the part of two or three to keep up the communication."

Six of the Masters objected to some of the books in general use in the School, using terms such as "very unfit", "imperfect", "objectionable", "deficient" and "so bad as to be injurious to the School". Not surprisingly the Masters had a number of suggestions for improvements. Mr Cock strongly urged making better provision for boys intended for commercial life: "where a Boy after leaving School is intended to be placed in a Merchant's Counting House it is desirable that he should obtain a practical knowledge of the different branches of Arithmetic to the various subjects which occur in commercial life, as for instance calculations of Interest, Exchanges of Money, Barter of Goods &c. and also that he should be able to read and write Letters both in the French and German languages." There were several suggestions for improving the system of promotion from one class to the next, in particular that this should always be done in consultation with the Masters of the classes concerned, and should take account of a boy's proficiency in mathematics as well as classics. Webster and Edkins returned to their familiar theme of the problems caused by the arrangements for the German class.

In their final encounter with Giles the Special Committee "were led, as well by his own evidence as by that received from other Masters, to press upon his attention, rather closely, several circumstances in which it was apparent his authority as <u>Head Master</u> had not been called into effectual exercise". Giles replied that the tight control exercised by the School Committee had deterred him from interfering as much as he perhaps otherwise should, and that representations which he had made to them had been neglected. He was asked for, and challenged on, specific examples, one concerning a resolution about the Masters' regular attendance, which he had failed to communicate to them, "upon which we thought it right to explain to him that being communicated to him as the <u>Head</u> Master, it was in our opinion his province to make the other Masters acquainted with it, as well as to see that they acted up to it."

Having made some recommendations about the organisation of the art classes, and with a reminder that the German class would be dealt separately, nine members[7] of the Special Committee signed their report, which in manuscript occupies 42 pages, and submitted it "to the judgement of this Worshipful Committee."

The Committee unanimously accepted it, and asked the Special Committee to suggest what to do next. Meeting on 10 December the Special Committee decided to ask Giles to forward any observations on the report he might wish to make, in writing, before their next meeting on Monday 16 December. Giles was called in and told this, and given a copy of the report.

On that Monday Mrs Sarah Hale sent a note to Brewer: "Mr Hale having been summon'd on the Special Jury and still being detain'd there will be prevented meeting the committee today."[8] Thomas Pewtress chaired the meeting (a very long one) until Hale arrived, and apparently Brewer became unwell during the meeting and had to leave; George Stacy then took the minutes. Having agreed to deliver the newly completed Report on the Examination of the German Class to the Grand Committee, the Special Committee heard that although Brewer had reminded Giles that morning that his written comments were needed by 12 noon for the meeting at 2 pm, and had separately requested him to return the copy of the Report he had been given[9], all that had been produced was this letter from Giles, dated 12 December.

> Gentlemen
>
> Under ordinary circumstances I should have thought it my duty to express regret that the Committee had carried on an inquiry among the Assistant Masters, for nearly three months secret and unknown to me: but circumstances which I have noticed in the Report placed before me have induced me to feel glad of an opportunity of making certain counter-statements and I respectfully request of the Committee to give me an immediate hearing. If they will allow a friend to accompany me to assist in conducting the evidence (but without speaking) and as a witness, I shall be obliged.
> I am, Gentlemen, your obedient Servant
>
> J.A.Giles

P.S. The above letter was intended to be submitted to the whole Committee which Mr Hale has now convened especially at 11 o'Clock. A Note from Mr Brewer states that the Special Committee at their meeting this Afternoon will require a written reply to their Report. I therefore address this letter to them in the first instance and afterwards to the Meeting for Wednesday. Allow me to request that the notice for that meeting should be specific in order to secure as large a Meeting as possible. My wish to have the attendance of a friend is simply this. Many persons (Clergymen and others) will know of these particulars and will not have an opportunity of hearing what takes place through the Common Councilmen who are present. I should wish to be able to refer them to a third party and by no means to have to make statement unsupported by such testimony. If the Special Committee will have the kindness to consider this point and give their reply, I shall be obliged. My friend the Reverend Dr Croly[10] has kindly promised to attend, but he is entirely ignorant of all particulars either on one side or the other, and would therefore be unbiassed. He lives at present in Hackney and I should like to know beforehand whether my request can be granted that I may inform him.

Giles's claim that he had not known about the inquiry is absurd. All twelve of his Assistant Masters had been called to give evidence, and even if the meetings were not held in the school their absences must have come to the Head Master's attention (unless he really was as ignorant of the day-to-day running of the school as some of his staff alleged). He himself had been "pressed rather closely" to give explanations to the Special Committee, so how could he have been unaware of the inquiry? Brewer despatched a note to Giles from the meeting "I have to request that you will have the goodness to return to me by the bearer the Report of the Special Committee which was submitted to you for perusal on the 10th Inst." In response Giles requested an interview with the Committee, which was granted. A "lengthened conversation" ensued, a glimpse of which is given in the notes of the meeting (written upside down in a different hand):

> Dr Giles: I must beg pardon. I must decline returning the Report. I have no objection to a copy being made.
> [Chairman]: The Report shall be placed in the hands of the Committee immediately.

After withdrawing, and apparently cooling off a bit, Giles then returned, produced the Report and also presented a second letter, headed "Monday evening".

> I am sorry that I should not before have known the formal mode of treating such business usually adopted by the City Committee. I have now only to say that I am perfectly ready to make any statement before the Special Committee, whenever they may think proper, although I should still prefer to go before the whole Committee.

But there was still nothing in writing, which is what the Special Committee wanted, and they therefore resolved that they were unable to prepare any recommendation upon the Report for the Grand Committee.

Hale was apprehensive about what might happen at the Grand Committee's Wednesday meeting, and on the day before sent Brewer a note:

> The committee yesterday after you left suggested the propriety of having a short hand writer present tomorrow. Pray give me your opinion by return of bearer. They think and I think to[o] that we should not be in the position to allow any one to say what they please.
>
> PS. I sincerely hope you are better.[11]

Brewer agreed, though in fact it was part of the Special Committee's meeting on Friday 20 December that was recorded verbatim.

When the Grand Committee met on 18 December Giles wrote to say he had decided to "waive his right" (did he have such a right?) to have a friend in attendance, but still wanted to give his observations on the Report orally to the Grand Committee. He was called in and asked directly whether he still declined to make a reply to the Special Committee in writing, and if so why. He replied that what he wanted to bring forward would be in the form of questions and answers. Giles left the meeting, and after further discussion was recalled to be told that, because the Special Committee might have to pass their Report to the Court of Common Council, they must first have his comments in writing, but that this did not preclude him from producing oral evidence later. This drew some candid remarks from Giles:

> I appeal to the Grand Committee because I feel that I am likely to have justice done to me to a greater extent by the Grand Committee than by the Special Committee. I believe that a secret influence has been employed in the Special Committee against me. There are at least two or three facts stated in the Report which could not have come to the knowledge of the Special Committee had they not been furnished by Members of that Special Committee. I disclaim any obligation to state what those facts are until I have heard whether my appeal is entertained.[12]

He withdrew again, and the Special Committee then presented its lengthy report on the German Class. At the end of the meeting it was agreed to inform Giles that the Special Committee would meet on Friday afternoon, 20 December, "when they would be ready to receive any communication from him in writing".

Who was this "secret influence"? The prime suspect is Thomas Brewer, who though not technically a member of the committee was present taking minutes at all their meetings. Brewer, Hale's protégé, was a constant and significant presence in the school; his sympathy for Bialloblotzky and willingness to communicate this to Hale have already been noted (pp.118–119). It is not clear what the "two or three facts" might be – perhaps the details of the damage done by indiscipline in the 6th Class, which Brewer would have had to rectify.

Preparing for the crucial meeting next day, Brewer wrote to Giles on Thursday 19 December to ask whether he intended to produce oral evidence at this meeting. "My reason for inquiring is that I may make arrangements to facilitate the taking down of such Evidence, in case I should be unequal to the task in my own person." He also wrote to W.B.Gurney Esq,[13] Abingdon St, Westminster, "I am directed to request the favour of your attendance upon a Committee of this Establishment, to take Notes of Evidence on an Inquiry before them, tomorrow, Friday the 20th Instant at Two o'Clock in the afternoon precisely."[14]

At that hour Hale, Stevens, Hardwick, Taylor, Pewtress and Lawrence gathered, with Brewer taking minutes. First the long-awaited written observations on the Report from Giles were read. These did not amount to much: he noted that almost all the Masters acknowledged that they had sufficient authority, accepted that some of the books in use were unsatisfactory (while disclaiming any personal interest in them and pointing out that they had all been approved by the Committee), and observed that Mr Cock's proposal concerning the commercial class quoted verbatim a paragraph that he (Giles) had written three years earlier. He flatly denied the more serious claims that he had not visited classes enough to be aware of what was going on, and had failed to support the authority of the Masters, asserting that "I am specifically acquainted with all that goes on with the Lessons and with the Classes and that I exercise as much inspection over them as is possible for me to do consistently with the care of a Class which the Committee formerly insisted on my taking under my own charge", adding that "I have always supported the authority of the Masters in all cases and at all risks." Giles confirmed in his written statement that he still wanted to produce oral evidence, and concluded: "I feel confident that I shall obtain a just sentence when I have produced such evidence, notwithstanding the acrimonious feelings which have been created and notwithstanding the difficulties which nothing but my own sense of justice induced me to throw in the way."

Giles was then called in and repeated that he wished to examine witnesses, whereupon Mr Gurney joined the meeting and began to take notes. His fascinating (and lengthy) verbatim record of the rest of the afternoon's proceedings is given in full in the Appendix.[15]

The first to be called was Charles Woodroffe, Master of the Second Class. Giles challenged Woodroffe's statement to the Special Committee that he would not appeal to the Head Master in any case of discipline, and cited "a very egregious case" when, in Giles's view, he had done so. The discussion centred on whether informing or consulting the Head Master was the same as appealing to him, and no agreement was reached on this. But the example cited as follows does give a sobering glimpse of the darker side of school life.

Some months earlier the Writing Master, Henry Manley, had found obscene words written on some of his copy slips; he identified the culprits and burnt the slips. Giles was informed and went to each class to give a general warning against such conduct. Then more recently Woodroffe had intercepted "a letter of a most disgraceful tendency thrown across the school by one boy to another". He consulted Manley, and found that one of the boys had been involved in the earlier copy slips case. In view of this they together took the letter to Giles, who agreed that it was obscene. "At half past three that afternoon the School were collected together and we gave the Boys castigation and they were in confinement for three days." Apparently the intended recipient of the letter was considered just as culpable as the writer, which seems rather harsh. Later Giles told Woodroffe that after two days being locked in solitary confinement one of the boys was unwell "in consequence of his being shut up in a room without fire",[16] and asked him whether he would let the boys off, to which Woodroffe replied "Really I am disposed to inflict the whole penalty."

Despite Pewtress twice disputing the relevance of his argument, Giles also reminded Woodroffe that, although "not an University-man", he had been promoted to his present position above other Masters who were graduates, and claimed that "that shewed such a good will on my part towards Mr Woodroffe that he had no right to say I would not support him in his authority." Hale was not persuaded: "Taking it for granted, what has that to do with the Report?" Woodroffe withdrew.

Charles Delille was then called in, and attention turned to the letter he had written on 12 September about Alfred Moul, the main part of which Delille read out to the meeting. He added "The Boy had not written the imposition, indeed it appeared to me as though he thought he was in a Divan[17] instead of a School. [...] I told him the object of the letter, and upon telling him that, I obtained a promise from him that the imposition should be done, and I either left the letter with Mr Brewer, or, having shewed it to him, I kept it; for these minor things have escaped my memory." Brewer then spoke up: "Mr Chairman, if I am in order I may be allowed perhaps to state how the fact is. Mr Delille when he had written that letter brought it to my office and shewed it to me, and requested me to go into the class room and witness Moul's contumacy. I did so. I went into the class room and saw that the description by Mr Delille with respect to the boy refusing to learn his imposition was correct. He was told in my presence that Mr Delille had written such a letter to the Chairman and that previously to sending it he would give him one more chance." Giles did not welcome the interruption ("I really think you should keep this back for the present"), perhaps realising that the fact that Delille preferred to confide in the School Secretary rather than the Head Master did not help his case. Delille confirmed that he stood by everything he had written, and withdrew.

Giles then started a new line of argument: "I distinctly deny knowing anything of Alfred Moul's punishment till two days after it began." The tempo of exchanges increased:

> *Dr Giles.* He never applied to me, he wrote to the Chairman. I should be glad Sir to see Alfred Moul.

> *Mr Deputy Stevens.* We must not have any of the Boys in the School examined.

> *Dr Giles.* He is not a Boy in the School, he has left the School.[18]

Mr Deputy Stevens. I should be sorry that any Boys should know anything of what takes place among ourselves.

Dr Giles. The Porter can give Evidence upon the subject.

Mr Hardwick. The Porter may be a good Witness but the Boy cannot know what passes between you and Mr Delille.

Mr Deputy Stevens. How can he prove a negative?

Dr Giles. I will read what [Moul] has signed.

Mr Deputy Pewtress. Excuse me Dr Giles we cannot hear that at present.

Dr Giles. This is the Case that has caused me more vexation than anything else.

Mr Deputy Pewtress. If you had pursued the examination of Mr Delille you might have procured his acknowledgement or denial of the fact which you state.

After further diffuse discussion Pewtress complained: "This is mere conversation and I cannot afford to spend my time here unless we stick to the points of this enquiry." Sticking to the points seems to have been difficult. Giles next questioned Abraham Sumner the Porter and then Delille again; Hale and Brewer also recounted their parts in the story.

Putting all this together, the sequence of events seems to be as follows. Alfred Moul claimed that on Friday 30 August his French books were stolen. Sumner confirmed that Henry Nathan[19], when later asked by Giles whether he had stolen them, said that "he believed he had". However, in the lists of books stolen Alfred Moul is not named, but his younger brother George (Nathan's classmate) is, losing books on Trigonometry and Conic Sections and a Greek Lexicon; there is no mention of French books. Whether or not his reason was genuine, Alfred Moul arrived at his French lesson the next day without books and unprepared. Delille did not accept the excuse, pointing out that George had the same French texts, so these were available in the home, and set Alfred an imposition. The next week Alfred was absent, at least on the Monday and Wednesday - according to Delille "He was very frequently absent." On Saturday 7 September Sumner saw Moul and another boy playing near the umbrella stand, when they should have been in the French lesson. Delille found them, and for this "misconduct and impertinence" told Sumner to lock Moul in the German Class Room at 12 o'clock. The boy refused to co-operate, so the conflict and confinement was repeated on the following Monday and Tuesday, though on one of these days (probably the Tuesday) Delille asked Sumner to provide the prisoner with a sandwich. On Wednesday 11 September there was another French lesson, during which Moul gained a second imposition for misconduct, which he again refused to write.

What happened from then on is disputed: first here is Delille's account. At 12 o'clock Delille left Moul in the German classroom, went down to the Head Master's library, and asked Giles to come to the classroom. Giles came up and told Moul that he must stay until the imposition was completed. Delille referred to the luncheon he had provided previously, saying that he would not do so again, at which point the boy "turned to us both and said 'I am accustomed to dine late' and threw himself back on the floor." By 1 pm on Wednesday the imposition had still not been done. On the following morning Giles spoke to Delille, saying that Alfred Moul would be leaving in a fortnight, and that his brother George had said that Alfred was "so impressed with a sense of the injustice of the imposition that he would stop away altogether". Giles therefore suggested to Delille there was need for "a little discretion". But since the imposition was for gross impertinence in class (rather than for the loss of books) Delille disagreed, and at noon confronted the boy again, who so annoyed him that he wrote his letter to Hale. He then took the letter to Brewer, who visited the classroom and "saw the Boy acting in that foolish way and not the way a Boy ought to be acting" – was he on the floor again? Delille told Moul that he had written to the Chairman; this seemed to bring the boy to his senses, and he was given one last chance. The letter was kept back, and the following day (Friday 13 September) the imposition was delivered. Delille wrote his postscript and the letter went to Hale. On receiving it Hale went to the school to see Delille "and told him that though it was not a part of his duty to call upon the Parents yet as he appeared to have an obstinate Scholar in this case I advised him to call upon the Parents and I met him in Fenchurch Street as he was going to Moul's house." So the whole affair was concluded on that Friday.

The evidence of Abraham Sumner is resolutely vague. Had he decided to stay on the fence since whichever side won he would have to live with the consequences? He confirmed supplying a sandwich to Moul "on a Tuesday, Wednesday or Thursday", and that at 12 on "a Wednesday" – the date of which he was unable to pin down even as to the month – he had been asked by Delille to fetch Giles, but had found Giles out. "Have you been sent by [...] any of the Masters on any occasion and found the Doctor out?" "Yes frequently."

The Doctor himself was much more definite. He asserted six times that he knew nothing of the Moul case "till two days after", by which he seems to have meant two days after Wednesday 11 September, when Delille said he asked him to come to the German classroom. Giles denied that had happened or that he went, saying that he was out of school by then. Two days later was the Friday on which the imposition was finally done and Delille's letter reached Hale. But according to Giles the matter continued over the weekend, and his conversation with Delille about "a little discretion" was not until Monday 16 September. This flatly contradicted the statements of Delille, Brewer and Hale, and was further undermined by Giles himself, for when Delille recounted yet again the "I am accustomed to dine late" episode, Pewtress asked "Was Dr Giles present at the time Mr Delille speaks of?" and Giles replied "Yes, but the words the boy used did not make that impression on my ear – I did not hear them." Giles appeared to be floundering. His final ploy was to ask again to hear evidence from Alfred Moul:

> *Mr Deputy Stevens.* How does the Boy know anything? I should be ashamed of any boy knowing anything of this transaction – it is not right that the Boys should know anything of this.
>
> *Dr Giles.* He is the best witness – the party concerned – he has said that he did the imposition because I advised him.
>
> *[Mr Delille].* Mr Brewer and myself are two witnesses to overthrow that.
>
> *Dr Giles.* The Boy can know his motives best.
>
> *Chairman.* We cannot examine the Boy.
>
> *Dr Giles.* Then I shall say no more on the subject. I shall abandon the subject altogether.
>
> *Dr Giles withdrew.*

After the abrupt departure of Giles and some further conversation with Delille the meeting was adjourned. In his *Memoirs* Giles gives his view of the proceedings:

> On the preceding Monday [*recte* Friday] I attended a meeting of the School Committee & the Chairman Mr Hale said that one of the boys had been disobedient to the master of his class, and had only been induced to submit by the intervention of Mr Hale himself, and he complained that I did not support the authority of the under-masters. This charge was in every respect untrue, and I requested that the boy (16 years old) should be examined. Mr Hale objected to this; upon which I rose from my seat and left the room, saying "Gentlemen, I will never again attend a meeting of this committee." [...] Thus ended the year 1839 and my Scholastic duties![20]

Christmas Day was the following Wednesday, and presumably Anna and the children had already gone ahead to spend Christmas with old Aunt Ann in Ware. Giles describes what happened after he walked out of the meeting:

> I was in a great heat from the closeness of the room, and within a quarter of an hour was on the top of a coach going to Ware. The next day I was in a burning fever, unable to rise, and kept my bed six weeks.[21]

This was a recurrence of the acute rheumatic fever which had attacked him at the age of 11 in Dorchester.[22] Giles was attended daily by a medical practitioner called Judson or his son; their bill for this and for a daily supply of medicine amounted to nine pounds.[23] On 22 December Giles wrote to Brewer asking for a copy of the shorthand writer's minutes. Brewer referred this to the Special Committee who met on the Friday, 27 December. The request for a copy was refused, but Giles was told that he could inspect the copy which was in the Secretary's office. At the same meeting a letter from William Giles Jr made clear why that was impossible:

City of London School
26th December 1839

Sir

I have just returned from Ware where I left my Brother the Revd Dr Giles confined to his bed by a severe illness from which there is no prospect of his immediate recovery. I understand that he had signified to you his intention of being in Town tomorrow - this of course has now become impossible.

I am Sir
Your obedt. Servt.

Wm Giles Jr
To the Secretary of the City of London School[24]

A suggested motion was drafted for this meeting (by Hale, or Brewer, or jointly?[25]) which makes it plain how strong the feelings against Giles were, at least in some quarters:

That after the most mature deliberation upon all the circumstances connected with this enquiry mentioned or referred to in the Report, the Special Committee is of opinion that it is apparent that the City of London School has not derived any advantage from the appointment of Dr Giles as Head Master but on the contrary that he has in many of the most essential requisites shewn great unfitness for the situation.

That this Committee is also of the opinion that in addition to the possession of the most ample classical and other literary attainments it is absolutely necessary that the Head Master of an Establishment like the City of London School should possess the most commanding weight and influence over every person connected with the Establishment – that he should be a person possessing a sound and ready discretion, systematic and methodical in all his arrangements and with a view of infusing a proper spirit of subordination it is above all essential that he should be a strict disciplinarian – the evidence however referred to in the Report unequivocally shows that in these and other qualifications Dr Giles has manifested a lamentable deficiency.

That this Committee considers it highly improbable that additional experience will in any material degree render Dr Giles a more efficient Head Master, and that under his superintendence there is no reasonable expectation that the City of London School will ever rise in public estimation, on the contrary that it must gradually sink into the position of a second if not a third rate establishment.

That this Committee from a sense of duty regrets to be impelled to recommend to the Grand Committee the imperative necessity of adopting measure to induce Dr Giles to resign his situation and that should he not see the propriety of adopting that recommendation, it will be necessary that an application should be made by the Grand Committee to the Court of Common Council to take such steps in the matter as the Court may deem necessary for placing the City of London School in a position to answer the just expectations of the Corporation and the Citizens of London.

That this Committee cannot conclude its labours without bearing testimony to the zeal and ability displayed by the second and junior Masters of the School and that in the progress of this investigation the Committee has not failed to observe a degree of efficiency and activity highly creditable to themselves and calculated to promote the reputation of the School.

The Special Committee did not pass this motion, and perhaps it was never put to them. Instead they adjourned until 1 January 1840 to wait for a Report of recent events for the Grand Committee, which Brewer was asked to draft (not much of a Festive Season for him). This stated that they had found nothing in the evidence recently put before them to invalidate what they said in their original Report, concluding with their conviction that "the interests of the School require that the present Head Master should no longer retain his situation." This was reinforced by the addition of a motion repeating the penultimate paragraph of the 27 December draft motion (as above). All this was agreed unanimously, for transmission to the Grand Committee on the following Wednesday, 8 January.

On that day the Grand Committee received the additional Report of the Special Inquiry, but did not have to express a view on its conclusion, as Brewer also presented this letter from Giles:[26]

Ware, Jany. 2nd 1840

Dear Sir

My continued serious illness renders it impossible for me to take any steps relative to the misunderstanding between the Committee and myself. I now write to tender my resignation, such resignation to take effect at such a time as may be most convenient to the Committee and myself. Had I not been taken so alarmingly ill I would have requested no delay at their hands but as my Medical Man gives me no hope of being restored to health during the vacation it would cause great disparagement to my property and great inconvenience, if not renewed illness, to myself to be too hastily ejected from my present residence. Under these circumstances I venture to request the Committee will allow my resignation to take effect at Lady Day next. This will give me two months to accomplish my removal and will also allow ample time to the Committee to appoint my successor.

I am Dear Sir

Yours truly
(signed) J.A.Giles

P.S. I have forwarded a letter of resignation to the Lord Mayor expressed in similar terms as the above, and containing the same request.

This letter makes sad reading: it is written in an unfamiliar hand, and signed by Giles, in a shaky parody of his normal fluent signature – he was obviously struggling to write at all. The resignation letter to the Lord Mayor[27], also dated 2 January 1840, was in similar terms, but added this explanation: "A severe illness which has recently attacked me and from which there is no immediate prospect of recovery prevents me from writing to your Lordship with my own hand and will most probably prevent my appearing before the Court on the day of re-election." The Court of Common Council at its meeting on 23 January accepted his resignation, delayed as requested, and instructed the Committee to look for a new Head Master.

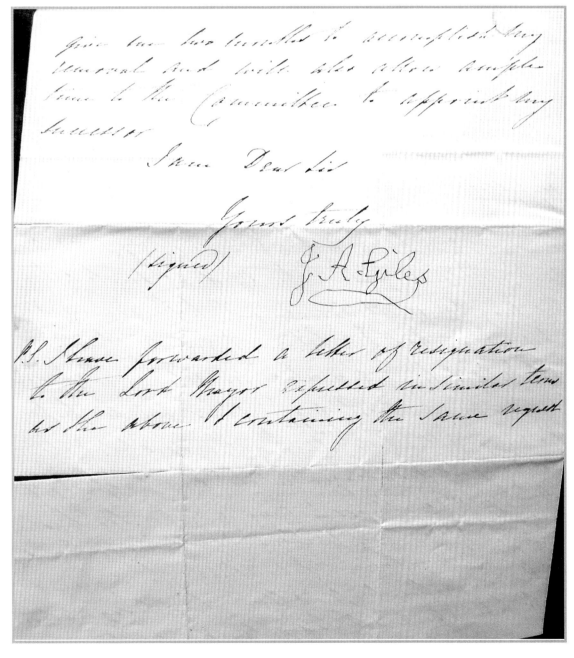

Giles's resignation letter of 2 January 1840.

10

CLS after Giles

School resumed on Monday 13 January 1840, without a Head Master. In a note from Ware dated 12 January J.H.Judson, Surgeon, certified that "The Revd Dr Giles has been confined by a severe attack of acute Rheumatism and that he remains unable to be removed and will for ten days or a fortnight be unfit to resume his duties."[1] In fact Giles did not return to London until about 7 February, two weeks after his resignation had been formally accepted, and then "was unable to take more than the lightest share of the duties which belonged to my office of Head Master."[2] There is no record of any special arrangements being made to cover his absence, so presumably the Second and Third Masters, Edkins and Webster, took charge, leaving Giles to concentrate on organising the removal of his household. After the Christmas conflicts a period of calm routine must have been welcome.

There was one urgent matter to deal with: who would look after the boarders? It was agreed that they should live with their parents, an arrangement which in March 1841 the Common Council made permanent, awarding each Foundation Scholar an annual allowance of £25 to cover living expenses, while continuing to pay for their clothing as before, and doubling the number of scholarships to eight. Thus ended the brief period for which the City of London School officially had boarders, though it was not the last time boys attending the school lived on the premises.

William Webster the Third Master, knowing the strange procedure prescribed for appointing a Head Master, did not delay. In January he wrote to the Committee that he intended to be a candidate, and pointed out that "although I cannot expect such a Testimonial as might be granted me if I were a Candidate for a Situation in another School, yet should I present myself to the Professors who nominate without any certificate from this Committee I fear I shall labour under a disadvantage which will not attach to my Competitors,"[3] and asked for some sort of statement about his appointment and conduct to serve in place of a Testimonial. The Committee "felt compelled under the circumstances to decline furnishing any person with a Testimonial with reference to the present vacancy."

On Monday 10 February Queen Victoria and Prince Albert of Saxe-Coburg and Gotha were married in the Chapel Royal at St James's Palace, the first wedding of a reigning British monarch since 1554. Though the bridal procession to the chapel from Buckingham Palace drew large crowds (in the rain), the celebrations were nothing like as lavish as when the Queen had first visited the City in November 1838. Nevertheless the whole school was given a holiday that day.

Having obtained a suspension of the standing order which said that a post could not be advertised until it was vacant (for Giles was technically in post until 25 March), the Committee announced the vacancy in the usual newspapers (ten of them, eight in London plus the Oxford Herald and the Cambridge Chronicle) on 22 February. By the deadline of 4 March fifteen applications had arrived, including those from Second Master Edkins, Webster as expected, and the headmasters of six grammar schools. As prescribed by the Act of Parliament the candidates' details and testimonials were passed to the six Professors for sifting. Their report was actually signed by five Professors. They were unanimous in selecting:

> The Revd B.W.Beatson[4]
> The Revd D.Coleridge[5]
> The Revd G.F.W.Mortimer

as "fit and proper persons to perform the duties of the First Master of the City of London School", adding that "in the opinion of the majority" these were the best qualified of all the candidates to discharge those duties. Sadly there is nothing to say who dissented from this view, and why. The Professors were awarded five guineas each for their services.

Although the Professors' report is dated 24 March their selection had clearly become known well before then, as by the time the Committee met the next day (Lady Day, the day Giles finished) Brewer had already been in touch with the three candidates. Beatson (from Cambridge) and Mortimer (already in London) were able to attend this Committee meeting, where they were informed that the Foundation Scholars would no longer reside with the Head Master, and asked whether, if elected, they could take up their duties within a week of the election – each said he had no doubt that he could. Coleridge in Cornwall was not invited, but Brewer was instructed to write to him to give the same information and put the same question. Also Coleridge's "friends in London" were informed that the other selected candidates had printed their Testimonials and distributed these among the Members of the Corporation "in order that, if they think it advisable, they may adopt a similar course on behalf of Mr Coleridge." So the canvassing for votes, which Giles had previously undertaken with relish, was still seen as a normal part of Corporation procedure, and two of the candidates had started campaigning before their selection was announced.

In 1840 neither the electric telegraph nor the railway had reached Cornwall. Letters between London and Helston were carried by fast mail coaches, and if all went well it was possible to send a letter and receive a reply within a week. Travelling the 280 miles to London by stage coach took three days. Whatever the sequence of communications, by Saturday 28 March Coleridge himself had arrived in London. Hale convened a special meeting so that the Committee could interview Coleridge on the same terms as the others. But having heard what Hale had to say, Coleridge

Derwent Coleridge, engraving, 1850.

"entered into an explanation of his views upon becoming a Candidate and of his intentions in the event of his being successful, and also of the disadvantages under which he laboured by reason of the votes of the Electors having been solicited and a large portion of them promised on behalf of the other Candidates before the Professors had made their Return, and, as he thought, before such a course could with propriety be adopted."[6] This, probably not the subservient response that had been expected, was followed a few days later by a powerful letter:[7]

To the Chairman of the Committee of the City of London School.

Sir – Having found the statement which I had the honour of laying before the Committee of Saturday last, was strictly correct, and that the contest was virtually decided before my canvass commenced, the only course left to me is to act upon the resolution of which I then gave notice, and to withdraw my name from the competition.

To you, Sir, who are truly interested in the welfare of the City of London School, and to whom, for your exertions in restoring that noble institution, the cause of education is deeply indebted, the following remarks may, I trust, be addressed without my incurring the charge of presumption. They are dictated by a sincere desire to promote the object which you have in view, and are grounded upon a long and practical intimacy with the subject.

On the present occasion, Sir, you will, there is every reason to believe, succeed in obtaining an able and estimable person to conduct your establishment; but speaking generally, and with reference to the future, can you expect again to light upon an individual calculated by station and character, as well as by talents and experience, to place your School in the position which on every account it ought to hold – who would be willing to involve himself in the annoyances, or to risk the uncertainty of a popular election, as hitherto conducted among you – who would consent to fight his way to your appointment by personal influence, priority of application, and importunacy of canvass – and on such a chance (supposing it the same to all, and not to bear unfavourably on those whom the Committee would most gladly see in the field, settled and successful schoolmasters, with strict professional engagements) to expose themselves to the inconvenience, perhaps the lasting injury, of a failure? The final election should, if possible, rest with the Committee alone, and probably a Common Council might not be indisposed to delegate a trust attended with high responsibility and some trouble: but, at all events, the competitors should be strictly prohibited from

154

communicating with the electors at large, either by letter or by personal visits, at any time previous to the election. The testimonials and circular-letters should be printed and forwarded by the Committee itself, before which, and before which <u>alone</u>, the candidates should be expected to make their personal appearance.

The provision by which three individuals are selected from the larger number of candidates, by a large and disinterested body of men, such as the London Professors, is a most wholesome one; but you, Sir, are well aware that this is but the first stage of the inquiry requisite to secure the <u>best</u> or even a <u>proper</u> appointment. The Professors judge from testimonials only; and with whatever judgment and fidelity they may execute their task, it may well happen, not merely that the pretensions of the several parties may be very unequal, but that some of the selected competitors may, from causes not brought under the cognizance of the Professors, be wholly disqualified for the office. Testimonials take no notice of defects, however just in their encomium they speak only to positive excellences, and these, however numerous, may conflict with some serious deficiency. Thus the duty of the electors commences when that of the Professors ends. As matters have been hitherto conducted this duty has not been merely neglected, but openly abandoned and disclaimed.

In conclusion, I must beg you, Sir, to convey an expression of my thanks to the Committee for the kind and courteous attention with which I was listened to last Saturday, and with every good wish for the success of the School, - I have the honour to be, Sir, your obedient servant,

Derwent Coleridge.

By Friday 3 April, when the Court of Common Council met, Benjamin Beatson had also retired from the contest, so the Court was presented with just one candidate, Mortimer, who was duly elected by show of hands. Beatson, who had never worked in a school and could hardly have been considered a strong candidate, went back to Cambridge, and stayed there until his death in 1874, at which time he was senior fellow of Pembroke College. By 1841 Coleridge was back in London as the first Principal of the newly founded College of St Mark in Chelsea, established by the National Society to train teachers. He held that post until 1864 and did much to shape the course of elementary education in England.

George Ferris Whidborne[8] Mortimer was born in 1805 at Bishopsteignton in Devon, where his father William, described as "a country gentleman" but with business interests in shipping and trading the local pottery clay, lived in a handsome villa called Delamore.[9] George was educated at Exeter School. He matriculated in Oxford at Balliol College in 1823, but then migrated to Queen's College, graduating with a first in classics in 1826. Giles describes him as "an old friend, Mortimer"[10] so presumably they knew each other in the two years they overlapped at Oxford. In 1828 (one year before he was ordained) Mortimer was appointed Head Master of the Newcastle Royal Grammar School, and in 1833 he moved to London to be Head Master of the Western Grammar School, Brompton.

Founded in 1828, the Western Grammar School was an independent proprietary school for about a hundred boys, initially free of any religious or denominational bias (the "proprietors", i.e. shareholders, included several prominent non-conformists). In 1836 it became linked with King's College, London (as the Camberwell Collegiate School had done), and adopted the stance of the established Anglican church. Its original premises were in Alexander Place, SW7[11], but in 1835 the foundation stone was laid for a new building nearby, at the end of North Terrace. This had a handsome portico in Greek Doric style which survives, though the rest of the building, used as a warehouse after the school closed in 1912, was converted to two houses in 1927-29. Mortimer probably moved the school into its new home in 1839.

Mortimer had wide scholarly and social interests. In 1833 he had written *The Immediate Abolition Of Slavery, Compatible With The Safety And Prosperity Of The Colonies,*[12] and on 17 November 1835 spoke to the Belgrave Institution on *Idumea and the Ruins of Patra* [i.e. southern Jordan and Petra]: "The Lecture by Mr Mortimer (the able head-master of the Brompton Grammar School) was marked by research, learning and the most refined taste."[13] Refined taste seemed to be important in Brompton, for when the celebrated comic actor and playwright John B. Buckstone[14] applied to become a proprietor in 1838 in order to obtain a place for his son he was turned down "on the ground that I am an actor, and that such a person in a public school would incite in the boys a desire to see plays, which would unsettle their minds." This policy does not seem to have worked with a later pupil, W.S.Gilbert.[15]

The French teacher at Western Grammar School was none other than Charles Delille.[16] According to the Census, in 1841 he was aged 32, living nearby in Michael's Place, Brompton Road,[17] with his wife Betsy (née Hale), 35, Frances Hale, 65, who was presumably Betsy's mother, and one house servant. No link has yet been found between Betsy or Frances Hale and Warren Stormes Hale, but there is at least a possibility that they were related, and therefore that Delille and Hale met socially. So could it have been that Delille, having found in Mortimer the "concentrated power [...] whose frown would be a punishment and whose smile would be a reward",[18] persuaded Hale that Mortimer was the right man to lead the City of London School, and that Hale then bent the rules to secure him by leaking the Professors' short list and encouraging Mortimer to canvass?

Whether or not there was any such plan, by 24 April the story behind Mortimer's "election" had reached the press:[19] "The City of London School Committee received a letter [the one from Coleridge quoted above], which has caused a sensation amongst the Members of the Corporation, from a gentleman who was candidate for the situation of First Master of the School, vacant by the resignation of the Rev. Doctor Giles. [...] The Committee are to report their opinion upon the letter." Coleridge had made three main criticisms of the appointment procedure: (i) that the sifting by the Professors relied solely on statements produced by the candidates, whom the Professors never met, (ii) that the election was by the whole Court of Common Council who again had no opportunity to interview the candidates in any significant way, and (iii) that the result of the election could be pre-determined by canvassing. The Committee eventually agreed on 8 June that issues (i) and (ii) were fixed in statute, and so could be changed only by amending the Act,[20] but that the premature canvassing could be stopped. This was achieved by the 62nd Standing Order of Common Council, agreed to 29th October 1840:

> That any person soliciting a Vote, or declaring himself in any manner to the Members of this Court a Candidate for either of the Offices of First or Second Master of the City of London School, before the Return is made by the Professors who are authorized by Act of Parliament to select the most eligible Candidates, shall by such conduct be deemed ineligible to fill the vacant Office; and that any Member of this Court soliciting a Vote for an Candidate before such Return is made be deemed ineligible to sit upon any Committee or Commission appointed by this Court.

After his unanimous election on Friday 3 April Mortimer met the Special Committee on the following Monday to discuss arrangements, and said that he proposed to begin work on Wednesday 22 April, immediately after the Easter vacation. On the issue of accommodation, Mortimer "stated that his family consisted of 13 persons, and he found on examining the House that there was a great deficiency in the number of Bedrooms, that he had therefore requested his friend Mr Donaldson, the Architect[21] to examine it, [...] who had prepared a sketch description, suggesting that 2 or 3 of the Rooms should be divided and Windows opened in two or three places – which, with some other slight alterations with a view to procuring additional light in the Basement, he estimated could be effected for about £80."[22] Donaldson's sketch was passed to Bunning for comment, though it seems that no immediate changes were made.

At the end of their meeting on Wednesday 8 April the Grand Committee and Mortimer proceeded to the Theatre, where Hale introduced their new Head Master to the assembled Masters and Boys. "The speech of Dr[23] Mortimer on the occasion was at once genial, fatherly and practical. When the speech was finished, one of the senior boys, Emery of the Sixth Class, was pressed by his schoolfellows into the Arena to welcome the Doctor in the name of the School and to beg at once his good offices with the Chairman and Committee for an extension of holidays at Easter beyond the three days given. It was a ticklish business, for the Chairman, for all his excellence and benevolence, thought holidays rather a waste of time. But the Doctor pleaded, the extension was promised for this time, and became hereafter a settled institution."[24] This initiative was not as spontaneous as Emery suggests: the gathering in the Theatre must have been announced earlier, and the astute sixth formers had seized their chance. The committee minutes say that Mortimer was presented with an address "signed by a number of Boys in the School entreating him to use his influence with the Committee to allow the approaching vacation to continue until the end of the Easter week," which he diplomatically handed to Hale. In 1841 the Easter holiday was again extended until the end of the week and the summer break put forward by a month, thus starting the current pattern of three terms instead of four quarters.

Mortimer's reign actually began on Monday 27 April 1840, and was to last 25 years. He started by enrolling two of his sons, George Gordon Mortimer, who was to drown accidentally at Newton Abbot in August 1843, and William Rogers Mortimer, who left at the end of 1845 and later managed the family estate in Devon. These were the first two of ten Mortimer brothers who attended the school, an amazing record not matched by any other family. Mortimer had married Jane, daughter of Alexander Gordon of Bishopsteignton, in 1830. They had sixteen children including five daughters and another son who was too young to attend CLS when his father retired in 1865.[25]

Mortimer also told the Committee that he wished to introduce into the school "a youth whose father being dead he had adopted into his own family with the intention of bringing him up and ultimately sending to one of the Universities."[26] This was Henry Stuart Fagan, then aged 12. But Fagan's family history was more complicated than that: his father Mitchell Henry Fagan was still alive – he died of "natural decay" in 1856, aged 76. Born near Dublin, Mitchell Fagan was an officer in the British Army, serving in the 2nd Ceylon Regiment and as Captain in the 2nd Staffordshire Regiment of Foot. Henry was born to Mitchell and Eliza Lucilla Evans[?] in 1827, followed by his sister Lucilla in 1830. Although Eliza was known as Mrs Fagan and described herself as "widow of Mitchell Fagan" there is no record of their marriage. Moreover, in 1836 Mitchell Fagan, describing himself as a bachelor, married Jane Irving, an army widow of somewhat dubious reputation. So either Mitchell and Eliza were never married, or Mitchell was a bigamist.[27] In 1840 Eliza was living with Henry and Lucilla at 63 Ebury Street, probably in lodgings. This is about 500m from Eccleston Square, which Thomas Cubitt was then constructing as part of his development of Pimlico. Here Mortimer, who had "a very comfortable independent fortune",[28] had taken one of the grand stucco houses, No.72. So the two families may well have met at church or elsewhere. How much Mortimer was aware of the family history is not known – he had no reason to lie to the Committee, and may well have believed that Henry's father was dead if that is what Eliza told him. At any rate he had decided that Henry needed his protection.

It seems that from Easter 1840 in term time Mortimer lived at the City of London School with his wife Jane, sons George and William, and Henry Fagan,[29] while their younger children, including sons Christian and Alexander, were looked after in Eccleston Square. A daughter Isabella and a son John were born in the school. In 1845 the family moved out of the school, and lived permanently in Eccleston Square (which in the school register is given as the home address for all the Mortimer boys). In Milk Street the basement, ground floor rooms and boarders' sitting room of the Head Master's house were then converted for school use, while the rest became an apartment for Thomas Brewer and his wife, where they lived until his sudden death on Christmas Day 1870.

Henry Fagan has left the only description of life as a boarder in Milk Street,[30] referring to the school as

> that little well, sunk down through the plateau of tall houses, round which always clings that indescribable odour which is made up of the butterfactor's smells at one corner, the fish and poultry man's at the other, the steams from the kitchen

of "His Lordship's Larder,"[31] and the sicklier scent that comes up out of the warehouse cellars. This last, we schoolboys always used to affirm, had a strong dash of "organic" in it. [...]

I remember how our Headmaster – I revere his memory too much to talk lightly about him – used to sit late into the night over heaps of school papers. His talk was always of boys – what some had done, what others were likely to do – and when years after I used to go and dine with him, he was always talking of boys of whom of course I knew little or nothing.

But it wasn't quite a healthy life, especially for a boarder. I remember how I hated the wood pavement then newly put down in Cheapside, because in the hot Julys, when we were panting for green fields and the great exam. of the year was coming on, the dust used to rise, palpable to taste and smell, higher than the first-floor windows, churned up by the perpetual whirl of carriages. No wonder a boy living there without a bit of playground, with no games but what we got up for ourselves – boxing until we were dustier than millers, or singlestick – should have worked by fits and starts, chiefly for exams. [...] In those great heats, the only thing was to get out on the leads at night, and by moonlight or lantern read Scott or Fenimore Cooper. [...]

How did I find time for [reading the French newspaper provided by Delille] and to do also a great many more "parties" than fall to the lot of most boys, for City people had not then quite giving up living in the City, and as I boarded at the School I was in a good central position? I also got out to the theatre pretty often.[32]

With his commitment and capacity for hard work Mortimer soon sorted out the long-standing problems that had defeated Giles. By 6 May he had produced a report on the state of the different departments of the school,[33] in which he proposed that the German and Drawing classes should be given on Wednesdays from 2 pm to 5 pm, and on Saturdays from 12 noon to 3 pm, and that these half days should be half holidays for the boys who did not take these subjects. Two of the regular masters should constantly attend these classes "for the purpose of maintaining order." He also suggested arrangements for "the full employment during School hours of the time of every Master, and the full employment of those Boys who do not learn Greek, and the attainment by them of considerable proficiency in Latin and Mathematics," and asked for the immediate replacement of Giles's Latin and Greek Grammars and other books which had been criticised in the evidence to the Special Inquiry.

Confidence was restored, and the decline in numbers reversed. From 1841 this was helped by the easing of the admissions regulations[34] and by doubling the number of Foundation Scholarships to eight. In 1847 there were 605 boys in the school, putting severe pressure on the available space, but the roll later settled to about 570. In 1842 William Emery became the first boy to proceed to university, at Corpus Christi, Cambridge, followed by Henry Judge Hose (Trinity, Cambridge 1845) and Henry Fagan (Pembroke, Oxford 1845). These early academic successes attracted an increasing number of gifts of prizes and scholarships, most notably those of Henry Beaufoy.[35]

While encouraging the highest standards for the academically gifted, Mortimer never lost interest in the needs of the majority of the boys, who were given a solid preparation for the world of business and commerce. This success in balancing the interests of all his boys was recognised in the Reports of two major Parliamentary Commissions: the Clarendon Report on Public Schools (published 1864) and the Taunton Report on Endowed Schools (published 1868) both included evidence submitted by Mortimer before he retired in 1865, and drew highly pleasing conclusions.

> The City of London School is a great day-school in the heart of London, having little connexion with the Universities, and educating, apparently with great success, a very large proportion of boys who are not intended for Oxford or Cambridge. At the same time the classical and mathematical education given there is so good that of those who do go to the Universities nearly all distinguish themselves; and in one year (1861) the four chief honours at Cambridge were gained by young men educated at this school.[36]

> Among schools of the first grade,[37] the City of London School is by far the best pattern of what a London school of that grade ought to be, and which more than any other school in this district will repay careful study and attention.[38]

The Beaufoy Scholarships by Eden Upton Eddis, oil on canvas, destroyed WW2. Hale seated in the Chairman's Chair to left, Brewer seated centre, Francis Hobler standing to the right. SEE NOTE 35.

It is requested that the Masters will be very careful not to omit sending the usual note to enquire into the absence of any of the boys, as one of those in the Junior Class has been detected playing the truant upwards of a week.

Further: the Porters have orders not to detain any of the boys after school-hours, unless under the eye of one of the masters; great inconvenience having arisen from the practice.

The practice of sending boys who behave ill, out of the class, must be modified in some way or other; as I sometimes find 10 or 12 such boys, playing in the passages, apparently heedless of the disgrace, and causing every kind of annoyance ~~to the~~ and interruption to the business of the School

J A Giles

Notices from Giles to the Masters.
CLS Archive.

Names and Dates of Election of Officers of the School, from the Commencement.

1836 Sept. 7.
Mr. Thos Brewer, of the Town Clerk's Office, elected Secretary.

... Nov 24.
Rev. John Allen Giles M.A. of Corpus Christi Coll: Oxford; Head Master of Camberwell Collegiate School, elected by Common Council Head Master.

Mr. Rob. Pitt Edkins M.A. of Trinity College Cambridge. Second Master of Kensington Proprietary Grammar School, elected by Common Council Second Master.

... Dec 7.
Abraham Sumner, elected Porter or Messenger.

... Dec 14.
Rev. William Webster, B.A. of Queen's College Cambridge, elected Third Master.

The first appointments as recorded in Brewer's Secretary's Book.
CLS Archive.

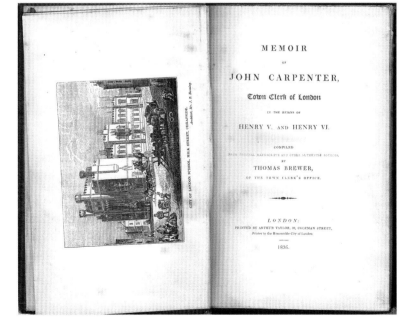

MEMOIR
OF
JOHN CARPENTER,
Town Clerk of London
IN THE REIGNS OF
HENRY V. AND HENRY VI.
COMPILED
FROM ORIGINAL MANUSCRIPTS AND OTHER AUTHENTIC SOURCES,
BY
THOMAS BREWER,
OF THE TOWN CLERK'S OFFICE.

LONDON:
PRINTED BY ARTHUR TAYLOR, 39, COLEMAN STREET,
Printer to the Honourable City of London.
1836.

CITY OF LONDON SCHOOL, MILK STREET, CHEAPSIDE.

Brewer's *Memoir of John Carpenter*, 1834. CLS Archive.

Dr John Allen Giles,
by Charles Grant, oil on
canvas, CLS Great Hall

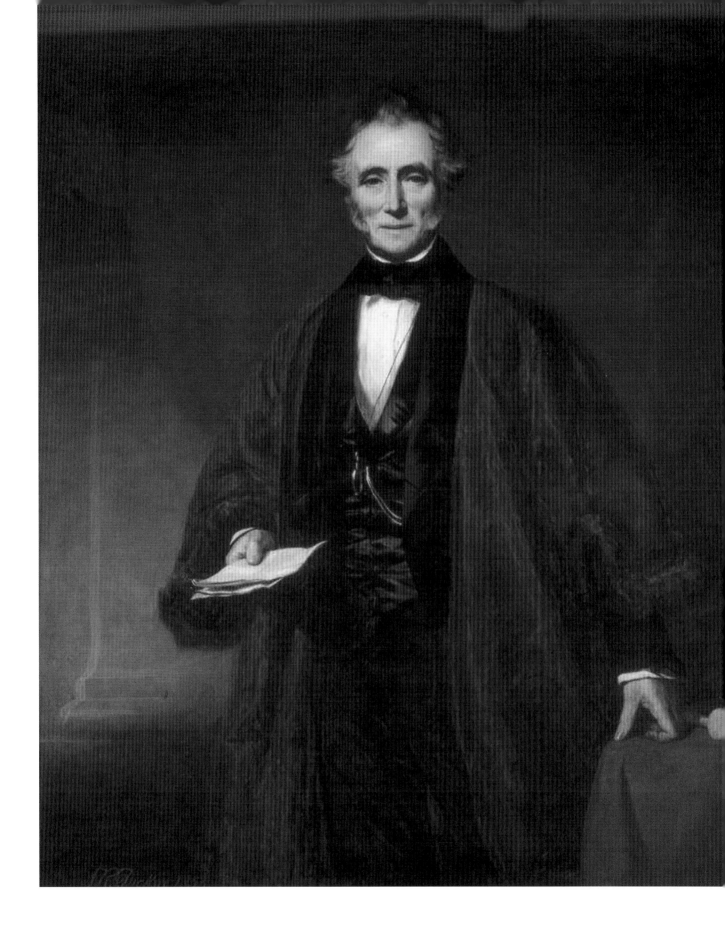

Warren Stormes Hale,
in his violet gown by John Robert Dicksee, CLS Drawing
Master, 1853, oil on canvas. Coll. Guildhall Art Gallery.

Dr Bialloblotzky's 'evil eye' letter. CLS Archive.

Delille's letter –1. CLS Archive.

Delille's letter –2. CLS Archive.

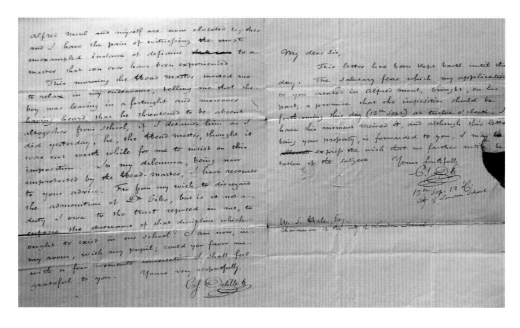

11

Giles after CLS: Bampton and Oxford

Giles was only 31 when he left the school, with 44 more years left of his complicated life, of which this chapter and the next can give only a brief summary. Further fascinating detail can be found in the *Diary & Memoirs*.

Fortunately by 1840 Windlesham Hall was just about complete, so Giles, Anna, Isabella and Arthur moved there. They took with them some of their furniture from the school residence, including two old chairs he had acquired from the Ashmolean Museum which had belonged to Oliver Cromwell[1] and John Bradshaw.[2] The print of John Knox, which Giles had bought for 15 guineas to secure the vote of Francis Moon, was sold to his printer friend Pickering for 4 guineas,[3] and a "mass of books" from his library at the school were sold by Sotheby for £700.[4] Some fittings also had to go to Windlesham: "Mortimer will not take the cornices which stand over the windows of the City of London School, so they must be sent down here."[5] And some furniture disappeared: "About the beginning of April, wishing to help Mrs Robinson, a widow of small means and mother of Jane Robinson an old schoolfellow of Anna's, I lent her the furniture which we removed from the City of London School, and placed it for her at a house in Great Ormond Street. She proposed to let part of it, but by her arbitrary conduct deterred every one from becoming her tenant, and before the end of the year I found I had lost all the furniture."[6]

Two days after Mortimer's first term started Brewer wrote to Giles at Windlesham on an urgent matter:

> We have not been able to find the general Register, which was kept by you, of the names and other particulars of the Boys admitted in the School, and, as some inconvenience is sustained by the want of it, I shall feel obliged if you can inform me where we are likely to find it, or what was done with it on your quitting the Establishment.
>
> Requesting the favour of an early reply
>
> I remain etc.

Chairs at Windlesham Hall belonging to John Bradshaw (upper) and Oliver Cromwell (lower).

By 5 May the problem had been resolved, as Brewer wrote to Giles's solicitor:

> F.T.Maxon Esq, 6 Little Friday St.
>
> Understanding that the Register belonging to this Establishment, which was taken away by mistake with Dr Giles's Books, is now in your hands, I have to request that you will deliver it to the bearer, who is one of the Porters of the School.

It may have been around this time, or later that year, that Giles called at Maxon's office "to receive a silver goblet presented to me by the boys of the 6th form in the City of London School."[7] Perhaps the Sixth Form felt somewhat guilty about their poor behaviour, which had been noted in the Special Inquiry report.

Giles's younger brother Charles (1822-81) had been lodging at the school since summer 1837, when at the age of 15 he started training as an architect with Henry Shaw. He later wrote his own memoirs,[8] which make clear his dismay at Giles's precipitate resignation.

> My brother's house was pleasant to a boy, but just the sphere to frustrate all efforts towards serious ends. In it pleasant society was to be found, a pretty warm hearted sister in law attracting all by vivacity, as my brother did himself by amiable temper and hospitality. The school was founded by the city common council and it might easily be predicted that with pride and money to back it there would be a great foundation one day of prizes and scholarship, and that the Head of such an establishment would find himself among the biggest of such Principals. All this my brother, in whom my father and others predicted ruin by want of common sense, failed to see; with an income at starting of some £1200 a year[9] he sacrificed a certainty of three fold that sum in a few years, and the honour and real good to be achieved by guiding the vulgar trading mind of London towards higher things, all he sacrificed to his mere dislike of vulgar minded intemperance by the school committee. He never showed the smallest desire to conciliate the men whose vote at the Annual Elections could remove him, and in fact courted his ruin by every means in his power. In two years he accomplished this and resigned his post with nothing to fall back upon save an active mind and body and his old Oxford reputation for scholarship, also with a heavy burthen of debt on his hands.

His mother was worried too, writing to Anna from Frome on 21 August.[10]

> You do not know how often I think of you all, and how anxious I am to hear of your welfare and happiness. How do you like living in the country? I hope your health and spirits are good: and the dear little ones also, how are they getting on? I was pleased to see Allen so cheerful, and I hope soon to hear that his prospects are brightening – Affluence I would not covet for any of my children, but I trust a competency will be granted them, and this with a contented mind is better than riches. [...]

Even "a competency" was hard to come by. Giles had ruled out seeking another Headmastership, writing to his brother-in-law "My connection with the City of London School was on the whole a bad thing for me, and although you think I might succeed in getting a similar appointment, I am very loath to try."[11] He occupied himself by revising his edition of Bede's *Ecclesiastical History*, and adding to it *The Works of Gildas and Nennius*[12] and *The Chronicle of Richard of Devizes*.[13] He invested £100 in preparing and sowing two of the fields he now owned, but the yield was poor and he soon gave up the idea of farming. His solicitor Frederick Maxon, by now also a personal friend, paid Giles £100 to take his son John Robert (JR) to stay with the family at Windlesham, both for the benefit of the country air and also for some tuition. The family enjoyed his company, though Giles told his father "he is slow to acquire a taste for reading in general, and will therefore never be a scholar."[14] In the autumn JR was joined by five other young men as boarders whom Giles tutored for various purposes.

In April 1841 Giles decided to let Windlesham Hall and take his family plus their maid Emma Carter, JR, and four of the boarders to France for the summer, if not longer. This clearly had educational advantages for the young men, but the prime motivation seems to have been financial. Frederick Maxon found a possible tenant in Samuel Bundy Williams, though further investigation cast doubt on his means. Williams had recently married the daughter of the minister in Charmouth, so Giles sent an enquiry to his uncle Robert, who lived there, and was told that her family were all respectable and supposed to be wealthy. On the strength of this, despite Maxon's misgivings, Giles went ahead and agreed to let Windlesham Hall to Williams for £100 for six months or £200 for one year. On 5 May Mr and Mrs Williams took possession, and the Giles entourage set off for Le Havre.

The party stayed in pleasant lodgings at Ingouville, between Le Havre and Dieppe, for a month before moving on to Paris. In mid July Giles and his pupils (one of whom had an examination to take, while two others did not like France) returned to London, leaving Anna, the children and Emma Carter ("she is a trump") in Paris. As the Williams were still in Windlesham Hall Giles decided to stay in London, and took a six weeks lease on 6 Claremont Terrace, Pentonville, furnished, for £24 from a Mr Bentley. Anna and the family arrived there from Paris on 1 September, and approved of the comfortable house. But next day bailiffs arrived to remove Bentley's furniture in settlement of a debt, and remained in occupation for three days until the matter was resolved. Then JR discovered that the cook, inherited from Bentley, had stolen some of Anna's jewellery; she was promptly dismissed.[15]

These were minor problems compared with what faced Giles at Windlesham Hall. He went there on 13 September, having earlier received a disconcerting letter from Williams asking him not to go.

> I went down to Windlesham, and soon perceived that there had not been much money spent there, and there were many signs that the present occupant had not much to spend. We had an early dinner on a leg of mutton, and afterwards I went to the cabinet in which I had locked up our plate, pointing out to Mr Williams

167

when we left him in possession on the 5th of May, that it would be quite safe there, as the lock (Chubb's patent) could not be picked. Mr Williams then anticipated what I was going to do, and told me he had removed the plate for safe custody in London. He said that as he came down stairs one morning, he observed that the bolt of the lock was outside the wood of the cabinet, having evidently been drawn out by lifting the wood by a screw driver or chisel, and he supposed the person who did it left off, hearing his steps overhead. I was however surprised to see that whilst every thing else was taken away, the silver cruet stand bearing my name, and given to me by my uncle John Allen at my christening, as also the Goblet and the Salver, given to me the one by the boys of the City of London School and the other by those of the Camberwell Collegiate School, were still remaining in the cabinet. Mr Williams assured me that every thing was right, and he promised to bring the abstracted articles to me in Claremont Terrace towards the end of the week. I was of course obliged to acquiesce; but on leaving the house was told by Mrs Harding my housekeeper who lived at the lodge, that she had never heard a word said about the supposed attempt to rob. I returned to London not very easy in my mind at what had happened.[16]

Unsurprisingly Williams failed to return the articles as promised. He disappeared, leaving Mrs Williams, close to her confinement, at Windlesham Hall, where she refused to see Giles. The trail went cold until 18 November when Mrs Harding gave Giles the address to which Mrs Williams had sent a parcel to her husband: a shop in Pickett Street,[17] near St Clement Danes church. Next day Giles went to see his old friend George Dawson at his chambers in Lincoln's Inn." 'What?' said he 'have you allowed this scoundrel to trifle with you so long? Come with me to Bow Street and we shall see what Mr Jardine[18] has to say about it.' We went straitway [sic] to Bow Street, Mr Jardine heartily approved of Mr Dawson's advice to take prompt measures & within half an hour Weston one of the Serjeants of Police in plain clothes was standing with me in Pickett Street in front of the house [...]" They took up their positions on this damp November day at about 3 o'clock, and had to wait over five hours before Williams appeared. Weston arrested him, and took him into custody at Bow Street.

The trial of Williams for theft of the silver, worth £200, and of Arthur Kirkham, a Strand pawnbroker, for receiving the goods knowing them to be stolen, took place before Jardine from 16 to 27 December, and was reported at length in the newspapers.[19] The silver was recovered, the charges against Kirkham were dropped, and Williams was found guilty and sentenced "to be transported beyond the seas for the term of seven years," though this was later reduced to two years imprisonment. Mrs Williams and her children were allowed to remain as visitors in Windlesham Hall until some arrangement could be made for them by her friends. Giles regained possession of the house just before the end of 1841, and the family spent Christmas in Ware with old Aunt Ann as usual.

Anna and the children returned to Windlesham on 5 January 1842, but Giles stayed in London for a few days to visit some old friends, lodging with his brother Charles in Everett Street. His return to Windlesham Hall on 12 January showed the problems of travelling in those days.

Went down to Staines in an omnibus which had lately been started, and walked thence to Windlesham 5 miles between 9 and 11 o'clock. On the road about a mile or two from my house I saw a gigantic mass moving towards me and was very much frightened for the moment: it was very dark and I could see no signs to tell me what it was; and only when I came nearer did I find out that it was an enormous elephant covered from head to foot with a cloth to protect it from the cold, and that its driver was sitting on its neck, also covered up so that it was difficult to see him. I afterwards learned that the creature was too large to be carried like the other wild beasts of the menagerie, and was always sent off on foot by night.[20]

By April Giles had decided to take the family and Emma Carter to Germany. He let the fields at Windlesham to a farmer called Scott, and allowed him to live in the Hall on condition of taking care of it. They went to Cologne, where after two weeks Giles fell gravely ill with typhus. His brother William was summoned from England to be with him. "At one moment all hope was given up, and it was a certain tenacity of life and elasticity of constitution that enabled me to survive. The doctor ordered me to drink any quantity of the best Bordeau[x] wine, and I felt pleasure in obeying his orders."[21] In June typhus came again, this time affecting Anna, Isabella and "Mr Pickwick" (their nickname for Arthur). They swiftly left their lodgings, later learning that two previous guests had died of typhus in the beds they had been using, and moved to Bonn. Giles relied on Anna's brother Henry Dickinson to help sort out his finances which were in confusion because of various unwise investments, writing to him on 15 June "[...] I hope not to trouble you much longer about my various affairs: they will, I hope, soon be settled, and notwithstanding the blows I have received during the last two years, it will all come right in the end. The fact is that I have invested every thing with what they call a *couleur de rose*,[22] and such a disposition is changed with much difficulty. [...]"[23]

By July 1842 Giles had found it impossible to deal with all these business matters from so far away, and they returned to England. Scott was still their tenant at Windlesham, but it seems the family stayed there too for a while, before enjoying Christmas at Ware and then making a prolonged visit to Exeter and Falmouth, returning to Windlesham on 15 April 1843. A week later Giles received a letter from Mrs Brockhurst, wife of J. Sumner Brockhurst, who by now was Head Master of Camberwell Collegiate School, asking him to take her husband's place, as he had "for the moment lost the use of his faculties from too great excitement." Giles went there next day: "I took the school in hand, and they fitted me up a bed-room in one of the class-rooms". Two weeks later he wrote to Henry Dickinson:

I am quite at a loss to conjecture what is the matter with Mr Brockhurst. His wife keeps me in the dark about it, and I shall stay here no longer. No one seems to know how he is or where he is. Some say he is not ill at all, but keeping out the way for debt: others say he is wholly out of his mind, with no hope of recovery. [...] Mr Scott has started to grumble at Windlesham: I shall go down tomorrow night. [...][24]

ABOVE
left –   William Giles, father
middle –   Sophia Giles, mother
right –   Ann Dickinson, aunt

CENTRE
left –   John Allen Giles
right –   Anna Sarah Giles

LOWER
left –   Charles Giles, brother
middle –   Arthur Giles, son, aged 12
right –   Herbert Giles, son

170

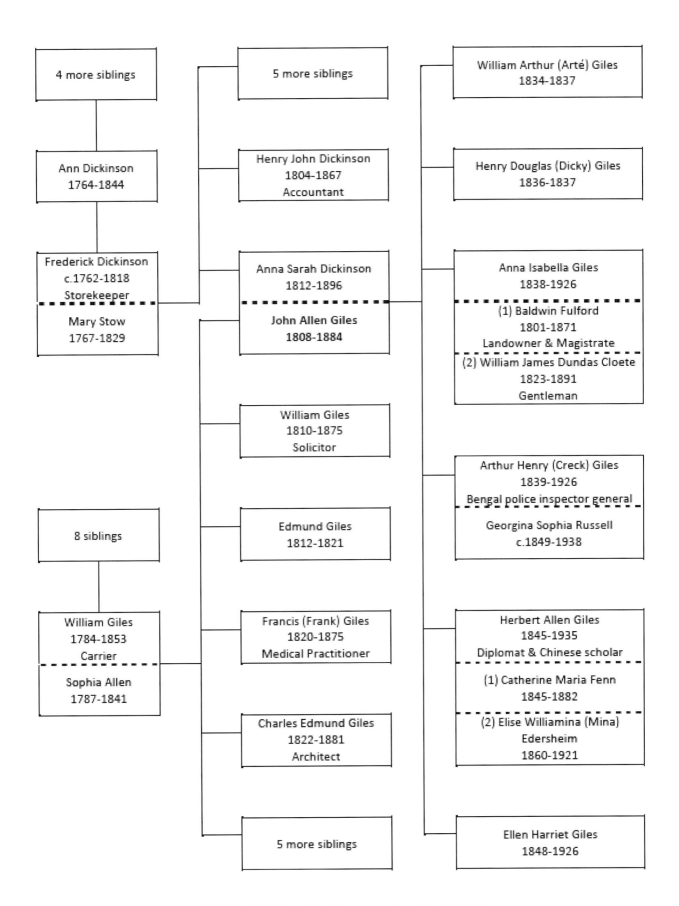

The Giles/Dickinson families as mentioned in the text.

Giles sorted out matters with Scott successfully, but his optimism that his affairs would soon be settled was also tinged with *couleur de rose*. His ongoing dispute with his publishers James Bohn and William Pickering, and others, dating back to dealings with the estate of the unfortunate Edmund Barker, was to rumble on for another fifteen months. The more immediate blow came on 26 July 1843 when William Dugmore, who had a £600 mortgage on part of Windlesham Hall, decided to foreclose on the mortgage. Giles had no way of paying him back, so the only option was to sell the house and estate. This seems to have been arranged swiftly, by mid- August. The purchaser was probably Mr Charles Law, the Recorder of London;[25] there is no mention of the price, though Giles does comment that most of their furniture, which had cost £1000, was sold for £200. Anna was not too upset: "I can now hardly be surprized at Anna's not wishing to live there any more. The neighbourhood is wild; and when your own manservant is taken for highway robbery and another man hangs himself at your front gate, you no doubt feel somewhat disposed to shudder at the idea of living in such a place."[26] Giles took Anna, the children and Emma Carter to live in Frome, and having settled them there he returned to London, and then set off for Boulogne by steamer on 24 August.

For the next four months Giles was in France, occupied with what he seems to have most enjoyed: searching in libraries and churches for manuscripts by Bede and other early English church fathers, which he transcribed in preparation for his planned series *Patres Ecclesiae Anglicanae*. He returned in late December so that the family could travel to Ware (by train now, as the railway had reached Ware in October 1843)[27] for Christmas with Aunt Ann Dickinson. It was the last time they saw her, for Aunt Ann died unexpectedly on 12 February, aged 80. She left one quarter of her estate to Anna, but had, at Giles's prudent request, put this in trust "not subject to the debts of her husband".[28]

Until the end of March Giles was collating and copying manuscripts in the Bodleian library; he then returned to France to continue his research. He was back in Oxford in July, renting "a nice little house on Headington Hill" where Anna joined him; apparently the children stayed with Emma Carter in Frome. By September his financial position in relation to Bohn, Pickering and other creditors had become untenable, and he was forced to petition for bankruptcy, stating that he had only ten shillings in his possession. The procedure in those days started with two weeks in prison[29] (in Giles's case in Oxford Castle) before an appearance in the Court of Bankruptcy in London. Here on 26 October Giles presented a schedule saying that his debts were £3,112 13s 4d, and his assets £1,070, though there was doubt that this sum could be realised. Anna's inheritance from Ann Dickinson was not under his control. The solicitor acting for the creditors drew attention to two boxes that Giles had moved from Oxford to an inn in Old Bailey, and claimed that they contained valuable manuscripts. Giles said the boxes contained only clothing and personal papers, and refused to hand them over. The Commissioner for Bankruptcy ordered the boxes to be deposited under the Court's supervision. Otherwise the petition for bankruptcy was unopposed, and the final discharge was given on 11 November.[30]

It was not Giles's nature to let setbacks such as bankruptcy get him down. By January 1845 resources had been found to allow the whole family (plus Emma) to leave for Belgium, and take comfortable lodgings in Bruges, where he found a rich collection of seven or eight hundred manuscripts. In May, having thoroughly explored the libraries of Belgium, Giles and his family returned to England. At the end of July he agreed to take charge of the churches of East Dean (he writes Dene) and Friston in Sussex for two months, and while he and the family were there enjoying living at Birling Gap (he writes Burling) he wrote the greater part of his two-volume *Life and Letters of Thomas à Becket*, which was published in 1846. At the end of September they returned to Oxford, to a house in North Parade, where on 8 December 1845 their fourth son Herbert[31] was born, though this is not mentioned in his diary.

The new year saw another move for the family, to the vicarage at Bampton, about 20 miles west of Oxford. St Mary's Church, Bampton, originally a 10th century Anglo-Saxon minster, had one of the largest parishes in Oxfordshire, which was divided between three vicars.[32] The senior of these, Mr Kerby, was old, and had agreed to let Giles perform his duties in return for allowing him to live in the vicarage (furnished) and £150 a year. "All this was clear gain to me."[33] The vicarage, now called Churchgate House, dates from 1546, with a large Georgian addition of 1799.[34] Their last child, Ellen Harriet,[35] was born there during the first quarter of 1848, but the birth is not recorded in the *Diary* and the exact date has not yet been traced. From 1849 to 1853 their elder son Arthur was a chorister at Magdalene College, Oxford. In autumn 1852 Anna took the fourteen year old Isabella to Worms in Germany, leaving her there to live happily for three years with the family of William Archer, an old friend who was acting as English Chaplain in Worms with leave of absence from his duties as Vicar of Churchill in Somerset.

Giles's duties, shared with the two other vicars and a curate, were not onerous, and left him plenty of time for research and writing, and long holidays such as six weeks in Paris in autumn 1846. As a matter of routine he seems to have applied for every vacant professorship that arose at Oxford, but without much enthusiasm and certainly without success: "it came to nothing and I took no thought about it, as I am much happier out of harness of every kind."[36]

His productivity during just over nine years at Bampton was prodigious. He produced 53 books (73 volumes allowing for multi-volume works), including old English chronicles translated from monkish Latin for the first time, biographies of Alfred the Great and Thomas à Becket, histories of Bampton and Whitney, and 17 out of 21 of "*Dr Giles's Juvenile Library: Dr Giles's First Lessons: a series of elementary treatises on every branch of literature and science, written in a simple language, and adapted to the capacity of children between the ages of six and twelve*".[37] Many of his translations of classical or medieval authors were pioneering works, but they were hastily done and lacked the customary support of notes and indices; within thirty years most of them had been superseded by more scholarly editions.

Soon his output was so large that he was having difficulty in finding printers of high quality who could keep up with him. So in 1847 he followed the example of his friend, the voracious bibliophile and manuscript collector Sir Thomas Phillipps,[38] and bought

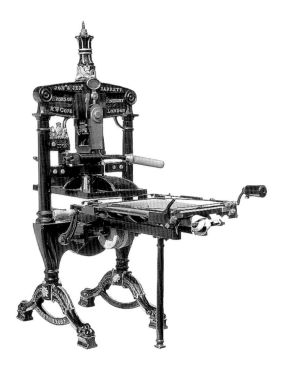

Albion Press

a new Albion printing press, with a huge quantity of type and all the furniture that was needed, which was set up in the vicarage. "Mr Black, a well known bookseller [...] suggested that I should employ young women, whose fingers being smaller would be better suited to picking up and setting the type. I at once caught at the idea, and between 1847 and 1854 taught no less than 24 girls, taken out of the Bampton National School, to become compositors. This attracted much notice: both Dr Pusey[39] and John Henry Newman[40] communicated with me [...]. I was invited to meet Lord Shaftesbury[41] and some ladies, who wished to obtain such information as I could give, seeing that they contemplated the establishment of a printing office in which none but women should be employed. Miss Emily Faithfull shortly afterwards established the Victoria Press in consequence of the favourable report I made at that meeting."[42] He also employed, for ten shillings a week plus board and lodging, an assistant, Charles Messiter, the son of a Frome solicitor. Despite being severely afflicted with what Giles calls St Vitus' Dance,[43] Messiter turned out to have great aptitude for Latin and for accurate transcription. He eventually married Sophia Tanner, one of the girl printers, "a young woman of elegant appearance and good manners, sufficient to have adorned a superior station."[44]

One of his original books was to cause Giles considerable problems. This was *Christian Records: an historical enquiry concerning the age, authorship and authenticity of the New Testament*, the sequel to the similar *Hebrew Records* dealing with the Old Testament, which had caused little comment when it was published in 1850. When *Christian Records* was close to publication in June 1854 proof sheets of the introduction reached Giles's diocesan bishop, Dr Samuel Wilberforce,[45] who reacted strongly by asking whether these gave "a true statement of the object and purport of your work", adding that "if it does so, I do not see how the putting forth of such views is reconcilable with maintaining your present position as a curate in my diocese."[46] A month's correspondence followed,[47] with Giles arguing that his book was historical and critical, but not doctrinal, and Wilberforce (who by then had read the whole work) adhering to his view that such questioning of the history and authorship of the Scriptures could not be reconciled with the teaching of the Church of England. Given the gulf between their positions it is not surprising that in the end Wilberforce simply closed down the argument and instructed Giles to recall the book. In response Giles could not resist some sarcasm, which he soon came to regret.

Bampton, Oxfordshire, July 8 [1854]

My lord

I submit to your decision, and enclose a copy of a letter which I will send by the next post to Messrs Whittaker, instructing them to suspend publication of my book. Thus, if I have offended against the doctrines of our church (which however I do not admit), I have at all events adhered to her discipline, and have obeyed your orders:- though I cannot but regret that your lordship had not sustained the noble votes you gave in the House of Lords, formerly in favour of free trade, and now in favour of free university education, by a third decision, more noble than either,- that enquiry into every thing touching our best interests should be free, and that you left my book to plead its own cause, and to stand or fall by its own merits- Will not some enemy, my lord, say of our church, what your lordship said of the House of Lords, on the occasion above alluded to, that it is to be feared that it may become stationary whilst every thing moves around it, and that it takes the lead, not of intelligence &c. but only of the backwardness of our age &c.?

I presume that I am at liberty to state the circumstances which have led to the suppression of my book – the public will expect it:- nothing however to be put forth that may in any way lessen the respect and good will with which your lordship will ever be regarded by

Your obedient servant,
J.A.Giles

The Rt Rev. the Lord Bishop of Oxford.

The self-inflicted calamity came two months later. Jane Green had been one of the compositors for five years when she was taken into the household as Anna's maid, a move which caused some resentment among the other girls. Richard Pratt had completed his apprenticeship with the Bampton shoemaker James Butler, but was still employed by and living with him. Richard and Jane had been engaged for six months when on Saturday 16 September Jane approached Giles to ask whether he would marry them without calling the banns as some of the young people in Bampton intended to make their wedding a rowdy occasion (a "shivaree"), and Richard's mother was unfriendly to her, so they wanted to avoid announcing the date of the wedding. Giles said she must get a licence, and offered to ask his son Arthur to drive her to Mr Goodlake, Rector of Bradwell, who could issue this. The vicarage household was in turmoil at this time, as nine-year old Herbert, who boarded in Oxford while attending Christ Church Grammar School, had been brought home seriously unwell on Tuesday 12 September, and by that Saturday was very ill with typhus fever. Giles was distracted, having taken turns with Anna throughout the night to look after Herbert, so his request to Arthur, who was only 15, was garbled, and no licence was obtained.

Jane asked for the marriage to be held at 8 o'clock on Tuesday morning, 3 October. Herbert was still dangerously ill, and Giles was up all night watching him. He got to the church just before 8 o'clock, and while he was waiting filled out the marriage certificate to save time, entering the names of Arthur and a servant Charlotte Lait as witnesses. But the bride and groom did not appear, so he went back to the vicarage where he was told that James Butler had refused to allow Richard Pratt to be absent from his work for even an hour.

The marriage was re-arranged for early on Thursday morning, before Richard had to start work. During the night of 4/5 October Herbert's fever reached its crisis and broke, so Giles and Anna got some sleep from about 1.30 a.m. Soon after 7 in the morning the couple were in church and the marriage was solemnised. Arthur was present and signed as a witness, but Charlotte Lait failed to appear, so Giles, knowing she was illiterate, put a cross next to her name, which he had already entered on the marriage certificate. As he later admitted, Giles had committed four offences that morning: 1. there was no licence; 2. the date on the marriage certificate was wrong; 3. the mark of the witness Charlotte Lait had been forged; 4. the ceremony had been conducted outside the hours permitted by law.[48] Of these the first three were, he claimed, due to his negligence and the strain of Herbert's illness, and he had never heard of the fourth.

Two days later Arthur left to join a ship for a voyage round the world; this had been arranged through a friend from Frome, but Arthur's departure was more sudden than expected. On the same day Butler complained to Giles that he had married his apprentice Pratt without his master's knowledge. Giles dismissed this, as Pratt was of age and could no longer be Butler's apprentice, whereupon Butler sent his version of events to the Bishop of Oxford.

Bishop Wilberforce acted immediately, writing on 9 October to his secretary John Marriott Davenport, a lawyer, and to Giles requiring an explanation. Before Giles had sent the bishop a reply he met Davenport's clerk, Robinson, who had been sent to Bampton to enquire into the marriage. Giles now realised he was in serious trouble, and consulted the local solicitor James Rose, who gave him the alarming information that the penalty prescribed for infringing the Marriage Act was 14 years' transportation. On Sunday afternoon, 22 October, superintendent constable Mitchell came from Witney to arrest Giles on the charge of having married the couple before 8 o'clock in the morning. Having spent the night in custody at Witney, Giles appeared before two magistrates the following morning, and was bailed, for £500 from himself and £250 from each of two friends, to appear at the next Oxford Assizes. He was also bailed for the same sums on a similar charge relating to another marriage two years earlier, and told to appear again that Friday. Giles's brother William, a lawyer, arrived from Taunton on Tuesday 24 October, and immediately went with Anna to see Davenport and argue that it was needlessly harsh to multiply cases in such a way. Davenport seemed to agree, and said he would consult the bishop. Wilberforce however was implacable, and insisted on the Friday hearing. William advised Giles not to appear at such short notice, so Giles, having posted two £500 cheques for his part of his bail, left for London on the Wednesday, took lodgings in Kentish Town and "remained in obscurity for some days."[49]

Anna stayed in the vicarage with Herbert and Ellen, and seems to have surprised Giles with her capability: "During this time I wrote every day to my wife, telling her how to arrange things, and she ably and faithfully did all I wished, and as satisfactorily as if I had still been at Bampton."[50] The manuscripts and proof sheets he had been working on were to be sent to him via a holding address, Bullock the Bampton blacksmith was to dismantle the printing press and send it to Mr Strong

Samuel Wilberforce, Bishop of Oxford
by George Richmond RA.
1868, oil on panel,
coll Royal Academy of Arts.

George F.W Mortimer
by Eden Upton Eddis, oil on
canvas, CLS Great Hall.

Soapy Sam, cartoon of
Samuel Wilberforce published
in *Vanity Fair*, 1869.

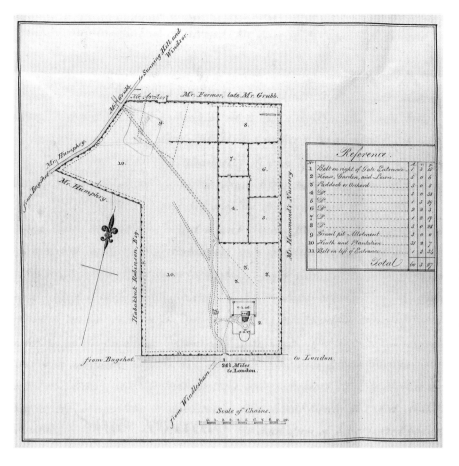

Churchgate House, Bampton.

Plan of Windlesham Hall and estate
prepared for its sale in 1843.

Perivale rectory and church.

Church of St Nicholas, Sutton.

Churchill Court.

Memorial tablet in the Mausoleum, Churchill.

The clock window in
Churchill Court.

The Giles memorial window in St John's Church, Churchill.

of 12 Pilgrim Street, Ludgate Hill for his use,[51] his library ("except what I mean to keep") was to be sent to Sotheby for immediate auction, and their own furniture was to be put into storage.

At this stage Giles seemed optimistic that he could avoid trial, writing to Anna "Depend on it I shall escape the snare, and will put you right again despite my enemies. I have no doubt that Mr Butler[52] the vicar of Wantage has caballed for a long time with the bishop to do me harm. Priestcraft is his pole-star, and I hope strait-forward [sic] dealing is mine."[53] Many of his friends and fellow scholars wrote similarly, believing that the prosecutions were out of all proportion to the offences, and that behind them was the bishop's animosity.

By the end of November Richard and Jane Pratt had set sail for Australia, so with Arthur also at sea there were no witnesses other than Giles to say what had happened at the marriage on 5 October. Anna and the children left Bampton and took lodgings in Ealing. Amid all this upheaval and ceaseless correspondence Giles did find time to note in his dairy for 4 December 1854 "I heard today that Edkins, second master at the City School, was dead." The sudden death of Edkins at the age of 49 had shocked the school, and he was widely mourned for his brilliant teaching, despite his eccentricities.

The next day Giles drove to Witney to appear before the magistrates on the second charge of conducting a marriage outside of canonical hours, to which was now added a further charge of not having a licence for this marriage. His total bail was increased to the enormous sum of £3200 (five times his annual salary as Head Master). These additional charges were eventually not pursued, partly because the Bampton church clock was often half an hour slow, and therefore nobody was sure of the exact time of this marriage ceremony. After this appearance Giles joined his family in Ealing, later moving to Islington and then to Enfield.

Three months later, on Tuesday 4 March 1855, Giles was tried at Oxford Assize Court by Lord Chief Justice Campbell.[54] The result of the trial was certain beforehand. Giles felt that Lord Campbell would have let him off altogether, but the breaches of the law were too many. Campbell gave judgement as follows:

> John Allen Giles, you have received from the University the highest honours it can confer, and are admitted on all hands to be a man of the greatest intellectual attainments; most distressing is it therefore to see you standing there to receive the sentence of the Court. I am still totally at a loss to account for the motives by which you have been actuated, but I am bound to say, in justice to you, that the suspicion which may have existed that you have been guilty of some immoral act, and for that reason wished to get this young woman out of the way, appears to me to be totally without foundation. The young man and young woman appear to have been attached to each other for months before, it was well known as an honourable courtship, and one which would no doubt result in marriage. I therefore acquit you of every suspicion of immorality. But I cannot imagine how it was possible that though you may not have been aware of its being a criminal offence to marry out

of canonical hours, that you should conceive otherwise than that it was a grossly improper thing to make a false entry of a marriage in this register, seeing how the safety of society depends upon the veracity of such entries. In this you have declared a marriage to have taken place on one day when in fact it took place on another. You have stated that it was by license when there was no license, and have said that it was witnessed by a person whom you knew was not present.[55]

Lord Chief Justice Campbell.

The sentence was 12 months imprisonment in Oxford Castle "but it was signified to me privately that I should be set free before that time. [...] I was accordingly released after a few weeks by order of the Secretary of State, with the concurrence of Lord Campbell himself."[56] After his release he and Campbell exchanged presents, Giles sending his *Sanctus Thomas Cantuariensis*, in 8 volumes, in response to Campbell's *Lives of the Chancellors*, in 10 volumes!

There was continued discussion of the role of Bishop Wilberforce in the case. Giles had written three times to him as his "father in God" "earnestly entreating him to treat my case more leniently; but instead of doing so, he handed the letters to his secretary Mr Davenport, who was solicitor to the prosecution, and they contained my acknowledgement of the whole affair."[57] Under cross-examination at the trial Wilberforce stated that, having received the complaint from James Butler and checked that no licence had been issued for the marriage, he had then left the affair entirely in the hands of the civic authorities and had nothing more to do with it. He agreed that he had handed the letters to Davenport, but said that this was because Davenport was officiating registrar of the diocese and acted as the bishop's secretary, and had nothing to do with his role in pursuing the prosecution. The widespread belief among Giles's friends and many Oxford academics was that this Pooh-Bah argument was disingenuous, and that others had encouraged the bishop not to relent. A letter James Butler wrote to the *Oxford Journal* on 21 March 1855 supported this:

[...] The Bishop of Oxford, when examined by Mr Clarkson, said <u>he certainly had not felt it his duty to take up this prosecution, nor had he anything to do with it;</u> thus conveying to the Court , and the world, that that the responsibility rested on another's shoulders rather than his own, and, as a matter of course, [...] it is generally supposed and believed that the affair originated with myself, and that I alone am responsible for it. [Butler repeats his reasons for writing to the Bishop] [...] I received a reply to my letter to his Lordship, in which he says "If the so-called marriage was celebrated before eight in the morning, Dr Giles is guilty of a felony, and liable to 14 years' transportation: this is so serious a matter that it should be examined by the Civil Magistrates, to whom YOU OUGHT at once to apply." This, however, <u>I did not do,</u> nor did I consult any legal adviser whatever. Previously to receiving the Bishop's letter, I had imagined the crime – if I may so speak – was an offence committed against an ecclesiastical authority, and would be reproved by the Bishop himself; but being undeceived on this point by his

Lordship's letter, I determined to have nothing more to do with the affair. [However, Davenport takes up the case and Butler is brought before the magistrate] where, before I was aware, I had laid information against Dr Giles, without so much as allowing me to choose whether I would do so or not; I, therefore, said to Mr Mitchell, on my way back, I had no idea they were going to make a tool of me in that way. [...] The Bishop of Oxford, in his evidence, produced my letter only, as the "accuser" of Dr Giles to him, which has led the public to believe that I only have made complaint to his Lordship, whereas Mr Robinson [Davenport's clerk] assured me that the Bishop had received letters from several Clergymen, calling his attention to Dr Giles's case.[58]

In one letter a cleric wrote to Wilberforce after the trial rejoicing "that we are freed for ever from the ministrations of one who for many reasons was quite unfitted for his office."[59]

Life for Giles in Oxford Castle was pleasant enough. Visiting appears to have been unrestricted, and he received calls from the Vice-Chancellor, the Heads of various colleges and many other friends. For example, Mark Pattison, Rector of Lincoln College, enquired, "I write therefore to ask if it would be convenient for you that I should come at 4 o'clock this afternoon?" There was also copious supportive correspondence from all around the country. Many offered to send him books, and once, while he was walking in the Castle garden, a piece of Cheddar cheese "folded nicely in a clean sheet of writing paper" was thrown to him from a window: "I have no doubt that some benevolent woman belonging to the Garrison took this mode of adding to my Commissariat, however contrary to the law it might be thought if told to the authorities."[60]

He exchanged letters every day with Anna and the children. In May they moved from Enfield to a cottage on Selsdon Road, Croydon; the postal service there was not so good, but with careful timing it was still possible for a letter to be sent and a reply received within the same day. On 20 May he wrote:

> You want to know how I spend the day: I will tell you. The man who waits on me comes a little before 8 o'clock and calls me: I am not long getting up, and have only to step across the passage into my sitting room, where indeed I generally go to dress by the fire, at the same time eating my breakfast, which consists of half a pound of bread and a large dish of coffee, or tea, generally the latter. No delicacies are allowed in this Royal Castle, and I want none. I then sit down at my desk and write or read the whole morning. [...] When I am tired of reading or writing, I walk up and down the passage, and I occasionally have a visit from the Chaplain. All the officers of the Castle treat me with great respect, and cannot see any connection between the supposed offences, for which I sojourn among them, and the deeds of the others who have lodgings here. I do not go much into the open air; but now and then walk in the Governor's garden. We dine at the medieval hour of 12, when I have about three quarters of a pound of mutton, 2 or 3 potatoes, half a pound of bread and a pint of soup, and I then return to my books until 6, when tea is brought me, and between 8 and 9 I go back to my bedroom, having

found the day long enough for every thing I may wish to do. The Governor looks in about 3 or 4 o'clock and generally sits half an hour with me. One of the wardens, named Smith, is a capital algebraist, for a man in his station of life, and I always get on some problem with him when he comes round. I have already taught him Logarithms, of which before he knew nothing. [...][61]

After serving three of his twelve months Giles was released on 3 June 1855, after a convivial breakfast with Governor Harrison and his beautiful wife. He did not go straight to Croydon, but hired a horse and rode to Bampton to visit and thank the many locals who had supported him. He was reunited with Anna, Herbert and Ellen at the Selsdon Road cottage on 6 June. In August they moved to 15 Clarendon Road Villas, Notting Hill, and were soon joined by Isabella and Arthur, who had returned from Worms and the sea respectively, and the younger son of Giles's friend John Cuninghame, who lived with them while he prepared for his Oxford examinations. The whole family lived quietly and happily there for the rest of 1855. Young Cuninghame got his place at Christ Church, and in January Arthur returned to sea. The printing press was retrieved and set up there, with some of the Bampton girls coming to operate it. Giles continued to work on the *Works of King Alfred* and his *First Lessons* series, but money was so tight that in March 1856 he had to apply to the Bankruptcy Court for protection under the Insolvent Debtors Act 1842;[62] the final hearing was on 16 April.[63]

In June 1855 Giles was offered the living of Draycot Foliat (Giles writes both Draycote Foliet and Draycote-Folliott) near Swindon, the advowson of which, i.e. the right of presentation to the benefice, had been purchased by his friend Mr Birch of Pudlicote, one of the two who had stood bail for him in Witney. The Rector's duties seemed tailor-made for Giles, as there was actually no church and only 27 parishioners, and the annual income was £170.[64] To secure the position it was necessary to have a testimonial signed by three beneficed clergymen and countersigned by each of their bishops. Unfortunately one of these was Bishop Wilberforce, who flatly refused to sign, though to do so was only to state that the incumbent who had signed was really what he professed to be, and said nothing about the suitability of the applicant. So Soapy Sam's obduracy put an end to this attractive proposition.

12

Giles after CLS: Perivale, Sutton and Churchill

Early in 1857 Giles was invited to preach at the church of St Mary, Perivale. "We liked Perivale and its funny little church very much. When I had preached two or three times there, I received a communication from Mr Conyers Berkeley offering me the curacy of Perivale if I liked to go and live there, as his father-in-law the rector Mr Lateward[1] was living on the continent. On the 16th of February I received a letter from Mr Lateward, dated from Friesenberg Baden-Baden, Germany; and to cut matters short I accepted the offer, not caring much for the stipend £50, which was all Mr Lateward could offer to pay, but we all wished to be in the country, and I saw we could make Perivale Rectory a very pretty residence."[2]

Giles went to see the Bishop of London, Archibald Tait,[3] "whose behaviour towards me was so polite and kind that I can never forget it." Tait said that he would issue a licence, but could not do so until two years had passed since the trial and conviction. But meanwhile Giles should go and take possession without a licence. By April they had relocated to the Perivale Rectory. The printing press went too, to be housed in the loft over the coach house, and Giles taught two or three local girls to work at composing the type. The village of Perivale was tiny; there were only five inhabited houses in the parish, with a total population of 32 in 1851.[4] But Giles was happy there, performing his parochial duties, writing and publishing, giving occasional talks to groups such as the Ealing Mutual Improvement Society, from time to time accommodating youths preparing for Oxford or Cambridge, and all within easy reach of London life.

At this time he started to produce Dr Giles's *Key to the Classics,* a series of word for word translations of standard Latin or Greek works, printed with the original texts – or, as many of his younger customers would say, "cribs". There were eventually 65 of these, the last appearing in 1876, and in September 1881 he spent a month revising and correcting them "in which there were lots of misprints and omissions, arising from the rapidity with which I was obliged to write them in order to meet the demand."[5] Unsurprisingly some schoolmasters disapproved: Frederick Calder, Headmaster of Chesterfield Grammar School, accused him of "causing my brother to offend" and hoped that "you may be induced to stay your hand in future from such work". Giles replied that "he'd better order a copy of my key for every boy in the school, and they would learn three times as much of Latin and Greek as they now do, and three times as fast."[6]

The large E-shaped Rectory at Perivale was a good place for parties:

> *Saturday, Jan. 29 [1859].* Anna came into the library at Perivale and said, "Well, we have got on well with our preparations for celebrating Isabella's birthday on Monday. I could only wish that Arthur was at home." An hour had not passed, when she said to me, "There is a carriage coming on the bridge over the Brent: I wonder who it can be." Ten minutes had not passed before the carriage drew up, and out jumped Arthur. He told us that he was in New York that day fortnight, and thinking suddenly that he would like to be at home on Isabella's 21st birthday, he immediately took a berth in the Steamship "City of Baltimore," and so got home in time. "And now, mother," said he, "I have not had my clothes off since we set sail, for fear of losing my money; we had such a rough lot of passengers on board: so let me relieve myself:" and saying so he turned out about forty or fifty sovereigns into her lap.

> *Monday, Jan. 31.* A large party, from 50 to 100 persons, celebrated Isabella's 21st birthday by dancing and singing nearly all the night.[7]

Life at Perivale continued in this pleasant way until Rector Lateward died in June 1861. The new Rector, Mr Hughes, suggested that Giles might rent the house from him and remain, but Giles declined and soon found another vicarage to occupy. Since 1844 the Revd Robert De Burgh had the livings of both St Martin's, West Drayton and St Mary's, Harmondsworth. He lived at West Drayton, and happened to need a curate to look after the Harmondsworth parish and live in the vicarage there. Giles and family (plus printing press) moved there on 7 September 1861.

The arrangement was not as easy-going as at Perivale: a year later "Mr De Burgh, instigated by his wife, who hated me as a liberal churchman, and later became a Roman Catholic, tried to eject me from the vicarage house at Harmondsworth. I of course resisted, and compelled him to consent to my remaining up to a certain time."[8] This turned out to be a year's notice, and in September 1863 the family rented a house in Cranford, just west of Harmondsworth. The highlight of their two years there was a chance encounter:

> *Wednesday, April 20* [1864]. This afternoon as I was walking towards the old coach road that passes Cranford, leading from London to Bath, young Mr Boyle told me that Garibaldi[9] had just gone by in the Duke of Sutherland's carriage, and that they probably would change horses at the Berkeley Arms. I immediately ran on as fast as I could and caught them just as they stopped at that inn. The duke and Menotti Garibaldi [Garibaldi's first son] went into the house, leaving the father and the duchess in the carriage. I placed my hand on the door of the open carriage, and said "I have the honour of speaking to General Garibaldi," to which

he bowed assent. "I should not have intruded on your notice, if I were not aware that one of your most intimate friends is related to our family." "May I ask who that is?" said Garibaldi. "Captain Roberts!"[10] said I. He seized my hand eagerly saying "Captain Roberts is indeed one of my dearest friends, and I am delighted to meet any of his family in England." I asked him where he was going, and turning to the duchess said, "I beg pardon, but I am so out of breath that I can hardly speak," at which she laughed outright. The General said, "I am going to Cliefdon[11] [Clivenden]." I told him my house was not above 200 yards from the main road: would he come and pay me a visit? He said he could not do so now, as he was engaged to the duke and duchess of Sutherland. I at once apologised to her Grace, and said that the General's achievements tempted persons to cut short all ceremony and must be so taken at present; at which her *Grace* was still more gracious. I added, "General, I hope to hear that Italian unity will soon be safely effected." He thanked me for my good wishes, and said if he came to England again, he would pay me a visit. I then asked the duchess if she would allow me to send something for Garibaldi to her house. She assented, the General shook hands with me, the duchess gave me a most polite bow: the duke and Menotti took off their hats to me, and we separated.

Next day two copies of *Alfred the Great* were sent to Clivenden, one for the duchess and one for Garibaldi, plus "a long letter comparing his achievements in reducing the paltry duchies of Italy into one monarchy with those of King Alfred who had consolidated the English Monarchy in the same manner." In her letter of thanks the duchess says she read the letter to Garibaldi, "which he listened to with gratification."[12]

Giuseppe Garibaldi, 1866

In November 1864 Giles became involved with a Mr Abbott[13] who had an ambitious scheme for developing an estate near Farnbrorough by building houses and a number of colleges, to be known as Brunswick University. Giles persuaded him and his colleagues to scale their scheme back to a collaboration with Mr Henry de Bruno Austin, a well-known building contractor, who agreed to include a single large college on the 230 acre estate he was already building at north Ealing. The college was to be called Alexandra College,[14] Giles was to be its President, *i.e.* Principal, and his brother Charles its architect. Austin provided two large houses already built on the estate as temporary accommodation, to one of which Giles and family moved in September 1865. This proved to be the end for the printing press: it was temporarily stored at another house in Ealing, and destroyed when that house caught fire.

The purpose of Alexandra College was to prepare young men for competitive entry to the Home or Indian Civil Service, Diplomatic Service, the Army, the Universities, or for Emigration and Colonial Pursuits or the Literary or Scientific Examinations required by the Inns of Court or Medical Schools. Each student would have his own room, with meals in the common hall with the tutors, and would be entitled to attend the lectures on all relevant subjects. The annual fee was to be 100 guineas.

Giles spent the last three months of 1865 working hard to get the college going, though "I took care to be provided with ample funds before I spent one penny in the cause."[15] He produced a very impressive prospectus,[16] with a list of distinguished professors and tutors. In addition to the standard subjects, they covered *Hindoo Law and the Hindoo and Bengalee Languages, Arabic Language, Fortification and general Drawing, and Animal and Vegetable Physiology applied to Farming and Colonial Purposes*. A few students were enrolled in 1866 and taught successfully in the other house Austin provided. But the contractor had over-stretched himself (he was at the same time building Cleveland Square in Bayswater) and in 1866 had to withdraw from the scheme; consequently Abbott pulled out too. Six years later Austin went bankrupt with only a few of the Ealing houses built. So the elaborate plans came to nothing, and once again Giles had to find what to do next.

For the past ten years Giles had been looking to purchase an advowson, and had asked ecclesiastical agents to look out for something suitable. Initially his idea was to secure Herbert's future, should he decide to follow his father into clerical life. But by now Herbert had very successfully passed his examination into the Chinese Department, and left in March 1867 to start his distinguished diplomatic and academic career in China. At about this time an agent named Wilson wrote that he was commissioned to sell the advowson of Sutton in Surrey. Giles was interested, but the present patron, Mr Padwick, told him that the living was currently vacant, and so the advowson could not be sold. However, Padwick was willing to present Giles to the living, and in June Giles took up office as Rector of St Nicholas, Sutton.

As one has come to expect, there were complications. Wilson claimed commission of £130 for his services, which Giles disputed as the advowson had not been available. The dispute reached the Croydon Home Circuit court on 13 August 1866. The court record[17] reveals that Giles had been prepared to pay up to £6,000 to purchase an advowson in the West of England, or between £4,000 and £5,000 for one in the London area; Padwick had recently paid £5,500 for Sutton, where the incumbent received £650 a year, plus a rectory "in a rather dilapidated condition". The vacancy was due to the retirement that year of the Revd Henry Hatch who had been rector since 1831, and "a Rev. Mr Hatch"[18] was given first refusal to succeed him, but decided not to. Judge Baron Martin soon intervened, saying that if any such arrangement as was asserted by the plaintiffs had been entered into it was illegal, and recommending the parties to come to a settlement. This they did: Wilson received £50 (which Giles paid) plus costs amounting to £200 (paid by Padwick). So instead of spending at least £5000 on the advowson Giles had gained a house and a job and £650 a year, all for £50 "which I willingly paid."

On New Year's Eve Giles and Anna started their annual custom of entertaining 200 of the parishioners in the National Schoolroom. "They danced, sang, and enjoyed themselves amazingly. There were present all the poor people who had pay from the Relieving Officer outside the Union workhouse, and many ladies and gentlemen. At midnight they went to the church, where they sang a hymn and waited for the clock to strike 12, and then they dispersed, leaving behind them the old year, and carrying with them the burdens and responsibilities of the new."[19]

Giles's first burden of 1868 came straight away:

> *Wednesday, January 1.* I felt this day a little pain in the lower part of my body behind. The pain increased so much that I lay in bed the third day, and evidently was suffering from an abscess. The surgeons Mr White and Dr Wilton came to see me, and at once pronounced it to be what the doctors call a Fistula. It gave me so much pain that I was happy as if I was in Elysium when Mr Clark's lancet was brought into operation. I was confined to my room 2 months, but was able to read and write letters [...]. I cannot refrain from recording the wonderful operation of chloroform. [...] Whilst I was lying on the side of the bed with the chloroform held to my nose, I turned my head to one side, and as I thought with the same movement turned it back again, saying "Well, when are you going to begin?" – "Begin? we have finished" – "Why I only turned my head to one side and back again" – "Ah, but a quarter of an hour perhaps may have passed before you turned it back again." I felt nothing whatever of the knife, and passed the whole of the day and the night comfortably as if nothing had been the matter with me at all. But the next morning, when they came to put fresh dressings I suffered the most awful agonies that can be conceived, and imbibed a greater objection to bodily pain than I ever before entertained.[20]

The medieval church of St Nicholas in Sutton, which was too small and in poor repair, had been replaced in 1862-64 by a new building in gothic style designed by Edwin Nash, incorporating the old monuments. The rectory however was, Giles thought, probably the oldest house in the parish, and over the years he spent more than £1000 on renovating it; it has since been replaced.

In the 25 years from the opening of the railway station in 1847 the population of Sutton grew from 1000 to 8000. "The increased population consists of well-to-do people rather than of poor. This is not usually the case with growing parishes, but it is so much so at Sutton, that I have heard it said that there are 700 men who take season tickets & go to London every day on business."[21] During his 16-year incumbency there was plenty of controversy over matters such as the establishment of a School Board (Giles opposed this, but had to accept it as there were latterly 1700 children to be educated), the provision of a cemetery as the churchyard became full, the construction of a carriageway to the church door across the churchyard, rows with the church wardens (leading to a court case in 1876, which Giles won), and a long-running dispute with a curate, Francis Grosvenor, whom he dismissed for his high church ideas on ritual - "I this day [9 October 1875] sent back his cassock and surplice, a kind of Poncho petticoat, such as Romanists use, but which I never liked, and accompanied it with a note stating that his duties were at an end."[22] Grosvenor dug his heels in and appealed to the Bishop, who ruled in January 1877 that the non-standard agreement Giles had made with Grosvenor in January 1874 was illegal.

Rather than incurring the costs of an appeal, Giles agreed to pay Grosvenor his salary for the fifteen months of the dispute. "So Grosvenor behaved like a scamp to get £100, and the title will stick to him as long as he lives."[23]

Despite these difficulties his qualities were recognised by some: "The Rector presided in his usual happy manner. We have never seen a gentleman more successful as a chairman. It does not matter what kind of meeting he presides over, our Rector is at home, and carries everything pleasantly before him. But we must remember that he is one of the greatest scholars of the day."[24]

Perhaps the most persistent problem was the provision of places of worship for the growing population. In 1872 some parishioners were in correspondence with a clergyman, Mr Phillips, who offered to fund the building of a district church. For a year Giles was kept in the dark about this, but eventually gave his assent. But by 1875 Mr Phillips had realised that various factions in the parish would make his scheme unworkable, and withdrew his offer. Giles decided to pursue the matter himself, and on 13 March 1876 a temporary Iron Church on the Brighton Road was opened. The *Sutton Advertiser* reported that "The building is large, clean, and well lighted, and warmed at each end. There is a small font, a small bell, pulpit and reading desk, and the whole has been erected, we understand, by the rector, at a cost of about £390."[25] The Iron Church was soon licensed for public worship, and Herbert Turner, a master at Whitgift School, Croydon, was appointed "to officiate there for a few months to see how they like him."[26] They did like him: the church proved so popular that after six years it had to be lengthened, and in 1881 transepts were added. In 1886 construction began on a permanent church nearby to replace it; two years later this became Christ Church, Sutton, with its own parish. Herbert

The Iron Church, Brighton Road, Sutton.

Turner followed Giles as Rector of St Nicholas from 1886 to 1922. In 1882 building started on another district church in Sutton New Town ("new" in the 1850s), about a mile east of St Nicholas, which became the parish church of St Barnabas.

When Giles moved there Sutton was in the diocese of Winchester,[27] whose bishop since 1827 was Charles Sumner, with whom Giles had been on friendly terms since his time at Camberwell. In 1869 Sumner had to retire, having had a stroke. In January 1870 Giles "was reasonably anxious" when he heard that Sumner's successor was to be Samuel Wilberforce, transferring from Oxford. After much deliberation Giles wrote him a conciliatory note of congratulation: "It is my duty to do all I can to promote the welfare of this growing parish, and it will be my pleasure to do all in my power to support your lordship's dignity and privileges on all occasions."

Wilberforce first visited Sutton for a confirmation service in the parish church on Monday 23 May 1870. He had changed the date, and then the start time, at very short notice, causing Giles difficulties with the complex arrangements, which involved ten of the local clergy and 160 confirmation candidates. The service went smoothly and was well reported in the local paper. "About 30 people came to lunch with the bishop at the rectory, and his lordship made himself very agreeable. [...] The bishop, seeing a gooseberry tart on the table, said, 'Mrs Giles, are your gooseberries yet fit for cooking?' – 'Oh yes, these are fresh from our garden.' – 'Dr Giles, I should like some of that fresh gooseberry tart. Please pass it to me; I won't trouble you to help me.' I passed it and he put half of it on his own plate. I then said, 'Will you help me too, if you please; for I like gooseberries.' He gave me half of the remainder, or a quarter of the whole original: but, when he had finished his former portion, he took the last quarter also."[28]

Giles considered the success of this first encounter with Soapy Sam in fifteen years something of a triumph, but things were different on his next visit, again for a confirmation service on 27 June 1871. "The bishop, having fixed three different times for it, came at last at a different hour from any that he had named in his letters [...]. He was in a pet and could not control his temper. He had come to the Station half an hour before his time, found no carriage waiting for him, and if Mr Crowther-Smith had not accidentally been there and called a fly, he would have been obliged to go to the church on foot.[29] As it was, he sat in the vestry 'fretting and fuming like a roasted apple,' as my father used to say so fitly on such occasions."[30] After that the relationship between rector and bishop reverted to its former courteous hostility, which lasted until "*Monday, July 21 [1873]*. The cook rushed into our bedroom before we were up, and told us that the bishop of Winchester had been thrown from his horse on Saturday evening, and killed on the spot."[31]

William Bingham, an old Oxford friend, wrote soon after:

> I dare say you were equally surprised and shocked at the sudden and violent death of your late diocesan. We have no right to judge mankind lest the remark about the tower of Siloam[32] should apply to us; but I own that with others I could not help feeling that a violent death was in some sort a retribution for a policy and line of conduct in the church that have caused much regret and excited great reprobation. I may be uncharitable and wrong, but I never saw him in the pulpit without a shudder. I hope you had no further cause to regret being again subjected to his sway. Any thing might be expected from a man who could reconcile it to his conscience to treat one of his clergy in a manner so tyrannical. [...][33]

When the news had reached China a letter came from Herbert in Ningpo giving an interesting glimpse of family life eighteen years earlier:

> My dear father,

> Another mighty victory you have gained – for how can you defeat an enemy more completely than by outliving him? To be still in the enjoyment of life and health while a foe is rotting in a vault is no trifle, and cancels whole years of insolence of office. *You* probably have long ago forgiven poor Soapy Sam, and Time may even have toned down the bitterness of the old lady's hate; but there are two

living beings who grew up cursing the Bishop of Oxford as they rose in the morning and lay down at night, making it their grace before dinner and their thanksgiving after – Ellen and I! No one taught us to curse the soapy prelate, and the old lady used to say *Hsh!* as we did so, though she enjoyed it all the time; but we learnt by instinct to hate and to curse the man who had sacrificed us and ours on the altar of bigotry and spite. I don't think we shall ever be able to do anything else than think of the old rascal thus; we began to hate too young and too hotly.[34]

Giles and his family spent July, August and September 1866 in Boulogne, interrupted only by his having to attend the court case about the advowson. In Boulogne they renewed acquaintance with Baldwin Fulford, J.P., a member of an old and distinguished Devonshire family whom Giles had first met some 40 years earlier. Baldwin and Isabella were attracted to each other despite the considerable difference in their ages: "We very soon noticed that he and Isabella had no objection to accompany one another to the market."[35] On 8 October 1868 they were married at Sutton: as the local newspaper reported it "Miss Giles, the eldest daughter of our worthy and respected rector, was led to the hymeneal altar at the parish church of St Nicholas, by Baldwin Fulford, of Fulford in the county of Devon, Esq., J.P."[36] The couple lived on the continent for two years, and then settled in the village of Churchill in North Somerset, which was well known to both the Giles and Fulford families. Their time there was happy but sadly brief, for Baldwin died on 2 May 1871 after a short illness, caused by a carbuncle on his head. After this Isabella travelled frequently, but kept her links with Churchill.

Meanwhile Arthur, having had enough of the seafarer's life, had joined the Bengal Police in 1863. He was appointed Deputy Commissioner of Police in Calcutta in 1870, and there on 8 June 1871 he married Georgina ("Georgie") Sophia, daughter of Colonel, later General, William Carmichael Russell. Herbert returned on leave from Tientsin in March 1870, and in June was married to Catherine (Kate) Fenn. The marriage was conducted by Giles at Kate's home village of Nayland in Suffolk. In September they left from Liverpool to return to China via America. Both sons produced large families: Arthur and Georgie had six daughters and two sons, while Herbert had three daughters and six sons with Kate, and a daughter and another child with his second wife Elise Williamina (Mina) Edersheim, whom he married in 1883, a year after Kate's death. Of these 17 children two boys and two girls died infancy. But it was reported that in 1935, at the end of Herbert's long life, he was on speaking terms with only one of his children. Ellen never married, but seems to have helped with the administration of the parish and in typical Victorian fashion stayed at home to care for her parents.

As the years passed Giles, who had always enjoyed long holidays, began to spend more time away from Sutton, leaving his parochial duties to his curate, by now a reliable one. He and Anna loved staying at Churchill, where Isabella still had a house. William Archer (with whose family she had stayed in Worms) was rector of St John's Church there until his death in 1872. The oldest house in the village, next to the church, was the old manor house Churchill Court.[37] This large L-shaped house had a 16th century core, with 17th and 19th century additions. Sir John Churchill had added barracks for a troop of cavalry which he led for Charles I, and there was a tradition that a member of the Giles family later owned part of the estate. The building had fallen into disrepair, and but as early as 1871 Giles made enquiries about buying it. Churchill Court was owned by George Cosserat[38] who had mortgaged it to William Brice. The Revd Mr Cosserat was difficult to pin down, and had a bad reputation among his fellow clergymen, bluntly summarised by the Bishop of Salisbury: "<u>Do not trust Mr Cosserat</u>. He is wandering about swindling tradespeople in place after place, running up bills and then disappearing. I have had at least a dozen cries from different neighbourhoods asking for his address. He cannot shew his face in this Diocese [...]"[39] Nevertheless, in June 1876 agreement was reached with Brice to sell Churchill Court to Giles and his son Arthur jointly for £1400, including seven acres of land. They soon bought 12 more acres for £1160. "This completes the circuit, and not only furnishes a way to the smaller pieces of land without going through the court-yard of the house, but renders the property compact and enclosed in a ring fence."[40]

The restoration of Churchill Court was tackled with great enthusiasm by the whole family. Charles Giles the architect made a detailed study of the building, identifying some of the stones as dating from the fourteenth century, and making many practical suggestions. Giles himself enjoyed the physical labour of knocking through openings and replacing stonework, tasks noted regularly in his diary. Isabella also made a financial contribution, let her house in Churchill, and moved into Churchill Court, and Arthur and Herbert and their families used it as their base when on leave. When Arthur retired from the Indian Police in 1897 Churchill Court became his permanent home.

The two volumes of *Hebrew & Christian Records*, which had caused so much trouble with Wilberforce, were republished in 1877, with extra material as Giles had originally intended. In the intervening twenty years Darwin's works on evolution had appeared and been widely accepted, and there had been corresponding changes in theological opinion. These two volumes by Giles were now seen as pioneering objective investigations, and widely praised as such. Of all his many books these are among the most important, and are still in print.

William Dundas Cloete[41] was a member of the Sutton School Board, which is presumably how he met the widowed Isabella. By April 1878 they were engaged, and he was visiting her at Churchill, where he had an attack of gout and was confined to bed for three weeks. Their marriage at Churchill on 25 June 1878, conducted by Giles, was a happy and unusual occasion, part of a double wedding, the other bride being Isabella's cousin Margaret Giles, son of Giles's late brother Frank.

> On Tuesday our village was all astir and "quite alive" on the occasion of so unusual an event as two weddings – which were solemnised at the parish church – while Churchill Court was gayer than it probably has been since the days of Charles I [...]. The service was choral, and the sacred edifice was crowded with spectators. Floral decorations were displayed in great abundance, and as the bridal parties left the church, the children of the parochial school took up their position in the churchyard, and strewed the pathway with flowers. The breakfast

was provided at Churchill Court, and was attended by a large number of relatives and friends. [...] The health of the happy pairs was proposed by an aged uncle of the two brides (Capt. Giles of Woodbury, Wells).[42]

With Giles now in his mid-seventies, deaths, funerals and obituaries inevitably occur with increasing frequency in his memoirs. Capt. Giles died aged 86 on 9 August 1879, to be followed six months later by his widow Maria and then in 1880 by his sister Maria Bowen. But there were enough left for another happy reunion at Burnham-on-Sea in September 1880, when 37 family members gathered, whom Giles took the trouble to list. Much sadness was caused by the death of Charles Giles on 16 June 1881. He had been in poor health for years, but had always wanted to see the antiquities of Rome; it was thought that when he finally got there he over-tasked himself in trying to do too much exploration. He was buried in Rome, but the family had a brass put in Frome church recording his birth in the town and his skilful restoration of its church.

On 26 October 1881 Giles was in reflective mood:

> My 73rd birthday! A very awful subject of contemplation. Few persons, born in a peaceful and quiet condition of life have had more ups and downs than I have had. The ups have been earned by my hard labour: the downs have been brought about by the enmity of bigots, who have taken advantage of small acts of rashness, to which I have always been liable. Notwithstanding all this, I have passed beyond the normal life of man, and am still in the soundest health.

Meanwhile in London the problems of the Milk Street building and the expansion of the City of London School to 680 pupils had caused its Headmaster Edwin Abbott to press for a new building, which after seven years was eventually achieved. There is no indication that Giles was aware of this, so to receive an invitation from the Corporation of London must have surprised him:

> *Tuesday Dec. 12 [1882]* Having received from the Common Council of London, through Alderman Sir Thomas Owden,[43] an invitation, I witnessed the ceremony of opening the new City of London School on the Thames Embankment. The Prince of Wales presided, and the proceedings did not last long, But the most wonderful thing was my presence. Nearly 50 years ago I was present as Head-master at the opening of the old building in Milk Street, and I have no doubt that I was the only one present at both ceremonies.

Pleased though he was with the idea of being sole survivor of the 1837 opening present, he was wrong. For example, Henry Lavington[44] had been there as a nine year old new boy, and attended in 1882 as a Common Councilman. His son recalled that "a few roughs" got into the playground on the latter opening day and his father's watch was stolen.[45] A 47 page booklet, *The History of the City of London School* by E.W.Linging was produced to mark the opening, for distribution to the guests. If Giles received and read this he would no doubt have noted, perhaps without much surprise, that his name was never mentioned, though Mortimer and Abbott received lavish praise.

In February 1883 a letter dated 24 December 1882 arrived from Herbert in China, telling them that his wife Kate had died that day from a liver tumour of which the first signs were only two months earlier. "This loss plunged us all into the greatest grief, for she was one of the most amiable, cheerful and happy women I ever met with, and Herbert's position, left with 6 little children so far away, was most lamented."[46]

The new City of London School when just completed in 1882. Photo by its architects, Davis & Emanuel.

For the rest of 1883 Giles split his time about equally between Sutton and Churchill Court, where he and Arthur were still busy planning and building. They added an extra storey with a "tower room" to the corner staircase, built a Mausoleum,[47] converted the Barracks building to a separate house (on 2 August Giles himself built up the gable for the stable there, and on 4 September put on its roof). All this was mixed with plenty of visits and visitors, much to his pleasure.

Back in Sutton, 17 December 1883 was a great day for Giles and Anna, their 50th wedding anniversary.

> The Rev. Dr and Mrs Giles were "at home" on Monday to a large number of their friends and parishioners, who assembled to congratulate them on their golden wedding. [...] Few couples are allowed to enjoy so long a period of wedded life,

and it was therefore no wonder that the congratulations offered to Dr and Mrs Giles were hearty and sincere. The large number of presents that commemorated the occasion had been arranged in the library, where they were inspected and admired by the visitors. Refreshments were served in the dining room, conspicuous among them being a wedding cake, bearing on flags the date of the marriage and of its fiftieth anniversary. Of this interesting memento the visitors, of course, all partook. Mrs Giles was naturally much affected on the occasion, and her emotion was not lessened by the many marks of esteem which were exhibited during the day. The Rector was unwearying in the discharge of his duties as host in spite of his burden of 75 years and the number of his guests. [...] No fewer than 120 persons called on Monday afternoon to offer their congratulations, among the number being Sir Thomas and Lady Owden [...]. In the evening was a quiet family party, at which sons and daughters, and many grandsons and granddaughters, were present.[48]

There is a pencilled note describing Giles, thought to be by Arthur, in the loose sheets at the end of the *Diary*:

In stature about 5'6", firmly built without any tendency to superfluous flesh. One shoulder was slightly lower than the other & he had a habit of hitching it forward which indicated energy. His head was abnormally large & his hat could be found down over head & face with ease. One of his eye-lids drooped slightly – the colour of his eyes was grey-blue. His hair originally brown became quite white and silvery in old age & covered his head to the last. His face was clean shaven. The sight of one eye was normal, with the other he was very short-sighted. One glass in his spectacles was plain & the other a powerful lens. He could read small print by firelight after he was 70 years of age. His speech had always slight traces of the Somerset dialect – which he could speak a little, & was very proud of it.[49]

Giles reading – "He could read small print by firelight"

As his physical labours at Churchill Court showed, during 1883 his health was still robust at the age of 75, except for some problems with his knees. But there are signs of change at the end of the year: Herbert married Mina Edersheim in Oxford on 28 December but Giles and Anna did not go as they were "too much afraid of catching cold." The last complete entry in his diary, for 22 February 1884, is "Went home to Sutton – and soon afterwards caught a severe chill, which made me cough violently for nearly two months."

John Allen Giles died at Sutton Rectory on Wednesday 24 September 1884, one month before his 76th birthday. His death was registered at Carshalton on the following Monday by Annie Potton "Present at the Death", with the cause of death "Insufficiency of Mitral Valves, Pneumonia, Exhaustion certified by J.Wilton, M.D." Notices of his death or obituaries (concentrating on his scholarly work) appeared in several local and regional papers, and also, surprisingly, in the *New York Times* of 26 September 1884. His death was recorded in the December 1884 issue of the *City of London School Magazine*, with a brief summary of his career but no further comment.

Giles is commemorated by a brass plaque in St Nicholas, Sutton, but was buried at Churchill, where a stained glass window in the church of St John the Baptist is dedicated to his memory. The three main figures in this are St Aegidius (the Latin name for St Giles), King Alfred and the Venerable Bede, the last two being the subjects of two of his major books, and beneath these are the Giles arms and those of Corpus Christi College, Oxford. There is no church record of his burial, though there is a memorial tablet in the churchyard erected by his wife. The parish burial register records that when Anna died (in Bath in 1896) she was "interred in the private vault of Churchill Court", which was presumably the Mausoleum Giles had built. So it seems that Giles built the Mausoleum for his family, and was interred there to be joined by his wife twelve years later, and in 1926 by Arthur.

The more one reads Giles's memoirs the more one comes to like his wry humour and tolerance. He was a loving husband and father, greatly enjoying his family life, his contacts with a large circle of friends and his wide-ranging travels. He was proud of his Somerset roots, and in the last ten years of his life did much to add to the physical stock and social wellbeing of his beloved Churchill. Yet his career was not a success, despite its brilliant Oxford start. He was not suited to be a clergyman, either by conviction or by temperament, and yielding to his parents' pressure for him to be ordained was the major mistake that sent his life on its erratic course. He broke new scholarly ground in collecting, collating and editing numerous classical and medieval manuscripts, though rising academic standards meant that many of his publications were soon superseded. Some of his original works have lasting value, but many of his books can only be classed as potboilers. His lively mind and independent character made it difficult for him to accept authority, whether of Corporation committees, bishops, parochial church councils or canon law. His inclination was always to think for himself and to challenge the arguments of others – just the qualities which would have made him a good lawyer, the career he had wanted to follow and always took an interest in. He was involved (as plaintiff, defendant or witness) in at least a dozen legal cases. But being a successful barrister would no doubt have deprived him of the leisure to pursue the wide variety of interests and contacts which gave his life its vivid character, and the City of London School would have lost the chance of having such an interesting First Master.

*　　*　　*

Appendix

GURNEY'S TRANSCRIPT OF THE FINAL MEETING

Proceedings
at
A Special Committee
of
The City of London School
Friday 20th December 1839

(Copy from Mr Gurney's short-hand notes)

Present
W.S.Hale Esqre in the Chair
Mr Deputy Stevens. Mr Taylor.
Mr Hardwicke [*sic*]. Mr Deputy Pewtress.
Mr Lawrence.

Dr Giles was called in.

Chairman. Doctor, the Committee are now prepared to hear any statement you may make supported by circumstances – and at the same time perhaps you will allow me to state that we have a Gentleman here who will take down any observations which may be made.
Dr Giles. It will be as well to take down the questions and answers.
Chairman. Yes.
Dr Giles. There are one or two questions I wish to put which bear upon the evidence of certain of the Masters and I think I had better see them first. I should like to see Mr Woodroffe if you would ask him to step in.
Chairman. Yes.
Mr Woodroffe, Master of the second class, was sent for.
Dr Giles. I will endeavour to be as short as I can, and for that reason I will not allude to trifling points which seem to me to be completely set aside by others more important.
Mr Woodroffe entered the room.
Dr Giles. Mr Woodroffe, I have one or two questions to put to you. I have this put in writing – whether it is from your own mouth or another person's copying your ideas I do not know – but you state that you had no reason to appeal to me, and that if you had reason you would not appeal to me.

A. I did.

Q. I beg to know what was your reason for not appealing to me?

A. I think if my memory serves me right the Chairman asked me if I had ever occasion to appeal to you, and I told him No – and then the Chairman asked whether if I had any case of discipline I should appeal to the Head Master. I said, No, I thought I should not appeal to the Head Master. Then the Chairman I think immediately asked me, Why? and I said that from the circumstances which had occurred with regard to Mr Delille and a boy of the name Moul, with which I supposed you were all familiar, I was warranted in supposing that we should not receive support from the Head Master. I think those were my very words.

Q. May I beg to know whether you did not appeal to me in a very egregious case indeed which occurred subsequently?

A. Yes, I informed you of the circumstances that had taken place.

Q. What was that case?

A. In consequence of some words that had been written.

Q. Was it not a letter of a most disgraceful tendency thrown across the school by one boy to another which you fortunately picked up and which, after having deliberated with Mr Manley, you brought to me?

A. Yes, I did.

Q. Then that must have been an appeal. Do you not consider that an appeal? I do not wish to put it strongly, because it does not appear to me that you gave it with much forethought, and therefore I put the best construction upon the case – but does it not appear that you did appeal to me?

A. I will state the reason for the appeal.

Mr Deputy Pewtress. Was that appeal before this enquiry?

A. Subsequently. Some time before this the Head Master came round the School and made an enquiry as to some boys who had been guilty of writing obscene words upon Mr Manley's copy slips – consequently immediately this information came to me and, in addition to the note having been written, one of those boys being the writer of obscene words in one of the copy slips, I judged it my duty immediately to give the Head Master the information he required.

Dr Giles. I did not apply to you in that case?

A. No – but you made that public throughout the school.

Q. Upon the former case occurring?

A. Yes.

Q. Did it appear that the parties concerned in the former case were concerned in the latter case?

A. I have not the least idea who were concerned in the former case – this boy who wrote upon the copy slip told me he had never written anything before.

Q. You said you thought you would not appeal to me. How long after was this?

A. I do not know.

Mr Lawrence. Was the observation of the principal Master when he went round the school in the way you mention previous to this enquiry or afterwards?

Dr Giles. It was previous, Sir. I have that case to mention because it will appear that in all such cases I have been appealed to by the Masters.

Mr Lawrence. Did you consider that in giving the information to the Doctor you were appealing to him?

A. No, I did not.

Dr Giles. My impression is that it was an appeal.

A. I do not regard it as an appeal. I should not appeal to you if I had a difficult case to deal with.

Dr Giles. Did you not say that it was a difficult case? Would it not be satisfactory Sir to read the words of the note? Because it appears to me that nothing more disgraceful could occur than this case, and therefore for a Master to say, when he tells the Head Master of it, that it was not an appeal is a confusion of terms.

Mr Deputy Pewtress. If I understand you he communicated the complaint in consequence of a prior complaint you had made.

Dr Giles. Yes, but preceding it a long time.

Mr Lawrence. Was this anything of an obscene nature?

Dr Giles. I was told that it was. I did not see it, because in fact the copy was burnt. (To Mr Woodroffe) I will not ask you any further questions, as it would take a long time if I were to ask you the other questions which I have written down.

Mr Lawrence. As Mr Woodroffe has stated in his former evidence that he should not think of appealing to Dr Giles, and the Doctor has brought this instance forward as a proof of his appealing. I should like this to be clearly understood, whether a Master giving information to the Head Master is to be considered as an appeal or not, that we may understand the Doctor.

Dr Giles. Yes. There appears to be no identity between the boy who threw this across and the former occasion.

Mr Lawrence. No, the question I put is this. You stated in your evidence before the Committee that in difficult cases you should not appeal to the Doctor.

A. In some difficult cases of discipline.

Q. It referred to discipline. Did you consider the case of these boys a case of that sort in which you were seeking advice or information or instruction of the Doctor?

A. I did not look at it as a case of discipline. I did not consider it a case of discipline.

Dr Giles. Will you allow me to state how I consider it? You came to me at two o'clock and said that you had discovered that one boy had thrown a most obscene letter to another across the school. Mr Manley came with you, and I looked at the letter and said that it was obscene, and I begged you to put it off for half an hour, and at half past three the school were collected together, and we gave the boys a castigation, and they were in confinement for three days. Was not that a case of discipline?

A. Yes, the giving the castigation was a case of discipline – but if I understood rightly the Chairman's former question was would I in a difficult case of discipline appeal to the Head Master.

Mr Deputy Stevens. Was this a case in which if Dr Giles had been absent you would have taken upon you to act for yourself?

A. I hardly know – I do not know what I should have done under such circumstances. I considered it my duty to mention it to Dr Giles immediately in consequence of his having come round the school sometime before, I do not recollect how long before, and mentioning this case. I considered it my duty to give him information upon the subject.

Chairman. Did you consider this an appeal to the Doctor, or did you consider that it was merely giving him information?

A. I beg to say that I do not consider it an appeal.

Dr Giles. Did I not two days after tell you of one of the boys being locked up in solitary confinement, and having undergone two days of the penance, and it appeared that one of them was unwell in consequence of his being shut up in a room without fire and there was great difficulty in enforcing that and I said to you, If you were disposed to mix mercy with justice you might let them off, that I thought they had suffered enough?

A. I beg your pardon, I did not hear you say that.

Dr Giles (To Mr Brewer). Did I not say that?

Mr Hardwick. I think you should finish with one witness before you call a second.

A. You asked if I was disposed to give way.

Dr Giles. I deny that. I did not use that word. I may have said "Are you disposed to let these boys off?", using a colloquial expression, and you said "Really Sir, I am disposed to inflict the whole penalty."

Mr Deputy Stevens. How does this apply?

Dr Giles. As a case of discipline it shews that the matter was in Mr Woodroffe's mind and in my mind, and that he knew how the punishment was proceeding. I should like to ask one more question. You were the Master of the Junior Class?

A. Yes.

Q. Did I not, when you left the junior class, when a new Master was appointed, put him under you?

A. No, the next new Master was Mr Cook.

Mr Deputy Pewtress. Really Mr Chairman, this does not apply to the question.

Dr Giles. This will be important.

Mr Deputy Pewtress. I must interpose. I cannot perceive the relevancy of these questions to this enquiry.

Dr Giles. You will see Sir in a moment. I want to prove that Mr Woodroffe had no reason to say he would not appeal to me by shewing that on one occasion, contrary to the opinion of the Chairman and contrary to the opinion of every Master, I put a Gentleman, not an University-man, above themselves and that that shewed such a good will on my part towards Mr Woodroffe that he had no right to say I would not support him in his authority.

Chairman. Taking it for granted, what has that to do with the Report?

Mr Woodroffe. I have stated my reason.

Dr Giles. Then I am satisfied with that, that will be sufficient.

Chairman. Doctor, excuse me, you assume from the report that the Masters have a personal feeling against you. Now I can state that in the examination that was gone into those were questions put to them by the Committee to which they were bound to give the answers.

Mr Delille was called in.

Dr Giles. Had you ever any reason to suppose that I should not support your authority as French Master in the School – did ever a case occur in which I did not shew a disposition to support your authority?

A. I cannot say that you did not shew a disposition – but I recollect a variety of instances where want of discipline has occurred of the most striking character in the 6th Class. I have been left unprotected in the 6th Class.

Q. Did you ever come to me and say that you had found a case occur, and I did not instantly say that whether right or wrong I would support you if possible – did I not say, do not put the matter into my hands, I wish the Masters to have the power, and I will support whatever step the Masters take with their pupils?

A. I have heard words to that effect used in a few instances. I should rather have some definite instance.

Q. You alluded the other day when you were asked certain questions by the Committee, to a letter which you wrote to Mr Hale – that letter was written it seems on the 12th of September, which was on the Thursday. On the preceding Wednesday, the 11th, you gave lessons to your class, did you not?

A. Exactly so.

Q. Will you state the particulars before I read the letter?

A. I do not know that I can tell you the dates.

Q. Shall I assist you with the dates? September the 12th the letter appears to be written – it says it took place on the 11th – the postscript says that it was kept back till the next day, Friday.

A. Will you be kind enough to allow me to look at the letter?

Dr Giles. (To the Chairman) I really think that I am not bound to shew the copy of the letter. I request Mr Delille to state the circumstances.

A. I want to see the postscript.

Mr Deputy Stevens. I think Mr Delille entitled to see anything that will refresh his memory.

Dr Giles. I say no more Sir.

Mr Deputy Stevens. I do not know whether the Committee agree with me.

Chairman. I think so.

Mr Brewer. Here is the letter itself. (*Handing it to Mr Delille*)

A. Shall I read the whole of the letter to you? I would rather, lest I should make a mistake in the dates.

Dr Giles. Will you stand by the letter?

A. Most assuredly.

Dr Giles. Then on that ground I meet the case.

A. "City of London School September 12th 1839

—My dear Sir

I apply to you under circumstances of importance to our School, namely discipline. One of the oldest of our boys, a pupil of Dr Giles, by name Alfred Moul, son of Mr Moul of 26 Brudnel Place, New North Road or 106 Fenchurch Street, has a lesson to write or translate for me, as an imposition for misconduct. This imposition was given to him by me yesterday."

Dr Giles. "Yesterday"? On Wednesday after the French lesson was over.

A. "This imposition was given to him by me yesterday, and ought to have been written by him on that day between the hours of twelve and one. The boy refused and still refuses to write the imposition, and, consequently, is now detained after school hours." There were two impositions – for the fact is that there had been a week's bad conduct. "I apprized the Head Master of the boy's conduct yesterday morning" If you remember I requested you to come upstairs and you came and you told Moul to do his lesson – "and, in my presence, Dr Giles told the boy that he should be detained until such imposition was written – the boy coolly turned to us both, and, alluding to the detention, said 'I am accustomed to dine late'." Now I am very glad to have this document, because I might incautiously commit myself.

Mr Deputy Stevens. I do not consider the dates of any importance.

Dr Giles. I consider them important.

A. He had been detained the previous day or the day before, I hardly remember which, and I had myself sent for luncheon for him – and I remember I mentioned to you the circumstances about his luncheon, but that in this case I wished the boy to be kept without any luncheon and then it was he turned round to us both and said "I am accustomed to dine late." Perhaps that will recall your recollection to it. I cannot help saying that I regret the letter and the circumstances that are now brought about. "I need not enter into the details of his misconduct, suffice it to say that Alfred Moul and myself are now closeted together, and I have the pain of witnessing the most unexampled instance of defiance to a Master that can ever have been experienced. This morning the Head Master invited me to relax in my endeavors" – I was then puzzled, I did not know how to act – "telling me that the boy was leaving in a fortnight and moreover having heard that he threatened to be absent altogether from school, if I detained him, as I did yesterday, he, the Head Master, thought it was not worthwhile for me to insist on this imposition. In my dilemma, being now unprotected by the Head Master, I have recourse to your advice." Those words I regret, I must say – those words were written under the pain that I was suffering from the boy.

Mr Deputy Pewtress. Is it true or not? That is the point.

A. It is true – we did not coincide in our views in regard to this case.

"Far from my wish to disregard the admonition of Dr Giles, but is it not a duty I owe to the trust reposed in me, to enforce the observance of that discipline which ought to exist in our School? I am now in my room, with my pupil; could you favour me with a few moments conversation I shall feel grateful to you. Yours very respectfully, C.J.Delille."
The moment that letter was written I communicated the letter to the boy – the boy had not written the imposition – indeed it appeared to me as though he thought he was in a Divan instead of a School – and I said "Alfred Moul, I am writing to the Chairman." I told him the object of the letter, and upon telling him that, I obtained a promise from him that the imposition should be done, and I either left the letter with Mr Brewer, or, having shewed it to him, I kept it; for these minor things have escaped my memory.

Mr Brewer. Mr Chairman, if I am in order I may be allowed perhaps to state how the fact is. Mr Delille when he had written that letter brought it to my office and shewed it to me, and requested me to go into the class room and witness Moul's contumacy. I did so. I went into the class room and saw that the description by Mr Delille with respect to the boy refusing to learn his imposition was correct. He was told in my presence that Mr Delille had written such a letter to the chairman and that previously to sending it he would give him one more chance.

Dr Giles. I really think you should keep this back for the present.

Mr Brewer. It was only in explanation.

A. "My Dear Sir, This letter has been kept back until this day. The salutary fear which application to you created in Alfred Moul brought, on his part, a promise that the imposition should be forthcoming this day (13th September) at twelve o'clock. I have this moment received it, and although this letter, being your property, is forwarded to you I may express the wish that no further notice be taken of the subject." And I assure that it is with deep regret that any further notice has been taken but I must stand by the letter, it is my duty to do that.

Dr Giles. You wished nothing to take place?

A. I wished that exceedingly and I only trust that if any of the remarks made should be of a severe kind that they will not prevent good feeling being again entertained and I trust that the end of this enquiry will make us to proceed together in as friendly a manner as possible.

Dr Giles. I am glad to hear that because I shall meet any opinion upon that subject with every possible candour.

Mr Deputy Pewtress. You had better pursue your examination.

Mr Hardwick. I do not know that the Committee would trouble Mr Delille any further as he has not travelled out of the letter unless the Doctor wishes to examine him further.

Dr Giles. I have no desire unless anything I may say should lead to any further examination.

Mr Delille withdrew.

Dr Giles. I have sent for the Boy to whom this imposition was given and I will tell you why. I distinctly deny knowing anything of Alfred Moul's punishment till two days after it began. Mr Delille came into my room two days after it began and told me that he had then written a letter to the Chairman. I was not aware of the Boy's being in disgrace until then.

Mr Deputy Stevens. But may we ask if any communication had taken place between you and Mr Delille previously?

Dr Giles. Not the slightest. Mr Delille gave lessons on Wednesday and Saturday.

Chairman. I beg pardon Mr Delille said the contest had been for a week. Did you not hear him say that the contest had been going on for a week and that he had given the Boy a sandwich on one occasion?

Dr Giles. Be so good Sir as to let me go into my case. I distinctly say that I knew nothing of the Boy's misbehaviour for two whole days after it began.

Mr Deputy Stevens. The Master would at first attempt to overcome the Boy's misbehaviour himself. It is only when it came to a certain pitch that he would apply to the Head Master.

Dr Giles. He never applied to me he wrote to the Chairman. I should be glad Sir to see Alfred Moul.

Mr Deputy Stevens. We must not have any of the Boys in the School examined.

Dr Giles. He is not a Boy in the School, he has left the School.

Mr Deputy Stevens. I should be sorry that any Boys should know anything of what takes place among ourselves.

Dr Giles. The Porter can give Evidence upon the subject.

Mr Hardwick. The Porter may be a good Witness but the Boy cannot know what passes between you and Mr Delille.

Mr Deputy Stevens. How can he prove a negative?

Dr Giles. I will read what he has signed.

Mr Deputy Pewtress. Excuse me Dr Giles we cannot hear that at present.

Dr Giles. This is the Case that has caused me more vexation than anything else.

Mr Deputy Pewtress. If you had pursued the examination of Mr Delille you might have procured his acknowledgement or denial of the fact which you state.

Dr Giles. He regrets the letter. If he is prepared to withdraw the letter or if you choose to let the matter rest it does not become me to say anything more.

Chairman. Do you suppose that I do not very much regret being called upon to sit here?

Dr Giles. But if it were the last thing I should say I would now say that I did not know of the case till two days after and I told him that I would support his authority whether right or wrong but having vindicated his authority in public some days afterwards I said to Mr Delille I want to talk to you privately, this was a confidential communication between him and myself and I then said I strongly suspect that the Boy had reason in saying I have lost my Books he replied I do not think he had and as the boy was about to leave in a fortnight I suggested to Mr Delille the propriety of relaxing in our endeavours but at the end of our conversation I observed "Mr Delille what I have now said is not to interfere with what I say publicly". I do distinctly say that I supported his authority in every way although in private I held a communication with him which he had no right to mention as Masters have a right to speak upon matters together in private particularly when they suspect they are in the wrong.

Mr Deputy Pewtress. Can not you examine Mr Delille to the facts in this Letter? He says "I apprized the Head Master yesterday morning".

Dr Giles. It was not so.

Chairman. He stands by that Letter.

Mr Deputy Stevens. He regrets this Letter and all the circumstances but he abided by the truth of the Letter. He regrets having written it.

Dr Giles. Did he write it as an appeal to the Committee?

Mr Deputy Pewtress. This is the point between you and Mr Delille. He asserts that he apprized the Head Master of the School of that circumstance yesterday morning. You had better question Mr Delille as to that fact.

Dr Giles. I was out on that day and the Porter came to my door and asked for me, it was five minutes to twelve and I had gone out. Mr Delille has mistaken the day of the transaction.

Chairman. I can state that in consequence of receiving that Letter I saw Mr Delille and I think said to him "Delille this Boy must have got a very unfavourable impression. If I were you I would see his Parents. Undoubtedly it is not a part of your duty to go to the Parents of any Boys but when you meet with a Case like this it is as well for the Master to see the Parents.

Dr Giles. But why Sir did you not tell me that you had an appeal from me?

Chairman. I considered that an appeal to the Committee.

Dr Giles. The Postscript is not an appeal.

Chairman. That is not a confidential communication.

Mr Deputy Stevens. The Postscript does not invalidate the former statement.

Mr Hardwick. If the Chairman received any communication he received it as Chairman of the Committee.

Dr Giles. If we were on hostile terms and the object was to get hold of everything against me I could no more expect the letter to be shewn to me than I could expect anything else that was improbable but up to that moment I should apply to you as the representative of the Committee on every Case and I should have thought it kind if he had said Mr Delille thinks that you have not supported him.

Mr Deputy Pewtress. This is mere conversation and I cannot afford to spend my time here unless we stick to the point of this enquiry.

Chairman. Then the question is whether you will have the Boy in or have Mr Delille examined again to that letter.

Dr Giles. I will have the Porter in.

The Porter Sumner is called in.

Dr Giles. Sumner, I call you in to state a fact Mr Delille has stated.

Mr Deputy Stevens. If you call the Porter you must ask him questions but I object to your telling him anything.

Dr Giles. Did you ever come to fetch me for Mr Delille?

A. I did one Wednesday morning at twelve o'clock.

Q. Did you find me in?

A. No I found you out.

Q. Do you recall the date?

A. I do not recall the date – all I know is that it was on one Wednesday.

Mr Deputy Stevens. Do you know whether it was two months back three months back or one month back?

A. No.

Dr Giles. Perhaps other facts will identify this. When did you hear of this Case?

A. I cannot tell – I was sent for by Mr Delille.

Q. That took place within a few days afterwards?

A. There was some disturbance between Moul and him on the Saturday but I cannot say that it was the following Saturday but on a Saturday soon after that Mr Delille came out and found Moul and another Boy playing at the umbrella stand – they were taken by Mr Delille somewhere and at 12 o'clock that Saturday Moul was locked up in the German Class Room.

Q. On the same Saturday?

A. Yes on the Saturday that I saw Moul at the umbrella stand.

Q. Do you remember afterwards providing a Luncheon?

A. I do.

Q. On that day?

A. One day the following week; I think it would have been from the Tuesday till the Thursday.

Q. Do you recollect Moul having stopped away and my sending for him?

A. I recollect his stopping away but I do not recollect your sending for him.

Q. When was Moul reinstated in his Class?

A. I cannot say.

Q. But it was not less than a week?

A. If I might be allowed to explain myself. I am not speaking from a certain knowledge of my own but from a belief that I have – the Boy Moul had two impositions – the one he had given him I believe on the first day of the disturbance whatever it was, that I believe he had on the Saturday [pencil note: Wednesday] he had another imposition for not going into the French Class. I do not know how that ended but I believe it ended rather seriously for him – I do not know from any knowledge of my own.

Chairman. You do not know it of yourself?

A. No I only know that I came on a Wednesday to Dr Giles and found him out.

Mr Deputy Stevens. Are you sure that it was at the request of Mr Delille that you went and found the Doctor out?

A. I am.

Q. Have you been sent by any other Master or any of the Masters on any occasion and found the Doctor out?

A. Yes frequently.

Q. You were sent by Mr Delille at that time?

A. Yes

Mr Hardwick. Were you sent by Mr Delille for the Doctor more than once?

A. No I think not.

Q. Never a second time?

A. No.

Dr Giles. Have you the French Register?

A. I have only one.

Chairman. You have no recollection as to what Wednesday it was?

A. No I have not – it might have been the Wednesday week previous to the Saturday or it might have been the same week.

Mr Lawrence. Was it before or after Moul was locked up?

A. I do not know. I have not made a note of the thing.

Q. Then if you were called upon to state whether it was before or after he was locked up you cannot say?

A. No.

Dr Giles. But you say you recollect providing a lunch and that was on Monday, Tuesday or Wednesday.

A. Yes.

Q. Do you recollect the remark of Moul that he dined late?

A. No I do not. I was not present on that occasion.

Mr Lawrence. Who told you he ever made such a remark?

A. Dr Giles told me that he made such a remark.

Dr Giles. It was Mr Delille told me that he made that remark – it seems that it was not until the 21st that he was sent to the lower class.

Mr Lawrence. The Doctor told you that Moul had stated to them that he was accustomed to dine late – was any other communication made to you besides the mere fact that the boy said he dined late?

A. Dr Giles called me in to his Library.

Dr Giles. The moment after this took place after I received this report knowing as I have said that I was not informed of this for two days it startled me and I spoke to Sumner. (To Sumner) Do you recollect my asking Nathan whether he had stolen Moul's books?

A. I do recollect.

Q. What was his answer?

A. That he believed that he had.

Q. Had the boy Nathan stolen them?

A. Yes.

Dr Giles. And he said that he stole them on the evening that the lessons were to be prepared and for which Mr Delille set him the imposition. This Register identifies the boy as having been absent that week – in my own register I have him absent on the Monday and on the Wednesday.

Chairman. Was not Moul often absent?

Dr Giles. I have his absence marked here whenever it took place – he was absent on the Monday and Wednesday afterwards, Monday being the German day. I said to Mr Delille "You may take him from my class in order to make him do the imposition" I having heard of it on the Saturday. Mr Delille came and took him out of the room and I believe that it was then that that took place which Sumner states and Moul is prepared to admit that it was solely in consequence of my advice that he did the imposition. I spoke seriously to him and I told him that I should insist upon his doing it and at the same time I advised him not to oblige us to proceed to extremities.

Mr Lawrence. You were aware he had an imposition?

Dr Giles. I did not know of it till two days after.

Mr Lawrence. You knew of the this circumstance of the disagreement between Moul and the French Master before the imposition was begun?

Dr Giles. I suppose it was before it was begun because he said he would not do it.

Mr Lawrence. How did you know the fact that the boy had offended the Master?

Dr Giles. Mr Delille told me that he had set this imposition which the boy would not do and that he had appealed to Mr Hale two days before – I knew nothing about it till then.

Mr Deputy Stevens. Do you mean to say that that is not true which is stated in Mr Delille's letter that in consequence of your not having enforced it he appealed to Mr Hale?

Dr Giles. I distinctly deny knowing of it till after he wrote to Mr Hale.

Mr Lawrence. Dr Giles states that prior to the boy's having the imposition to write he knew of the fact.

Dr Giles. No I did not know of the fact.

Mr Lawrence. You stated that you advised the boy to write the imposition.

Dr Giles. That was afterwards.

Mr Lawrence. But the letter was not sent to the Chairman before the boy had written the imposition.

Dr Giles. I say again that I did not know till two days after the imposition was given that it had been given and that when Mr Delille told me of it he said I have written to the Chairman about it.

Chairman. Mr Delille says there were two impositions.

Mr Deputy Pewtress. Mr Chairman, Sumner ought to withdraw and Mr Delille ought to be present during this cross examination.

Chairman. Mr Delille says there were two impositions.

Mr Deputy Pewtress. It is an important circumstance to ascertain the truth of the statement in Mr Delille's letter.

Mr Deputy Stevens. "This morning the Head Master invited me to relax in my endeavors."

Dr Giles. I did not do so. The two Masters were then holding a conference and I said "Are you quite certain Mr Delille that he committed the offence?"

Mr Deputy Stevens. He says "Being now unprotected by the Head Master I have recourse to your advice."

Dr Giles. Would you say that if it was true it bears any proof of his being unprotected by me?

Mr Deputy Pewtress. Yes if it was true.

Dr Giles. Which part?

Mr Deputy Pewtress. The whole of it.

Mr Delille was again called in

Chairman. Can you explain something about the dates: that is your letter and there is your class book. Does the minute in the class book bear out the dates of those letters?

A. I assure you Gentlemen that I hardly understand the circumstances of the case with regard to these dates – this boy on the 7th was suspended from my class – it was on the 7th if the 7th was a Saturday. I may very likely mistake the dates.

Mr Brewer. We have ascertained the 11th to be Wednesday which was your day for the 6th class.

Mr Delille. The boy's misconduct and impertinence took place on the 7th on which day at 12 o'clock he was locked up by me. On the 11th the Wednesday afterwards I applied to the Head Master.

Dr Giles. I had just gone out; it was five minutes to 12 o'clock and I had gone out and there is the misunderstanding.

Chairman. In your absence the Doctor has denied the truth of your statement that you applied to him.

Dr Giles. Do not suppose by that that I meant to say that you intentionally put a falsehood upon paper. I suppose that on finding me out you applied to Mr Hale. Sumner said that he came to me from you and found me out.

A. I am totally unprepared with the dates.

Mr Deputy Stevens. But I put this question to Sumner: you say you went to Dr Giles and found him out and that that was on a Wednesday – was it on a Wednesday a month or two weeks or three months ago? – and he said he could not tell. Therefore you now know the exact answer of the Porter. I believe I am correct.

Dr Giles. He said a few days afterwards the affair of Moul took place.

Mr Deputy Stevens. No.

Mr Delille. I should be apprehensive of answering in any manner that would deteriorate any part connected with this disagreeable affair but on the 7th the boy made use of a very impertinent expression and at 12 o'clock he was detained. The imposition was not done at one o'clock – he was detained again the next day – then there came the next lesson which was the 11th, the Wednesday, at one o'clock – the lesson was not even then done. I assure you Gentlemen I am annoyed now in not being prepared with these things.

Mr Deputy Pewtress. Go on.

Dr Giles. Gentlemen I must request the same candour to be shown to me. I am subject to a complaint which Mr Delille is willing to withdraw. Mr Delille hesitates in saying because it took place so long ago.

Mr Delille. Without referring to these trifling things which I consider trifling for they are unconnected with the grand question, this letter was written to the Chairman after my application to Dr Giles – distinctly so.

Mr Lawrence. In what way did you apply to Dr Giles?

A. I went to him and requested him to come up to the boy. I said the boy Moul has refused to do an imposition I have given him, will you come up stairs and insist upon it being done. Dr Giles came.

Q. What did Dr Giles say to you in the presence of the boy?

A. He went up to the boy and told him that he should do the imposition, and it was then that I made use of the expression that I should not provide him with luncheon and he then turned to us both and said "I am accustomed to dine late" and threw himself back on the floor.

Q. Are you sure Dr Giles was present?

A. He was present and I turned to Dr Giles at the time.

Dr Giles. You say you had provided luncheon. I did not know anything of that.

A. Yes I had.

Mr Deputy Pewtress. Was Dr Giles present at the time Mr Delille speaks of?

Dr Giles. Yes, but the words that the boy used did not make that impression upon my ear – I did not hear them.

Mr Lawrence. After this took place of course you proceeded in enforcing your imposition.

A. Most assuredly.

Dr Giles. Did I not hear you out the morning afterwards they had a hint from me.

Mr Deputy Pewtress. You had better finish this interview before you go to any other.

A. There it ended, we retired.

Mr Lawrence. Had you written that letter then?

A. Most assuredly not.

Dr Giles. You told me that before I went into the German room you had applied to the Chairman.

A. No.

Dr Giles. I mentioned it in the evening in my own family. I thought it a breach of rule but an inadvertence, my own Brother heard me make the remark. I said that the French Master had written a letter to the Chairman or applied to him and I had not heard of it previously.

A. I beg to assure you that this letter was written after the circumstances of your coming up stairs into the German room.

Mr Lawrence. After you had attempted to enforce the imposition on the boy what took place that induced you to write this letter?

A. At the next opportunity that boy was detained for I had mentioned to him in the presence of Dr Giles that he would be detained till it was done. At one o'clock I went in and it was not done. At the next time I had him down stairs and it was then that the boy so annoyed me that I wrote this letter.

Dr Giles. How many days now, I say that a Sunday passed over.

A. No I beg your pardon.

Dr Giles. A Sunday intervened between the first mention of the subject and the final step and one day the boy stayed away and I sent for him and gave him advice.

A. Now that I am getting prepared for this I can tell you the whole of the affair. This 13th of September was of course on Friday. On that day I received that imposition and all was ended and it was on Friday that I added the postscript and that it was sent to you immediately.

Dr Giles. On what day did he stay away from school?

A. Previously.

Q. What day?

A. I cannot say.

Q. On Thursday?

A. No he was with me on Thursday.

Mr Lawrence. You seem to be losing sight of the first part of the letter in which you say the Doctor had not supported you.

Mr Deputy Pewtress. We want an explanation - in what way did that occur?

A. When the boy was under circumstances of detention previous to this letter having been written it was then in the conversation we had upon the subject of the affair that Dr Giles alluded to the boy's leaving and that it was not worth while to insist upon this. It was under that impression that I considered myself unprotected.

Dr Giles. You put the matter in a false view. Will you allow me to put my interpretation? You allow that I said publicly that I should support your authority. I afterwards called you aside and said "Mr Delille, this boy has stopped away from school and I find he is going to leave in a fortnight and his Brother says he is so impressed with a sense of the injustice of the imposition that he will stop away altogether." I said that the punishment must be enforced "but as he is going to leave the School and as I think there is a plea of justice in what he says about having lost his books there is need for a little discretion in setting the boy an imposition."

A. That was not the cause – it was for gross impertinence in the class.

Dr Giles. Then I am more in the dark than ever.

A. The letter was written when I had given up your assistance.

Mr Lawrence. I think questions should be asked and answered but if we have a cross-fire it answers no purpose.

A. If I am to explain the imposition, it had no reference to the books, the boy had not prepared his lessons twice, but his Brother had a set of books in his own family. Therefore when he came in and said his lessons were unprepared "I have not books and I am not to provide books every time I come" his Brother having books he might have been prepared.

Mr Lawrence. But the main point is that the Doctor denies ever being with you in the Class room when the Boy said that he did not mind being detained for he dined late.

Dr Giles. No it was on Monday morning that I took him out of the Class room – it was the German day – in order that Mr Delille might take him. Do you recollect that?

A. No, whenever we were together in the German room it was at my request that you should come.

Dr Giles. You said that you kept him in the German room and that you had provided him with Luncheon but you would not do so again.

A. I said that he had better provide himself with Luncheon.

Mr Deputy Pewtress. But the main fact lies there. Dr Giles positively denies the statement you have made in the Letter and says he did not know of the circumstance till two days after it occurred.

Mr Deputy Stevens. And that the letter was sent to the Chairman before he knew of it.

A. Here is something that will explain it: there is the date of the 18th which is the Saturday [recte Wednesday] week afterwards.

Dr Giles. And my impression is that the matter was not ended till the Friday week.

A. The Boy was present then and he is marked fourteen and if you refer to the Second Class Register you will find him inscribed in one instance before he was degraded and sent to the lower division of the French Class. Without entering into the minutiae which I must say that I have not been studying in order to quibble about the dates, I fully declare that this was written after my communication with the Head Master.

Chairman. I can state that this was written on Friday and I saw Mr Delille and told him that though it was not a part of his duty to call upon the Parents yet as he appeared to have an obstinate Scholar in this case I advised him to call upon the Parents and I met him in Fenchurch Street as he was gong to Moul's house.

Dr Giles. But be so good as to notice the end of this postscript: "I have this moment received it and although this Letter being your property" – I deny it was your property.

Mr Hardwick. That is not the Chairman's observation it is Mr Delille's. Mr Delille gives this as his opinion "although this letter being your property I may express the wish that no further notice be taken of the subject."

Mr Lawrence. Suppose it was not the Chairman's property it does not affect the matter.

Dr Giles. No, but surely if you were to hear the boy and he were to state that he submitted in consequence of my having ordered him to submit that would affect the enquiry.

A. Let us have the boy in.

Dr Giles. He has left the School.

Mr Deputy Stevens. How does the boy know anything? I should be ashamed of any boy knowing anything of this transaction – it is not right that the boys should know anything of this.

Dr Giles. He is the best witness – the party concerned – he has said that he did the imposition because I advised him.

A. Mr Brewer and myself are two witnesses to overthrow that.

Dr Giles. The Boy can know his motives best.

Chairman. We cannot examine the Boy.

Dr Giles. Then I shall say no more on the subject. I shall abandon the subject altogether.

Dr Giles withdrew

Mr Delille. If you will allow me to say a single word on the observation of Dr Giles I can only say that Mr Brewer was present when I told Moul that I had applied to the Chairman and I shewed him the letter and I mentioned to him that by applying to the Chairman this would bring sorrow to his family, that he might consider that this would be public. I have several times mentioned to the Boys that I should obtain the protection of the Committee. I can only express my regret that this should have taken place.

Mr Hardwick. On the 12th of September you make the observation "I apprized the Head Master of the Boy's conduct yesterday morning". The 12th of September was a Thursday. Then the interview you had with Dr Giles was on Wednesday the 11th. Will you allow me to ask what time of the day on Wednesday you had your interview with Dr Giles?

A. It was of course in the morning but I am trying to tell you the very precise hour. I fully recollect that I requested the Head Master to come up stairs to me to speak to Moul which was precisely 12 o'clock.

Q. Did you send to him?

A. I went in myself to his Library.

Mr Deputy Pewtress. Did you ever send Sumner?

A. No I do not remember that.

Q. And Sumner bringing word that he was gone out?

A. No.

Mr Lawrence. Are you in the habit of sending messages to Dr Giles?

A. I have sometimes sent messages of a very trifling character.

Mr Hardwick. Do you recollect ever having sent Sumner to Dr Giles's Library to see if he was in?

A. Never. I do not recollect having done so.

Mr Deputy Pewtress. But such a thing might have occurred?

A. It might have occurred.

Chairman. But you are sure that it was not on this occasion?

A. No.

Mr Hardwick. When this interview took place it was in consequence of your having sought Dr Giles in his Library?

A. Yes, he came a few minutes afterwards.

Mr Lawrence. Was he long with you?

A. Not very long.

Mr Hardwick. In the latter part of this letter you state "this morning the Head Master invited me to relax my endeavours telling me that the Boy was leaving in a fortnight." Where did that take place?

A. In the passage.

Q. Is it possible that you could have made a mistake that that is a true statement?

A. That is a true statement.

Q. Did all this happen before you wrote the Letter?

A. Yes. I stake my whole life to that.

Chairman (To Mr Brewer). Mr Secretary, Mr Delille wrote this letter and he shewed it to you?

A. He did. I saw him in the act of writing part of it.

Mr Lawrence. Did you know what he was writing?

A. Yes. I saw it when it was complete.

Chairman. Then you accompanied Mr Delille into the Class and saw the Boy acting in that foolish way and not the way in which a Boy ought to be acting?

A. Yes I saw him acting in the way described by Mr Delille.

Mr Deputy Pewtress. Was Dr Giles present.

A. No.

Mr Delille. He may have been absent.

Mr_____. [sic] But you say that very morning he had advised you to relax?

Mr Delille. Yes, but at that hour he might not have been present.

Mr Lawrence. When was it written?

Mr Delille. The first part was written in school hours.

Chairman. Was not Moul frequently absent?

A. Very frequently absent.

Q. Do you know the cause?

A. No, but I have ascertained the cause of another Boy's absence on whose Parents I have called.

— Adjourned.

Chapter Notes

Chapter 1

[1] John Carpenter (*c.* 1370-1442) was Town Clerk of London from 1417 to 1438, and represented London in the parliaments of 1437 and 1439. He compiled the *Liber Albus*, the first book of English Common Law, and was an executor of Sir Richard (Dick) Whittington's will.

[2] Richard Taylor (1781-1858), originally from Norwich, was a printer with premises in Red Lion Square. His firm, later Taylor & Francis, produced many fine editions of the classics and works on natural history. He represented the ward of Farringdon Without for 35 years, always supporting educational causes.

[3] "An Act for establishing a School on the Site of Honey Lane Market in the City of London". Anno Quarto & Quinto Guglielmi IV Regis. Cap. 35.

[4] *Memoir of the Life and Times of John Carpenter* by Thomas Brewer (London: Arthur Taylor 1856); *The City of London School* by A.E.Douglas-Smith (2nd edition, Oxford: Basil Blackwell, 1965); *Carpenter's Children* by Thomas Hinde (London: James & James, 1995).

[5] Warren Stormes Hale (1791-1872) came as an orphan to London from Hertfordshire in 1804 to be apprenticed to his brother Ford Hale (also a member of the School Committee). He set up a successful business as a wax chandler, being the first to utilize recent discoveries of French chemists. He retained a humble and rather puritanical approach throughout his life, but was dedicated to advancing the cause of education, not only in steering the City of London School Act through parliament, but in 1854 playing a similar role in setting up the City of London Freemen's Orphan School in Brixton (since 1926 the City of London Freemen's School in Ashtead, Surrey).

[6] William Venables (1785-1840) was a wholesale paper maker and stationer. He had liberal views, supporting Electoral Reform and Catholic Emancipation. By 1834 he was an Alderman "past the chair", having been Lord Mayor in 1825-26.

[7] When Hale resigned the Court of Common Council conferred on him the honorary title of President of the City of London School, which he held until his death.

[8] In 1838 Highgate School had only 19 pupils, and from 1843 to 1865 the Master of Whitgift School had not a single pupil (though the school building was used by a National school).

[9] John Richardson Major (1797-1876), Headmaster 1830-1866.

[10] Henry Malden (1800-1876), Professor of Greek at University College London 1831-1876, and joint Headmaster 1833-1846.

[11] The Town Clerk.

[12] Now kept in the London Metropolitan Archives.

[13] Henry Brougham (1778-1868) was a Scottish barrister who was elected as a Whig MP in 1810 and was soon recognised as one of the most forceful members of the House of Commons. In 1820 his reputation was enhanced by his very able defence of Queen Caroline (see p.35). Always a strong supporter of popular education, he took a leading part in the foundation of London University in 1826. From 1830 to 1834 he was Lord Chancellor in Lord Grey's government, being raised to the peerage as Baron Brougham and Vaux; under this radical government the 1832 Reform Act and the 1833 Abolition of Slavery Act were passed. But Lord Melbourne thought his eccentric conduct was a main reason for the fall of that government in 1834, and did not reappoint him when the Whigs regained power in 1835. Brougham never again held public office.

[14] Fulford, *Royal Dukes* (Collins/Fontana 1973) p.259.

[15] An ancient and usually unsuccessful surgical technique for treating cataract; in the Duke's case the operation in late 1835 restored his sight.

[16] Still kept in the School archive.

[17] These are still used by the School Governors.

[18] Winchester ran a stationery business in the Strand, and was closely involved with the Tory party. He became Sheriff in 1826, and MP for Maidstone in 1830, though he withdrew from the 1831 election when he got very short shrift from his constituents. As Lord Mayor he was unpopular for refusing to allow Guildhall to be used for political meetings.

[19] David Salomons (1797-1873), banker and barrister, was the first Jew to be elected Sheriff and later Lord Mayor. He was for many years MP for Greenwich. In 1845 he gave a scholarship, unusually to be held by a boy during his school days rather than at university. His marble bust by William Behnes is in the lobby of the present school's Great Hall.

[20] George Birkbeck (1776-1841), physician and academic, came to London from Glasgow, and worked with Jeremy Bentham, Henry Brougham and John Hobhouse to improve the education of working men. To this end they opened the London Mechanics Institute (now Birkbeck College) in 1823.

[21] See Douglas-Smith pp.53-57 for the details.

[22] Gresham College; see Chapter 5.

[23] He had been elected Sheriff, but as a Jew was unable to take office until the Sheriff's Declaration Act, passed in August 1835, removed the requirement to swear "upon the true Faith of a Christian".

[24] See http://www.histparl.ac.uk/volume/1820-1832/member/winchester-henry-1777-1838.

[25] Brewer did later discover a will of John Carpenter, full of interesting detail but not mentioning his charitable bequest. The full story, set out in another will, came to light only in 1961: see Douglas-Smith pp. 22-26.

CHAPTER 2

[1] The current spelling. Giles uses Bridgewater.

[2] *The Diary and Memoirs of John Allen Giles*, ed. David Bromwich (Somerset Record Society, 2000). Hereafter referred to as D&M.

[3] D&M, p.20.

[4] *The Castle Spectre* by Matthew "Monk" Lewis, author of the celebrated Gothic novel *The Monk*, was a dramatic romance set in Conway. It was first performed at the Theatre Royal, Drury Lane in 1797, where it had a long and successful run, remaining in the repertory until the 1820s. *The Castle Spectre* opened in New York in 1798, and was a staple of English touring companies in the early 19th century.

[5] *Pigot's Directory for Frome*, 1822, includes "Giles and Hooper, carrier to London through Trowbridge, Bradford & Co., Monday & Thursday. To Bourton, Bruton, Castle Cary and Wincanton, Wed. & Saturday mornings. To Bristol, Monday & Thursday."

[6] D&M, p.24.

[7] D&M, p.25.

[8] D&M, p.27.

[9] Founded by Thomas Hardye in 1579, though possibly based on an earlier foundation of Edward VI.

[10] D&M, p.31.

[11] Mr Pococke, who "gave up pedagogizing and made carriages drawn by kites, in which he made many journeys on the high roads of Somersetshire, whenever there was enough wind to make his wheels go round." D&M, p.32.

[12] D&M, p.33.

[13] *Ibid*

[14] D&M, p.35.

[15] D&M, p.36.

[16] D&M, p.37,38.

[17] D&M, p.38.

[18] *Ibid*

[19] This Fiji (Feejee) Mermaid was bought from Japanese sailors by an American sea captain, Samuel Barrett Edes, for $6000 in 1822; it was exhibited that year in London, and then elsewhere, including Frome. After Edes's death it was sold to Moses Kimball of Boston in 1842, from whom the showman P.T.Barnum (1810-91) leased it for $12.50 per week, and exhibited it.

[20] D&M, pp.40-42. Giles dates this visit to 1819, but it must have been 1823 when Beckford left Fonthill and visitors were admitted to view the contents before they were sold.

[21] The Charterhouse was originally a Carthusian monastery, built in 1371 between the Barbican and Clerkenwell. After the reformation it became a private mansion, later bought by Thomas Sutton who in 1611 endowed almshouses for 80 'Brothers' and a school. The school moved to new premises near Godalming in 1872.

[22] Dr John Russell (1787-1863) became Headmaster of Charterhouse School (where he had been as a boy) in 1811. Under his administration the school became extremely popular. He resigned from Charterhouse in 1832 on becoming Rector of St Botolph's, Bishopsgate.

[23] D&M, p.47.

[24] D&M, p.50.

[25] Allen kept in touch with some of the other candidates, two of whom later became Headmasters: John Bradley Dyne, Highgate School 1838-78, John Bidgood Bennett, Queen Elizabeth Grammar School Blackburn 1845-55.

[26] D&M, p.55.

[27] D&M, p.60.

[28] D&M, p.58.

[29] Henry later became senior wrangler, then Bishop of Grahamstown and a bishop in the Church of Scotland.

[30] The building, dating from 1677, was converted to The Devereux public house in 1843.

[31] D&M, p.91.

[32] The premier law scholarship at Oxford, endowed by the jurist Charles Viner (1678-1756) and first awarded in 1758.

[33] D&M, p.93.

[34] William Astell (1774-1847) was one of Bridgwater's two MPs from 1807 to 1832.

[35] D&M, p.95

[36] Obituary in Proceedings of the Somerset Archaeological and Natural History Society, vol 30 (1884) pp.166-168.

[37] D&M, p.140.

[38] D&M, p.117.

[39] All fellows except the medical fellow had to be ordained. Information supplied by Mr Julian Reid, archivist of Corpus Christi College.

[40] John Dalley (1785-1851) was the local Collector of Customs. His wife Maria (1799-1871) was 13 years older than her sister Anna Dickinson.

[41] Anna Sarah Dickinson (1812-96) was born in the Victualling Yard of HM Dockyard, Deptford, where her father Frederick Dickinson (1762-1818) was store keeper. By 1833 both her parents were dead, which is presumably why she was living with Mr and Mrs Dalley.

[42] D&M, p.121.

[43] D&M, p.126.

[44] D&M, p.129.

[45] St Giles Camberwell register of baptisms.

[46] But before this, on 16 October 1834, Allen and Anna had seen the Houses of Parliament burning as they dined with Mr Myers in his house at the top of Camberwell Grove.

⁴⁷ D&M, p.127.
⁴⁸ Wilson's Grammar School, founded 1616 in Camberwell, moved to Sutton in 1975.
⁴⁹ See p.169.
⁵⁰ D&M, p.150.
⁵¹ D&M, p.151.

CHAPTER 3

¹ *The Times, Morning Herald, Morning Chronicle, Morning Post, Courier, Standard, Globe.*
² The position Giles might have been occupying if his plans had not changed.
³ Not related to Thomas Brewer as far as is known.
⁴ It is right to learn even from the enemy (Ovid, *Metamorphoses*, IV, 428).
⁵ Francis Graham Moon (1796-1871) was London's leading print publisher, with premises in the Royal Exchange. Elected to the Common Council in 1831, he was Lord Mayor in 1854-55.
⁶ D&M, p.151. A 'proof before the letters' is made before the title is added.
⁷ He quotes Lucretius (D&M, p.152): *Medio de fonte leporum surgit amari aliquid* (From the midst of the fountain of delight something bitter arises).
⁸ D&M, p.152.
⁹ Widened in 1845 to form part of what is now Gresham Street.
¹⁰ This description is of the building as originally designed. There were many later alterations, some of which are shown in the plans between pages 72 and 73 of Douglas-Smith *City of London School.*
¹¹ See Chapter 5.
¹² The plan in Douglas-Smith has Secretary's and Porter's rooms interchanged, and does not show the cloakrooms.
¹³ Minutes, 30 Nov 1836.
¹⁴ Douglas-Smith, p.75–76.
¹⁵ D&M, p.7.
¹⁶ D&M, p.152.
¹⁷ The title was revived for a few years from 1980.
¹⁸ Listed at the back of Thomas Brewer's Secretary's Book, City of London School Archive.
¹⁹ The Socinians (followers of Faustus Socinus, 1539-1604), like the Unitarians, rejected the orthodox theology of the Trinity.
²⁰ For example by Brougham at the foundation stone dinner, see p.25.
²¹ *Morning Chronicle*, 12 January 1837, p.1.
²² *Morning Chronicle*, 14 January 1837, p.1.
²³ Douglas-Smith, p.81.
²⁴ D&M, p.153.
²⁵ These were light chairs which could be hired for use at a "rout" or large party or reception.
²⁶ Douglas-Smith, p.70.
²⁷ p.74 and p.26 respectively.
²⁸ See Chapter 9.
²⁹ *City of London School Magazine*, No.100, November 1892, p.313.
³⁰ Available online at http://cityoflondonschoolheritage.daisy.websds.net/Registers/Main; hard copies of the Register are kept at the London Metropolitan Archives and in the City of London School Archive.
³¹ For 113 entries no occupation is given.
³² Built in 1701 for the community of Portuguese and Spanish Sephardi Jews in London.
³³ Thus the claim in Douglas-Smith (p.95) that "Jews had not attended the School in Dr Giles' day" is wrong. There are eight more names – including Levy four times - which strongly suggest further Jewish connections, but these have not been confirmed.

[34] Some of them presumably on the rout chairs.

[35] William Ritchie was Professor of Natural Philosophy at University College, London, from 1832 to 1837.

[36] See Chapter 5.

[37] D&M, p.154.

[38] John Tricker Conquest (1789-1866), obstetrician, was lecturer in midwifery at St Bartholomew's Hospital until he resigned in 1834 and changed to homeopathy. In addition to texts on midwifery, paediatrics and homeopathy he produced in 1841 a new translation of the Bible "with twenty thousand emendations".

CHAPTER 4

[1] Minutes, 19 September 1839.

[2] It is not known whether this was done, or whether the change was suggested by Bunning or later by Mortimer's architect Thomas Donaldson (see p.157).

[3] Minutes, 8 August 1839.

[4] Minutes, 8 August 1837.

[5] This proved to be an intractable problem, to which there are periodic references throughout the life of the building.

[6] The firm of R.W. Herring traded in Fleet Street between 1769-1839 and are recorded as cabinet-makers, upholsterers, appraisers and undertakers.

[7] CLS Archive.

[8] There are later examples of this practice when Edwin Abbott was Head Master, with each master initialling the notice to indicate that he had seen it.

[9] D&M p.154

[10] Founded in 1830, a precursor of the current Philological Society which dates from 1842.

[11] D&M, p.154.

[12] Perhaps the servants' bedroom, if that was not in use. There was no other "spare bedroom".

[13] D&M, p.157.

[14] D&M, p.159.

[15] The pattern of the school year was changed from four quarters to the present three terms, with half-holidays on Wednesdays, in 1840.

[16] Minutes, 19 April 1837.

[17] Secretary's notice of 14 June 1837, in CLS Digital Archive.

[18] Henry Shaw, 1800-73, produced many antiquarian books on architecture, furniture, and graphic and decorative arts, all superbly illustrated by his drawings.

[19] D&M, p. 181.

[20] D&M, p. 165.

[21] Described in detail in D&M, pp. 161–164.

[22] In which the NW room is the boarders' sitting room, and the SW room is the Head Master's sitting room.

[23] D&M, p.165.

[24] The following is drawn from Giles's draft in the CLS Archive.

[25] Benjamin Wyon (1802-58), engraver of seals and medals, was appointed chief engraver of the seals in 1831 and made William IV's great seal. In addition to the 1837 City of London School medal he designed and engraved the very fine CLS Beaufoy Shakespeare medal of 1851.

[26] Why 1447? Brewer in his Memoir gives the year of Carpenter's death as 1441 or 1442, and Douglas-Smith (p.17) supplies evidence that the latter is correct.

[27] In his *Memories and Reflections*, quoted in Douglas-Smith p.xiv.

[28] CLS Archive.
[29] CLS Archive.
[30] CLS Archive.
[31] *Morning Post*, 10 November 1837.
[32] Sub Committee minutes, 8 December 1837.
[33] "to the verge of madness" according to Edwin Abbott (Douglas-Smith, p.125).
[34] Minutes, 20 December 1837.
[35] Ann Dickinson (1764-1844) was a sister of Anna's father Frederick Dickinson (*c*.1762-1812).
[36] D&M, p.168. Again one wonders where they all slept.
[37] *A Christmas Carol* would be published in 1843.

Chapter 5

[1] Where Tower 42 (formerly the NatWest Tower) now stands.
[2] The Royal Society of London for Improving Natural Knowledge.
[3] Edward Taylor, *Three Inaugural Lectures* (London: Richard and John Edward Taylor, 1838,) pp.56, 69.
[4] In 1799 it was agreed "to provide a finger board pointing the way to the lecture room".
[5] The Keeper of the Gresham Lecture Room during this period was Uriah Yarrow, who was paid £35 per annum.
[6] *The Public Ledger and Daily Advertiser*, 21 February 1834.
[7] *Ibid.*
[8] The London Institution was founded in 1806 to promote the diffusion of Science, Literature and the Arts. In 1812 it moved to an elegant new building in Finsbury Circus with a library, reading rooms, lecture rooms and a laboratory. The Institution was particularly known for its promotion of chemistry. It closed in 1912, and the building, having then housed the School of Oriental Studies, was demolished in 1936.
[9] Report of the City of London School Committee, March 1838, p.19.
[10] Following the passing of the 1832 Reform Act, which had introduced wide-ranging changes of the parliamentary electoral system, Lord Grey's government turned its attention to local government. A Royal Commission was set up to inquire into the Municipal Corporations of England, Wales and Northern Ireland and to make recommendations, which eventually led to the Municipal Corporations Act 1835.
[11] The same report as had drawn attention to the Carpenter Bequest's large surplus of income over expenditure. It was this which started the discussions that led to establishing the City of London School.
[12] *The Public Ledger and Daily Advertiser*, 21 February 1834.
[13] *The Times*, 9 December 1836
[14] Report of the City of London School Committee, March 1838, p.18.
[15] *The Times*, 9 December 1836.
[16] Samuel Baylis was a founder in 1833 of the Radical Club, precursor of the Liberal Party. He lived in Whitecross Street, where there is now a plaque commemorating him.
[17] Interjections as in the original.
[18] *The Courier*, 16 December 1836.
[19] *The Public Ledger and Daily Advertiser*, 16 December 1836.
[20] Probably William Thomas Brande (1788-1866), who had just given the Royal Institution Christmas Lectures on *The Chemistry of Gases*. See p. 121.
[21] Thomas Gray, *The Bard* II,iii, referring to the legend that Julius Caesar built the Tower of London.

[22] School Committee minutes, 19 December 1836

[23] *The Times*, 6 October 1837

[24] William Horsley (1774-1858) was a composer and organist, and a pupil and friend of Mendelssohn. He composed oratorios and symphonies but is now remembered (if at all) for his five volumes of glees. In 1838 he became organist at the Charterhouse. His daughter Mary married Isambard Kingdom Brunel.

[25] Edward Taylor (1784-1863) was a bass singer and choral conductor who directed the Norwich triennial festival for many years and toured the country lecturing on musical topics.

[26] Frederick William Collard (1772-1860) and his brother William Frederick Collard (1776-1866) both contributed technical innovations to piano manufacture. In partnership with various others, including Muzio Clementi, they conducted business from 26 Cheapside from 1791 to at least 1860.

[27] JGGC minutes, 13 October 1837.

[28] D&M, p.166.

[29] The first time live music was heard in the school.

[30] *The Times*, 18 October 1837.

[31] *The Times*, 25 October 1837. Presumably Bishop and Gauntlett gained no votes.

[32] JGGC minutes, 11 January 1838.

[33] *Morning Post*, 16 January 1838.

[34] *London Dispatch*, 28 January 1838.

[35] School Committee minutes, 2 May 1838.

[36] *London Evening Standard*, 25 May 1838.

[37] *London Evening Standard*, 18 May 1838.

[38] Gresham Committee minutes, 4 February 1839.

[39] In the Mercers' Company archive.

[40] *The London Courier and Evening Gazette*, 27 November 1839.

[41] Crosby Hall in Bishopsgate was the great hall of a mansion built in 1466 by the wool merchant Sir John Crosby; later occupants included Richard Duke of Gloucester (later Richard III), Sir Thomas More, Sir Walter Raleigh and the East India Company. Most of the house was destroyed by fire in 1672, and later the remainder was converted to a warehouse. In 1910 Crosby Hall was moved to Chelsea, where it is now part of a private home.

[42] *The London Courier and Evening Gazette*, 27 November 1839.

[43] The building was replaced by a larger one in 1912, which still stands, though Gresham College moved elsewhere in 1961.

[44] There have been links from time to time since then: the Second Master Robert Pitt Edkins became the Gresham Professor of Geometry on the death of Samuel Birch in 1848, until his own death in 1854; his successor as Second Master, his pupil Francis Cuthbertson, often deputised to read the Gresham geometry lectures; in the 1980s two later Professors of Geometry, Clive Kilmister and Christopher Zeeman, used the school as the venue for their lectures, which were aimed at sixth formers and attracted audiences of up to two hundred.

CHAPTER 6

[1] Probably a Polygraph, patented by J.I.Hawkins in 1803, and used extensively by US President Thomas Jefferson.

[2] The Oxford friend with whom Giles had toured the continent in 1830.

[3] D&M, p.169.

[4] Committee minutes, 7 February 1838.

[5] Committee Minutes, 7 November 1838. Regular chemistry lessons (as an optional extra, 7 shillings per term) started in March 1847, given by Thomas Hall.

[6] This first happened in 1840.

[7] D&M, p.170.

[8] Committee Minutes, 3 April 1838.

[9] Letter Book, CLS Archive.

[10] *Ibid.*

[11] Minutes, 2 May 1838.

[12] Minutes, 29 October 1838.

[13] See *Raised in the Scale of Civilisation* by T.J.Heard in the *Old Citizens' Gazette* #295 (2008).

[14] The Third Master, William Webster, was an unsuccessful candidate for this job.

[15] D&M, p. 580.

[16] D&M, pp 173–175.

[17] The Steam Train was then a new and amazingly rapid form of transport.

[18] The London to Birmingham railway was then operating in two sections, Euston to Denbigh Hall (near Bletchley) and Rugby to Birmingham, with the gap filled by a stagecoach shuttle. The full London to Birmingham service opened in September 1838. The Great Western Railway from London to Oxford opened in 1844.

[19] 6 September 1838, presumably a quiet day for news.

[20] "who had risen from being a music-master to be a doctor of divinity [and] was very vain, but a good-tempered man" D&M, p.166.

[21] D&M, p.175.

[22] A portrait painter who exhibited at the Royal Academy between 1825 and 1839.

[23] Minutes, 1 August 1838. Augustus Keppel Gifford was a tobacconist of Holborn Hill; his son Augustus Robert did indeed leave the school then.

[24] Minutes, 5 September 1838.

[25] This second charter expired with the death of William IV, but was renewed by Queen Victoria in December 1837. The first London University degrees, all to students of University College or King's College, were awarded in 1839.

[26] The City University was incorporated in 1966, and became a constituent college of the University of London in 2016.

[27] Minutes, 18 December 1838.

[28] D&M, p.177.

[29] *A Topographical History of Surrey* by E.W.Brayley (Dorking, Robert Brest Ede 1841), Vol 1, Part 2, p.470.

[30] D&M, pp.141, 172.

[31] D&M, p.173. The Giles arms are "Gules, a cross between four chalices or, on a chief of the last three pelicans vulning themselves proper".

[32] The Revd George Walton Onslow (1768-1844), a great-nephew of the 1st Earl of Onslow, was rector of Wisley in Surrey; he and his wife Elizabeth had six children. D&M, p.177.

CHAPTER 7

[1] This brief account of Bialloblotzky's life before he became involved with the school summarises the detailed study *Transnational Evangelicalism: The Case of Friedrich Bialloblotzky (1799-1869)* by Nicholas M.Railton (Vandenhoeck & Ruprecht, Göttingen 2002), pp. 44 – 171; hereafter cited as Railton. No image of Bialloblotzky has been found.

[2] The Continental Society for the Diffusion of Religious Knowledge over the Continent of Europe, founded 1819.

[3] Revd Walter Oke Croggan (1791-1854), Wesleyan Methodist minister.

[4] In 1828 the Greek War of Independence (1821-29) sparked the Russo-Turkish War, which ended in the Treaty of Adrianople (September 1829), in which Greek independence was finally confirmed.

[5] Founded in 1768 in Trevecca, Breckonshire, by Selina, Countess of Huntingdon to train Methodist ministers, the college moved to Cheshunt in 1792 and then to Cambridge in 1906; it merged with Westminster College, Cambridge, in 1967.

[6] Opened in October 1834, by 1836 the school had about 80 pupils; it is now Forest School, on the same site with over 1300 students.

[7] Built in 1623 to provide a place of worship for the Spanish infanta Maria Anna who was to have married Charles Prince of Wales, and later serving the same purpose for Queen Henrietta Maria. Known then and now as the Queen's Chapel, and used from late 18th to late 19th centuries by both French and German protestants.

[8] Some of the correspondence relating to the German Class survives in the City of London School archive, and a full account appears in the *Proceedings of an Inquiry Instituted by the Committee into the State of the School 1839 – 40*. There are several manuscript copies of this in the archive; references here are taken from the hard-back fair copy dated 18/9/40, hereafter referred to as PI. The section dealing with the German Class runs from p.91 to p.134.

[9] Sub Committee minutes, 20 September 1837.

[10] All underlinings as in the original.

[11] Adolphus Bernays obtained his doctorate from the University of Giessen in 1833.

[12] Wittich, who had worked at University College School for three years, was appointed Professor of German at University College in June 1837. Bialloblotzky had also been a candidate for this post.

[13] Author of a standard German Grammar published in 1842.

[14] PI, p.124.

[15] PI, p.129.

[16] Railton, p.179.

[17] Wrongly given as Hagan in Railton.

[18] Published in the magazine *All the Year Round*, quoted in Douglas-Smith, p.92.

[19] An ecclesiastical court dating back to the Norman conquest, which by this time retained only a few residual powers relating to non-ecclesiastical matters. In 1857 the Divorce Court was set up and replaced the Consistory Court's jurisdiction over matrimonial cases.

[20] One of the two major tributaries of the Nile. It starts in Ethiopia at Lake Tana, and joins the White Nile at Khartoum.

[21] Charles T Beke: *The Sources of the Nile* (London, James Madden, 1860), p.152.

[22] Bialloblotzky's plan had been sound, and was essentially adopted by Richard Burton, John Hanning Speke and James Grant in their various expeditions from Zanzibar in 1857, 1858 and 1860, which led to the discoveries of Lake Tanganyika and Lake Victoria, and the identification of Lake Victoria as the source of the White Nile.

[23] Railton, pp 212-213. Bialloblotzky's handwriting, shown on p.164, does not seem to deserve this.

[24] The *Gesellschaft Deutscher Naturforscher und Ärzte*, founded 1822, and British Association for the Advancement of Science, founded in 1831, renamed as British Science Association 2009.

[25] T. von Lyra, quoted in Railton, p.213.

CHAPTER 8

[1] James George Stuart Burges Bohn, 1803-80, of 12 King William Street, Strand.

[2] 1796-1854, of 177 Piccadilly.

[3] D&M, p.182.

[4] Lower Darwen was then a village south of Blackburn. The parish of St James Lower Darwen had been created from part of the parish of Blackburn in 1830. The living was worth £150 p.a.

[5] D&M, p.179.

[6] D&M, p.180.

[7] Quoted in Douglas-Smith, pp.90, 91. *Le Bourgeois gentilhomme* and *Les Plaideurs* are comedies by Molière and Racine respectively. 'Theatrical scenes' seem to have been introduced after Giles had departed.

[8] Edmund Henry Barker (1788 – 1839) was a noted classical scholar, prolific author and lexicographer. He was a scholar of Trinity College, Cambridge, and university prize winner, but he refused to take the Oath of Supremacy, and so never graduated. He married and spent about 25 years in Thetford, Norfolk, later moving to London.

[9] D&M, p.153.

[10] D&M, p.154.

[11] 16 March 1838; D&M, p.171.

[12] George William MacArthur Reynolds (1814-79), prolific and immensely successful writer of popular fiction.

[13] D&M, p.179.

[14] Minutes, 6 August 1839.

[15] Of these six boys, Hose, Watson and Emery were all later ordained, had distinguished careers in the church or education, and were Presidents of the John Carpenter Club, which Hose founded.

[16] In 1840 and 1841 the prizes were presented by the Lord Mayor. This should have happened in 1842 also, but the Lord Mayor cancelled at short noticed. The Committee then secured agreement that the annual presentation of prizes is part of the Lord Mayor's official calendar of engagements.

[17] This seems to be misremembered. The Municipal Corporations Act of 1835 (which applied the principles of the 1832 Great Reform Act to local authorities) specifically excluded the Corporation of London from reform.

[18] John Hoard had been a member of the School Committee since its first meeting in September 1834, so could not have been one of the "noisy persons". He was one of the Committee of Visitors from September to November 1839.

[19] D&M, p.182.

[20] D&M, p.182.

[21] PI p.1.

[22] The Unwin family's connection with the school continued despite this tragedy: three more brothers, a half-brother and three nephews were pupils.

[23] PI, p.17.

[24] PI, p.27. This fudge lasted until 16 December 1841, when the Court of Common Council gave the Committee discretion to admit "other parties" as Pupils if nominated by a member of the Common Council, provided that those complying with the regulation received preference.

[25] Henry Nathan had been in the school for two years. His father was N. Nathan of 9 Bury Court, St Mary Axe.

[26] In the CLS Archive are lists of items stolen from eight classes, collected on 4 October. Nathan's class lost most: 26 books and 3 sets of geometry instruments – with Nathan himself listed as losing a German Dictionary and a History of England.

[27] Minutes, 6 November 1839.

[28] "As wave comes over wave". D&M, p.185.

[29] D&M, p.186. Kennedy's celebrated *Elementary Latin Primer* was published in 1843, but his *Elementary Greek Grammar* did not appear until 1866.

CHAPTER 9

[1] Alfred Moul and his brother George, sons of James Moul, Tea Broker of Brudenell Place in Islington, both joined the school in the Easter quarter of 1837. Alfred did indeed leave at Michaelmas 1839, aged 16, and George stayed until Lady Day 1841.

[2] The others were Stevens (joined the Committee in October 1838), Hardwick (December 1838) and Corney (March 1839).

[3] Brewer's rough but comprehensive notes of the evidence given on 10 and 14 October are in the CLS Archive.

[4] SI pp. 39-80. The separate report on the German class has been covered in Chapter 8. Underlinings are as in the original.

[5] William Huggins recalled that "Too frequently the business of the school and other calls took Dr Giles from the class, and the boys were very often left to their own devices – not always too edifying." *City of London School Magazine*, No.100, November 1892, p.313.

[6] In the CLS Archive there is a note in Brewer's handwriting giving these figures, with the additional figure of 12 panes broken in the Boarders Sleeping Room.

[7] The absentees were Thomas Corney and Samuel Baylis.

[8] CLS Archive.

[9] Copies in the Letter Book, CLS Archive.

[10] George Croly (1780 – 1860) was a well-known figure in the City. Irish by birth he was unable to obtain church preferment when he moved to London around 1810, and therefore pursued a literary career, becoming a prominent contributor to the *Literary Gazette* and *Blackwood's Magazine*, a theatre critic and foreign correspondent. In 1835, through the influence of Lord Brougham (a distant relative of his wife) he was appointed Rector of St Stephen's, Walbrook, a position he held until his death. His preaching, which attracted large congregations, was said to have "a sort of rude and indeed angry eloquence that would have stood him in better stead at the bar than in the pulpit".

[11] CLS Archive.

[12] Minutes, 18 December 1839.

[13] William Brodie Gurney (1777-1855) was a famed shorthand writer, using the system of stenography, *Brachygraphy*, invented by his grandfather Thomas Gurney. W.B Gurney recorded and published many famous trials, including the proceedings against Queen Caroline in Westminster Hall (see p. 35), and from 1813 was official shorthand writer to the Houses of Parliament.

[14] Letter Book, CLS Archive. 19 December 1839.

[15] Gurney's transcript is in the CLS Archive, and was copied into the PI compilation (pp.137–176). References given here are to the PI copy.

[16] Was this in the "narrow place" of confinement in the basement described on p.58? One hopes that the daily incarceration was for the two hour lunch break only.

[17] A smoking room attached to a cigar shop.

[18] At Michaelmas, 29 September.

[19] See p. 133–134.

[20] D&M, p.186.

[21] *Ibid.*

[22] See p.33.

[23] D&M, p.187.

[24] Original in CLS Archive, transcribed in SI p.177.

[25] The draft in the CLS Archive is in Brewer's handwriting.

[26] Original in CLS Archive, transcribed in SI p.192.

[27] CLS Archive.

CHAPTER 10

[1] CLS Archive.

[2] D&M, p.187.

[3] CLS Minutes 28 January 1840.

[4] Benjamin Wrigglesworth Beatson (1803-74), classical scholar, was born in London, the son of a Cheapside merchant, educated at Merchant Taylors' School and Pembroke College, Cambridge.

He became a Fellow of Pembroke soon after his graduation, and remained so until his death.

[5] Derwent Coleridge (1800-83) was the third son of the poet Samuel Taylor Coleridge. He was educated in Ambleside and at St John's College Cambridge, and became Master of Helston Grammar School in 1826.

[6] CLS Minutes, 28 March 1840.

[7] Quoted in *The Sun* (London), 24 April 1840.

[8] It is likely, though not certain, that his mother was from the Whidborne family in the Teign estuary area. Several generations of this family bore the names George Ferris Whidborne, most notably the palaeontologist (1845-1910) who described the fauna of south Devon.

[9] Listed Grade II in 1987: "Delamore is a particularly fine and unaltered example of a large villa in substantial grounds".

[10] D&M, p.187.

[11] Between Brompton Road and Thurloe Place, south of the present Victoria and Albert Museum.

[12] "A Letter to the Representatives of the Southern Part of Northumbria and of the Town and County of Newcastle on Tyne."

[13] *Literary and Scientific Intelligence*, February 1836.

[14] John Baldwin Buckstone (1802-79) had a long and successful career at the Haymarket and Adelphi Theatres, and was later the lessee of the Haymarket, where his ghost is said to make occasional appearances. This account is from his letter to *The Times* of 13 February 1838.

[15] Sir William Schwenck Gilbert (1836-1911), playwright best known for his collaboration with Sir Arthur Sullivan, attended Western Grammar School from 1846 to 1849.

[16] In his *French Grammar* of 1840 Delille is described as "Professor of the French Language in Christ's Hospital, the City of London School, the Western Proprietary Grammar School, the City of London and Marylebone Literary and Scientific Institutions, etc., Honorary French Master at King's College, and French Examiner in the University of London."

[17] Michael's Place was a terrace of houses opposite the Brompton Oratory built in the 1790s by the Polish/Italian architect Michael Novosielski (1750 – 95) and demolished for redevelopment in the 1880s.

[18] See p.140.

[19] *The Sun* (London), 24 April 1840.

[20] Something which did not happen until 1968.

[21] Thomas Leverton Donaldson (1795-1885), architect of Holy Trinity Church, Brompton, first Professor of Architecture at University College, London, whose Flaxman Gallery and Library he designed.

[22] CLS Minutes, 6 April 1840.

[23] Mortimer was not yet a Doctor. He was to gain his higher degree the following year, even more rapidly than Giles, becoming a Bachelor in Divinity at Oxford on 18 November 1841, and Doctor in Divinity the next day. *The British Magazine of Religious and Ecclesiastical Information*, 1841, p.702.

[24] Related by William Emery (CLS 1837-43), later Archdeacon of Ely and founder of the Church Congress, in Douglas-Smith, p.86.

[25] The Mortimer boys at CLS were George Gordon (CLS 1840-43), William Rogers (1840-45), Christian (1842-54), Alexander (1845-56), Brooke Cunliffe (1851-52), John Camden (1852-54), George Ferris Whidborne (1853-61), Frederick Crofton (1857-64), Henry Beaufoy (1860-70) and Lewis Gordon (1862-71).

[26] CLS Minutes, 6 April 1840.

[27] There is much detail about all this in Taylor, Michael A (2014) '*A very able man, of somewhat explosive ... opinions': the Reverend Henry Stuart Fagan (1827-1890), Church of England parson, Headmaster of Bath Grammar School, literary man, and Irish Home Ruler*, and the *Supplementary Notes*, both available at http://repository.nms.ac.uk/1185.

[28] Douglas-Smith, p.155.

[29] In the 1841 Census, on 6 June the residents at the City of London School were Mortimer, Jane, sons George and William, daughter Isabella (aged 6 months) and three house servants Mary Hockley and Ann and Jane Cormack. Henry Fagan was not there, but nor was he at 63 Ebury Street where only a servant was in residence.

³⁰ In *All the Year Round*, May 1883, pp. 448-452.
³¹ A popular dining room on the corner of Cheapside and Russia Row, which was still operating in 1862 and later became Magog's public house.
³² Perhaps in the company of his contemporary John Lawrence Toole (1830-1906, CLS 1841-45) who was to become a celebrated comic actor, actor-manager and theatrical producer.
³³ CLS Minutes, 6 May 1840.
³⁴ See p.133.
³⁵ See Douglas-Smith, *passim*, especially pp.96-100. This large group portrait, painted in 1845 by E.U.Eddis to commemorate the gift of the Beaufoy scholarships, gives a rare glimpse of the school's interior. It shows Hale (in the Chairman's chair which is now in the Asquith Room of the present school), Brewer (the only known image of him), Francis Hobler (Beaufoy's solicitor, Beaufoy himself being too reclusive to attend) and Mortimer. The original painting was sadly destroyed in the Second World War, having been removed from the school 'for safe keeping'.
³⁶ Clarendon Report, p.37. The 'young men' were William Steadman Aldis, Senior Wrangler and First Smith's Prizeman, and Edwin Abbott Abbott, Senior Classic and Senior Chancellor's Medallist, who would succeed Mortimer as Headmaster four years later.
³⁷ *i.e.* taking pupils to the age of 18 and preparing them for university.
³⁸ Taunton Report, quoted in Douglas-Smith, p.153.

CHAPTER 11

¹ 1599-1658, Lord Protector of England.
² 1602-1659, Lord President of the High Court of Justice for the trial of King Charles I.
³ D&M, p.152.
⁴ D&M, p.199.
⁵ D&M, p.190.
⁶ D&M, p.189.
⁷ D&M, p.192.
⁸ Quoted in D&M, p.x.
⁹ A considerable exaggeration: in 1838 Giles received £700, including the allowance for care of the boarders.
¹⁰ D&M, p.190. This was the last letter Sophia Giles was able to write, as she became crippled by arthritis. She died on 20 September 1841, aged 54.
¹¹ D&M, p.217.
¹² British monks of the 6th and 9th centuries respectively; Giles received £50 for this book.
¹³ A 12th century Winchester monk who chronicled the first three years of King Richard I's reign.
¹⁴ D&M, p.190.
¹⁵ D&M, pp 200, 201.
¹⁶ D&M, p.201.
¹⁷ Named after Alderman William Pickett (d.1796), who successfully campaigned for The Strand to be widened at this point in the 1790s. The whole area was cleared in 1870 for the construction of the Royal Courts of Justice.
¹⁸ David Jardine (1794-1860) was appointed senior Bow Street magistrate in 1839.
¹⁹ D&M, pp. 204-209.
²⁰ D&M, p.211.
²¹ D&M, p.216.
²² "through rose-tinted spectacles".
²³ D&M, p.217.
²⁴ D&M, p.225. In October 1858 Giles came across Mr and Mrs Brockhurst in Oxford Street. "His wife was with him and seemed to be keeping guard over him."

[25] The Hon Charles Ewan Law, QC (1792-1850) was Recorder of London from 1835 and an MP for the University of Cambridge from 1833 until his death.

[26] D&M, p.227.

[27] Giles recalls a joke which would not have made sense five years earlier: "Why is a boy just flogged like a railway engine? – Because he has a tender behind." D&M, p.286.

[28] D&M, p.236.

[29] This requirement, dating from Insolvent Debtors (England) Act 1813, was abolished in the Bankruptcy Law Consolidation Act 1849.

[30] *Jackson's Oxford Journal*, 16 October 1844.

[31] Herbert Allen Giles (1845-1935) became a diplomat in China and was then Professor of Chinese at Cambridge University for 35 years.

[32] In 1857 the parish was split into three separate parishes.

[33] D&M, p.252.

[34] Used as the location of Crawley House in the *Downton Abbey* television series.

[35] Ellen Harriet Giles (1848-1926) did not marry and had no children.

[36] D&M, p.262.

[37] For details see D&M, pp. xii-xviii.

[38] Giles knew Sir Thomas Phillipps (1792-1872) through his researches into medieval manuscripts. Phillipps lived at Middle Hill, Worcestershire, where sixteen of the twenty rooms of the house were given over to books. His printing press was housed in Broadway Tower, a nearby folly. After his death the disposal of his vast collection was not completed until 2006.

[39] Edward Bouverie Pusey (1800-1882), Professor of Hebrew at Oxford and a leading member of the Oxford Movement.

[40] Saint John Henry Newman (1801-1890), theologian and poet, leader of the Oxford Movement before converting to Roman Catholicism in 1845. Canonised in 2019.

[41] Anthony Ashley-Cooper, 7th Earl of Shaftesbury (1801-1885), politician, philanthropist and reformer. Shaftesbury had presented the report on the City of London School Bill to the House of Lords.

[42] D&M, p.302. This could not have been "shortly afterwards" as Emily Faithfull (1835-1895), women's rights activist and publisher, did not become politically active until 1858, and the Victoria Press was not established until 1860, staffed mainly by women but with a few men to do the heavy tasks.

[43] Sydenham's chorea, characterised by rapid, uncoordinated jerking movements primarily affecting the face, hands and feet.

[44] D&M, p.268.

[45] Samuel Wilberforce (1805-1873) was the fifth child of the reformer William Wilberforce. He was appointed Bishop of Oxford in 1845. He was later famous for clashing with Thomas Huxley in the debate on evolution at the 1860 Oxford meeting of the British Association. He was nicknamed "Soapy Sam" for his habit of wringing his hands as he spoke. Disraeli was more imaginative, calling Wiberforce's manner "unctuous, oleaginous, saponaceous".

[46] D&M, p.299.

[47] Which Giles published as *The lord bishop of Oxford's letters to the Rev. Dr Giles for suspending the publication of "Christion Records" with Dr Giles's letters in reply.* (London, Whitaker, 1854).

[48] Under Hardwicke's Marriage Act of 1753 marriages had to be conducted between 8 a.m. and 12 noon (later extended to 3 p.m., and now 6 p.m.)

[49] D&M, p.305.

[50] D&M, p.306.

[51] Later Sir Thomas Phillipps offered to house both Giles and the printing press at Broadway, but by then it had been moved to London.

[52] William John Butler (1818-1894) became vicar of Wantage in 1846, and first clashed with Giles in 1849 over the elaborate plans Giles proposed for celebrating the 1000th anniversary of Alfred the Great (born in Wantage). Butler was a staunch high churchman; he founded the Anglican Community of St Mary the Virgin in Wantage in 1848, and became Dean of Lincoln in 1885.

[53] D&M, p.306.

[54] John Campbell, 1st Baron Campbell (1779-1861) was a liberal reforming politician and lawyer who worked with Lord Brougham. He was Chief Justice of the Queen's Bench 1850-59, and then Lord Chancellor until his death.

[55] Quoted in D&M, p.313.

[56] D&M, p.312

[57] D&M, p.308.

[58] Quoted in D&M, p.313. Italics as in the original.

[59] Oxford Record Office, CPZ, 1/22.

[60] D&M, p.319.

[61] D&M, p.323.

[62] Under this Act any person not being a trader, or being a trader and owing less than £300, could obtain a protection order from the Court of Bankruptcy or a District Court of Bankruptcy staying all process against him on condition of vesting all his property in an official assignee.

[63] *Daily News & Morning Chronicle*, 13 March 1856. There is no mention of this in D&M.

[64] Draycot Foliat church, then ruinous, was demolished in 1572, and its materials used to repair and extend the church at Chiseldon, about a mile away, where the Draycot Foliat parishioners then worshipped. But, after a brief period of union, the benefices of Draycot Foliat and Chiseldon remained separate until 1923. (https://www.british-history.ac.uk/vch/wilts/vol9/pp 43-49, accessed 31.12.20.)

CHAPTER 12

[1] The Lateward family had been Lords of the Manor of Perivale since 1767. James Frederick Lateward (1787-1861) became Rector in 1812, with an annual stipend of £310, but was largely an absentee incumbent employing curates to perform his duties. From 1853-60 he was British Chaplain at Berne, Switzerland.

[2] D&M, p.337.

[3] Archibald Campbell Tait (1811-82) was Bishop of London from 1856 to 1868, and then Archbishop of Canterbury until his death.

[4] 1851 census.

[5] D&M, p.591.

[6] D&M, p.381.

[7] D&M, p.346.

[8] D&M, p.356.

[9] Giuseppe Garibaldi (1802-82), Italian general, patriot and republican, who played a major part in achieving Italian unification.

[10] Captain Daniel Roberts RN (1789-1869), having retired from the navy in 1817, lived in the south of France and then on the island of La Maddalena, north of Sardinia, and was well known throughout the archipelago. Garibaldi lived on the neighbouring island of Caprera from 1854. The family connection between Roberts and Giles has not been clarified.

[11] Cliveden, the country house and estate in Buckinghamshire, which the Duke of Sutherland had bought in 1849.

[12] D&M, p.363.

[13] No known connection with Edwin Abbott Abbott, a pupil of George Mortimer and his successor as Headmaster of the City of London School in 1865.

[14] Princess Alexandra of Denmark had married the Albert Edward, Prince of Wales, in 1863, and was very popular.

[15] D&M, p.367.

[16] Reprinted in D&M, pp. 367-368.

[17] Reprinted in D&M, p.375.

[18] The Hatch family had strong connections with Sutton for many years. Henry Hatch was brother of Revd Thomas Hatch (1788-1851), vicar of Walton-on-Thames and Lord of the Manor of Sutton, who was father of Revd Henry John Hatch (1818-95). In 1859 Henry John, then chaplain of Wandsworth Prison, was involved in a notorious trial for indecently assaulting two sisters aged 11 and 7. He was convicted and sentenced to 4 years hard labour; in 1860 the older sister was successfully prosecuted for perjury and Henry John was released. He took the living of Little Stambridge, Essex, but may well have considered returning to family territory in Sutton.

[19] D&M, p.378.

[20] D&M, p.378.

[21] D&M, p.521.

[22] D&M, p.510.

[23] D&M, p.525.

[24] D&M, p.557.

[25] Quoted in D&M, p.515. Giles shared the cost with his daughter Isabella, £200 each. He found the structure in London, bought it for £200, paid £100 to have it moved to Sutton, and then had it fitted out.

[26] D&M, p.516.

[27] In 1877 Sutton was transferred to the diocese of Rochester, and then in 1905 to the newly created diocese of Southwark.

[28] D&M, p.388.

[29] A distance of less than half a mile.

[30] D&M, p.400.

[31] D&M, p.454.

[32] See Luke 13:1-5.

[33] D&M, p.454.

[34] D&M, p.460.

[35] D&M, p.375.

[36] D&M, p.380.

[37] Now listed Grade II, Source ID 1320945.

[38] George Peloquin Graham Cosserat (c.1806-89), rector of Winfrith Newburgh, Dorset.

[39] D&M, p.541.

[40] D&M, p.521.

[41] William James Dundas Cloete (1823-91) was born in Cape Town, son of Sir Henry Cloete, and went to Magdalen Hall, Oxford. In D&M his name also appears as Cloeté and Clöete.

[42] *Weston Mercury*, quoted in D&M, p.548. Captain Joseph Giles (1792-1879) was a brother of Giles's father, so actually a great uncle of the brides.

[43] Sir Thomas Scambler Owden (1808-89), Lord Mayor of London 1877-78.

[44] Henry Hugh Lavington (1828-92), railway contractor, member of Common Council 1882-87, Master of the Innholders' Company 1890, started a unique family connection with CLS, attended by three of his sons, three grandsons, one great grandson, two great great grandsons, and one great great great grandson, who left the school in 1973.

[45] Douglas-Smith, p.240.

[46] D&M, p.600.

[47] There is no sign at Churchill Court of any structure that might have enclosed an interment space or burial chamber, so it seems that by "Mausoleum" Giles meant the sunken walled private family burial plot in the SE corner of the churchyard, which had access through gates from the Churchill Court garden.

[48] *Sutton Advertiser*, 22 December 1883.

[49] D&M, p. x.

LIST OF SUBSCRIBERS

Scott Aaron, 1987–1994

Zain Ahsan, 2001–2008

Zia Ahsan, 1968–1976

David Bartle, 1970–1979

Geoff Bates, 1955–1962

Martin Biltcliffe, *Staff*, 2003–

Peter Butt, *Staff*, 1974–1998

Jonathan Cohen, 1970–1977

Andrew Davis, 1967–1973

Peter Donaldson, 1941–1950

Timi Dorgu, 1998–2006, *Governor*

Neil Edwards, 1977–1982

Richard Edwards, *Staff*, 1966–2005

Keith Eyeons, 1982–1989

Sheldon Fernandes, *Staff*, 2003–

James Fraser, 1986–1990

Vernon Gamester, 1959–1965

David Gerecht, 1983–1992

Chris Gooderidge, 1954–1962

Anthony Hudson, 1951–1958

Neville March Hunnings, 1939–1948

Jamil Husain, 1969–1977

Martin Israel, 1965–1973

Russell Jones, 1972–1977

Dov Katz, 1985–1992

Stephen Kelly, 1979–1984

Lionel Knight, 1952–1959, *Staff*, 1969–2005

Mike Knight, 1976–1984

Peter Levene, 1951–1960

Tim Levene, 1983–1991, *Chair of Governors*

Ryan McDonagh, 1994–2001

Richard Oblath, 1970–1972

George Phillipson, *Staff*, 1987–2014

Simon Platt, 1981–1988

Philip Powell, *Staff*, 1980–1990

Benjamin Reisman, 1984–1991

Dan Roman, 1988–1990

Bernard Silverman, 1961–1969

Jonathan Silverman, 1959–1967

David Smith, 1965–1972

Chris Southgate, 1956–1965

Richard Steele, 1970–1979, *CCF Staff*, 1979–

Keith Stella, 1965–1972

Mark Stockton, 1968–1976

Bruce Todd, 1961–1968

Vagish Vela, 2000–2007

Brian Ward, 1956–1961

Alan Willis, 1961–1968

and 13 anonymous subscribers.

Index

Illustrations in *bold italic*

Jackson, George 70, 71
Jardine, David 168, 226
Joint Grand Gresham Committee 81, 82, 83, 88, 89, 90
Jones, Richard Lambert 86
Joseph, Walter 133, 134
Judson, J.H. 148, 152

Kennedy, Benjamin Hall 134, 223
Kerby, Charles Lancelot 173
King George IV 35
King William IV 9, 71, 72
King's College 12, 41, 43, 115, 221
    School 15, 17, 115, 132

Lait, Charlotte 175, 176
Lamerte, George 117
Lateward, James Frederick 185, 186, 228
Lavington, Henry 194, 229
Law, Charles 172, 227
Lawrence, William 121, 144, 199-203 *passim*
Ledger, Alfred 70
Leeds Grammar School 11
Lindo, Elias Haim & Raphael 64
Linging, E.W., *History of CLS* 194
London Institution 82, 88
London University 12, 24, 105
    School 15, 17

MacDougal, Thomas St Clair 59-61
Major, John Richardson 15, 214
Malden, Henry 15, 214
Manley, Henry 59, 61, 144, 145, 200, 201
Marshall, Chapman 28

Maxon, Frederick Thomas 129, 166, 167
Maxon, John Robert (JR) 167
Melvill, Henry 53
Mercers' Company 12, 13, 81, 83
    School 12
Merchant Taylors' School 12
Messiter, Charles 174, 227
Middleton, John 42, 71
Middleton, William 40
Milk Street 9
Mill Hill School 17
Mitchell (superintendent constable) 176, 182
Mitchell, Joseph 105
Moon, Francis Graham 48, *52*, 165, 217
Mortimer, George Ferris Whidborne 123, 153-160, *160, 177*, 194, 225
Mortimer, George Gordon 157
Mortimer, Jane (née Gordon) 158
Mortimer, William Rogers 158
Moul, Alfred 135, 145, 203-213 *passim*, 223
Myers, Revd 43, 44, 216

Nash, Edwin 189
Nathan, George 146, 147
Nathan, Henry 117, 133, 134, 223
National Society for Promoting the Education of the Poor 11, 31
Newcastle Royal Grammar School 155
Newland, Abraham 68, 75
Newman, John Henry 174, 227

Obbard, Robert 98, 99
Onslow, George Walton 109, 221
Otter, William 47
Owden, Thomas 194, 196, 229
Owen, Edward 92, 93

Taylor (Oxford bedmaker) 39
Taylor, Edward 89, *89*, 90, 92-95, 99, 137, 219
Taylor, Richard 9, *12*, 13, 83, 125, 144, 199-203 *passim*, 214
Tegg, Thomas 103
The Castle Spectre 32, 215
Tholuck, Friedrich 110
Thorp, John Leslie *17*, 18
Thorpe, Robert Alder 100
Tonbridge School 11, 69
Turner, Herbert 190

University College 105, 221
    School 15, 97

Venables, William 11, 15, 214
Vinerian Scholarship 41, 216

Ward, Thomas 76, 107, 108
Watson, Henry 130, 223
Webster, William 48, 53, 58, 79, 108, 116, 120, 138, 152, 153, 221
Were, William Davy 70
Western Grammar School 12, 155, 156, 225
White, G.J.P. 47
White, William H. 20
Wilberforce, Samuel 125, 174, 176, *177*, 182, 184, 190, 191, 227
Wilberforce, William 13, 227
Willemont, Thomas 109
Williams, Samuel Bundy 167
Williams, William M.H. 34, 36
Wilson, Mr 188
Wilson, Richard 48, 53, 70

Wilton, John 189, 196
Winchester, Henry 20, *22*, 22, 27, 215
Windlesham 72, 97, 103, 109, 169
    Hall 109, 131, 165, 167, 168, *178*
Wire, Under Sheriff 87, 103
Wittich, William (Wilhelm) 121, 222
Wood, Matthew 60
Woodroffe, Charles Nathaniel 59, 76, 99, 128, 199-202
Woodthorpe, Henry 18, 82
Wren, Christopher 81
Wright, Joseph Henry 77, 79
Wyon, Benjamin 74, *74*, 218

Yarrow, Uriah 89, 91, 94, 219
Yates, James 121
Yealden, Mr 33